ILEX FOUNDATION SERIES 15

GLOBAL MEDIEVAL

Also in the Ilex Foundation Series

Dreaming across Boundaries: The Interpretation of Dreams in Islamic Lands
edited by Louise Marlow

Strī: Women in Epic Mahābhārata
by Kevin McGRATH

Persian Literature and Judeo-Persian Culture: Collected Writings of Sorour S. Soroudi
edited by H. E. Chehabi

The Rhetoric of Biography: Narrating Lives in Persianate Societies
edited by L. Marlow

Jaya: Performance in Epic Mahābhārata
by Kevin McGRATH

The History *of Beyhaqi (The History of Sultan Masʿud of Ghazna, 1030–1041) by Abu'l-Fażl Beyhaqi*
translated and with commentaries by Clifford Edmund Bosworth
fully revised and with further commentary by Mohsen Ashtiany

The Last of the Rephaim: Conquest and Cataclysm in the Heroic Ages of Ancient Israel
by Brian R. Doak

Ruse and Wit: The Humorous in Arabic, Turkish, and Persian Narrative
edited by Dominic Parvis Brookshaw

Kṛṣṇa: Friendship in Epic Mahābhārata
by Kevin McGRATH

On the Wonders of Land and Sea: Persianate Travel Writing
edited by Roberta Micallef and Sunil Sharma

Poet and Hero in the Persian Book of Kings
third edition
by Olga M. Davidson

Comparative Literature and Classical Persian Poetics
second edition
by Olga M. Davidson

Ferdowsi's Shāhnāma: *Millennial Perspectives*
edited by Olga M. Davidson and Marianna Shreve Simpson

Mirror of Dew: The Poetry of Ālam-tāj Zhāle Qā'em-Maqāmi
translated with an introduction by Asghar Seyed-Gohrab

GLOBAL MEDIEVAL

MIRRORS FOR PRINCES RECONSIDERED

Edited by
Regula Forster and Neguin Yavari

Ilex Foundation
Boston, Massachusetts

Center for Hellenic Studies
Trustees for Harvard University
Washington, D. C.

Distributed by Harvard University Press
Cambridge, Massachusetts, and London, England

Global Medieval: Mirrors for Princes Reconsidered
Edited by Regula Forster and Neguin Yavari

Published by Ilex Foundation, Boston, Massachusetts and The Center for Hellenic Studies, Trustees for Harvard University, Washington, D.C.

Distributed by Harvard University Press, Cambridge, Massachusetts and London, England

Production editor: Christopher Dadian
Cover design: Joni Godlove
Printed in the United States of America

Cover image: From *Fragment of a manuscript. 26 leaves with 19 paintings (page T, Recto)*. Ca. 1450. Opaque watercolor and gold on paper. From the Edwin Binney 3rd Collection, San Diego Museum of Art.

Library of Congress Cataloging-in-Publication Data

Global medieval : Mirrors for princes reconsidered / edited by Regula Forster and Neguin Yavari.
pages cm -- (Ilex Foundation series ; 15)
Includes bibliographical references and index.
ISBN 978-0-674-08827-6 (alk. paper)
1. Education of princes--Islamic Empire. 2. Education of princes--Europe. 3. Islamic Empire--Kings and rulers--Conduct of life. 4. Europe--Kings and rulers--Conduct of life. 5. Political science--Philosophy. I. Forster, Regula, editor. II. Yavari, Neguin, editor.
JC393.G57 2015
320.1--dc23

2015017906

CONTENTS

Introduction

Neguin Yavari
Regula Forster

Is a genuine history – as in genuinely historical – of political thought in the premodern period possible, and can premodern traditions of political thought be compared with each other fruitfully? Is global only modern; or, does the past have a history unmediated by the present – at least insofar as political and intellectual history is concerned? Current approaches to comparative history and to global political thought neglect a substantial portion of medieval and early modern political writing, including a genre (loosely defined) commonly known as mirrors for princes.

The genesis of a good number of mirrors for princes is a pseudo-Aristotelian treatise of advice supposedly written for Alexander the Great, and in wide circulation in Europe by the thirteenth century. Known as the *Secretum secretorum*, the Latin mirror version of this text is based on a tenth-century Arabic original, *Kitāb Sirr al-asrār*, itself a confluence of a number of traditions of political propriety, with an "international" cast of heroes, packaged as advice for Alexander by Aristotle. As illustrated in this account, multiple contexts is a salient feature of mirrors for princes, marked as they are by the integration of Greek, pre-Islamic Iranian, Indian, and Arabic materials alike. In both form and content, mirrors are exemplars of comparative and global political thought. Reconsidering this literature could address important questions regarding the history of political thought through engagement with non-Western traditions, as well as with those European strands of thought that have been neglected or undervalued by modern historians as factors influential in shaping modern political institutions and intellectual currents.

This book brings together eleven essays that cut across temporal, geographical and cultural divides to address ideas about power, and inquire into the relationship between different intellectual traditions. We hope to raise seminal questions and to stimulate further debate on the utility of notions such as context, exchange and translation and transnational in the study of medieval political thought. The introductory chapter provides a brief overview of the current state of the debate in international intellectual history and comparative political thought.

A Genuine History of Medieval Political Thought

The history of political thought is often conceived as a genealogy of modern political concepts and debates.[1] The quest for origins takes place to a large extent within borders defined by that which separates the past from the present, and the West from the rest, implying a teleological approach. It is contingent upon an implicit notion of progress ushering in the modern world, a world which is, or ought to be, more democratic, just, and equitable than the prior orders which it has supplanted. Thus, most histories of political thought reiterate the connections between the European present and incipient indications of progress in its past history. By reciting the familiar tale of the emergence of luminaries whose conceptual and linguistic innovations brought about change in the social world itself, histories of political thought tend to reify divides and consolidate barriers. They undermine genuinely comparative inquiries. Paradoxically, there is simultaneously a vociferous demand for internationalizing and globalizing intellectual history in the Western academy.[2]

Many a delimitation to the pursuit of non-Western or comparative political thought is justified in terms of methodological and conceptual rigor. Practitioners agree that in the absence of such safeguards, intellectual history will dissolve into a study of "flotsam and jetsam," with little in the way of contribution to explaining historical change that cannot be gleaned otherwise. The centrality of context to the practice of intellectual history is a particularly consequential barrier for the study of non-Western and premodern political thought, and subsequently, a serious critique is elusive. Against textual autonomy, Quentin Skinner suggests that "the understanding of texts presupposes the grasp both of what they were intended to mean, and how this meaning was intended to be taken."[3] As a corollary, therefore, Skinner also insists that rather than the pursuit of "perennial problems" and "universal truths," intellectual histories must approach texts and statements as "the embodiment of a particular intention, on a particular occasion, addressed to solution of a particular problem, and thus specific to its situation in a way that it can only be naïve to try to transcend."[4] Genuine histories of political thought, therefore, maintain both a sharp distinction between past and present, and a focus on those past concepts that are in a continuum with

1. Grafton 2006; Gordon n. d.

2. Rüsen 2002; Dallmayr 2004; Kelley 2005; Armitage 2013; Jordan with Nederman 2013; Moyn and Sartori 2013.

3. Skinner 1969, 48.

4. Skinner 1969, 50.

present values, that is, that are found to be influential in shaping the social world. In J. G. A. Pocock's estimation, a history of political thought exists in those societies that enjoy continuity with their past – even if their present is radically different, it is nevertheless, shaped by ideas that have arisen in another age.[5] Tracing the history of parliamentarianism, for example, is of little consequence in the study of political thought in a specific oikoumene – bordered along religious, civilizational, or geographical lines – unless those discursive deliberations have had demonstrable effect on the society in which they have originated. Such concerns bear also on the thorny question of transmission, for what does a common intellectual heritage mean, if a singular source or a vehicle of transmission cannot be documented? What does it exactly mean to learn, for instance, that the wheel of fortune is used metaphorically in mirrors from the Islamic and Christian worlds, ranging from the eleventh to at least the sixteenth century, amidst spectacularly divergent social, economic, and political conditions?

The wicked problem of similar pasts and different presents, or commonalities in political thought amidst incongruous historical contexts in comparative frameworks is on display in a recent article by three political scientists at Stanford: Lisa Blaydes, Justin Grimmer, and Alison McQueen, in which they have subjected several Christian and Islamic mirrors to automated text analysis, to shed light on the issue of "speaking truth to power."[6] The authors find that as early as the ninth century, and as feudalism took hold in Europe, Christian mirrors displayed more explicitly political language. In the Islamic world, in contrast, "mamlukism" undermined genuine political critique.[7] Feudalism itself is problematic enough as a moniker with no fixed meaning,[8] but "mamlukism" holds little analytical promise if it is used as blanket term to describe political and social orders in effect throughout the Islamic world from the ninth century to, presumably, the present. What this approach has yielded does not surpass the tired claim that sharp divisions separate the contemporary Western and Islamic worlds in spite of their equally prosperous pasts.

Context, transmission, and the propriety of comparison are also addressed – if implicitly – in Linda Darling's study on mirrors for princes in the Middle Eastern and European contexts. In her view, comparison of the two types of mirrors has been undermined by a "historiographical or critical

5. Pocock 2004, 549–50.

6. Blaydes, Grimmer and McQueen 2013, 2.

7. Blaydes, Grimmer and McQueen 2013, 3.

8. The authors would have benefitted from, among many such, Chris Wickham's 1985 study in which he argues for the fluidity of feudalism and against its absence from the non-European world, specifically, in China and the Islamic world (Wickham 1985).

tradition [that] has taken two extremely similar phenomena and rendered them incommensurable."[9] European mirrors are primarily classified along national lines, according to Darling, whereas on the Middle Eastern side, a general rubric, charting the ascent from non-Islamic founts in the ninth century to full-fledged Islamic political thought by the eleventh century, prevails. The author identifies Spain as a possible site for cultural encounter, to suggest that similarities between European and Middle Eastern mirrors may have a more material history than hitherto acknowledged.[10] Although "strong resemblances" between European and Middle Eastern mirrors may suggest a "transnational phenomenon," she cedes that "actual contacts have yet to be traced." By the early modern period, however, Darling sees with the authors above, "a divergence between the two traditions, with European ones becoming increasingly theoretical and philosophical."[11]

Incommensurability is also at the heart of another valence of difference that merits address in the present discussion, again regarding the differences – perhaps innumerable – between the West and the Islamic world, past and present. A proper comparative approach to political thought, Andrew March has argued, is bound to be a study in difference: "Comparative political theory needs to explain why it is not merely expanding the canon to include non-Western texts and why a certain non-Western text is "alien," thus justifying the moniker *comparative*."[12] The contribution of a Muslim theorist to political thought is not sufficient to qualify the enterprise as "comparative," for it is no different than proclamations by a Norwegian or a Buddhist, or even a Marxist thinker on the subject. March sets out ten theses to conclude that comparative political theory must be engaged, that is, it must study "the contestations of norms, values, and principles between distinct and coherent doctrines of thought."[13] Consequently, comparative political thought, where the Islamic world is concerned, must be limited to the standoff between religious political thought and Western traditions of liberal and secular norms and values. In his words, "a genuinely comparative political theory (as opposed to a better political theory or a better universalism) must have a conception of what makes a tradition distinct from another (a role, I argue, that is best filled by religion)."[14]

9. Darling 2013, 225.
10. Darling 2013, 226.
11. Darling 2013, 241–2.
12. March 2009, 531.
13. March 2009, 531.
14. March 2009, 564. A less prohibitive view of difference is de rigueur among intellectual historians; see Bevir 1999; Burke 2002; Brett and Tully 2006; Printy 2009; Felski 2011; Holsinger 2011; Jay 2011; and Tucker 2011.

Modern history, as we have seen, is central to the study of past political thought. The chronology of globalization – if indeed a prerequisite for global thought – is itself fraught with controversy. In *Global Muslims in the Age of Steam and Print,* for example, James Gelvin and Nile Green argue that exchange and transmission between and within cultures and civilizations is only feasible in a globalized world, which is coeval with the technologies of steam and print, whose heyday lasted from around 1850 to 1930. In this period, Euro-American societies become connected to others, including Muslims, for whom "it was also an age of discovery and differentiation. Muslims discovered both other Muslim and non-Muslim societies, defined themselves in relation to these contacts, and synthesized new ideologies and rethought older doctrines. The Age of Steam and Print was the foundational sine qua non of the contemporary Islamic world."[15] Moreover, although "Muslim thinkers may have always thought in universal terms, such as a universal Muslim community or *'umma,* the intellectual genealogy of "Islamic world," is of much more recent provenance and cannot be equated with its antecedent."[16]

If the velocity of exchange and contact is the hallmark of the global, then according to David Armitage, international thought is datable to at least as far back as Hobbes,[17] while Samuel Moyn and Andrew Sartori insist on modern and capitalist social formations for the spread of "concept global,"[18] and in the case of a concept generated in non-Western societies, "it would need to be fully intelligible within the European intellectual context."[19] Global intellectual history for Sartori and others is predicated upon translatability, or the potential to formulate a political claim that, explicitly or not, reflects, illuminates, and addresses that which is already in existence, that is, European articulations of the political. In this vein, however, one may ask if the works of those non-Western intellectuals who ascend to globality are themselves in any ways significant even in the very longue durée, or are primarily objects of fascination for the tired but unfortunately still true orientalist gaze. Can a minority position, or a failed project, politically speaking, become the object of study if it was not of much consequence in its own historical context? And is such a reading an instance of *autopoesis,*[20] a distinguished thinker writing for and responding to other thinkers, but not in a conversation beyond the academy with laymen or political stakeholders?

15. Gelvin and Green 2014, 2.
16. Gelvin and Green 2014, 4.
17. Armitage 2012, 33–45.
18. Moyn 2013.
19. Sartori 2010, 322.
20. Steinmetz 2008, 550, note 2; Steinmetz has borrowed Niklas Luhmann's term.

An authentic alternative universalist claim, one better suited to the global world than European models, is the subject of a collection of essays on the *Bhagavad Gita* in modern Indian history. Shruti Kapila and Faisal Devji, the volume's editors, suggest in their introduction that thought is global when it is read as such. Beginning in the nineteenth century, and as part of an effort "to think of politics beyond and after imperialism," India's political and literary leaders read the Gita in new ways, and they:

> were participating in a transnational conversation, one that detached India from its own neighborhood to link it with a community of readers and writers in America and Europe...For the Gita, and with it Hinduism itself achieved a kind of territorial transcendence, by forsaking the rest of Asia to join a debate with the West alone, given that the book attracted little attention in other parts of the world. This debate, moreover, broke with the exegetical tradition within which the text had previously been studied.[21]

The claim here is that the Gita is read in India as a global text, that is, as a text that lays an authentic claim to the political. Whether or not the Gita was born in an Indian context, it was made global by Indian thinkers who interpreted it in radically new ways. One is left to wonder, however, if the outward journey of the Gita is historically significant because the new reading was *in* India, or, that the Gita *itself* is translatable, that is, it can speak to the West, or better yet, is made to speak to the West?

Toward a Comparative Medieval Framework

As is the case with the study of nationalism, for example, where modernists insist that the nation as the fundamental basis of politics is a strictly modern phenomenon, and medievalists argue for a much longer history of nation and of nationalism, many historians of medieval political thought cast a qualitatively wider net in defining that which constitutes context, exchange, percolation, and historicity. In response to new currents in intellectual history, Paul Strohm has suggested a turn to "historicity" without "historicism," toward an analytical conception of history that reflects "the unruly multiplicity of ways in which history can manifest itself within a text."[22] Concurrent cultures may be non-synchronous, and "influence" and "reaction" are perhaps not the best ways of talking about cultural encounter. It may be impossible to know the "history" in a medieval text, or to gain knowledge of

21. Kapila and Devji 2013, xii.
22. Strohm 2010, 383–4.

the truth of a historical claim, but that only means "that there's no finality in our interpretations, that we never nail it once and for all."[23]

With these debates in mind, the contributors to this volume (along with several other participants who chose not to include their work in the proceedings) met at the Freie Universität Berlin in 2012 to explore possibilities for a genuine comparative framework to study the works of authors from disparate cultural origins and in the distant past. We sought to think beyond agents and sites of transmission and translation, for it seems to us that the notion of cordoning off of the medieval past from global intellectual history is useful only as a crutch to the kind of modern intellectual histories of non-Western traditions that find the challenges posed by the complexities of context, modes of exchange and agents of transmission that characterize premodern thought as cumbersome and unrewarding, and premodern thought itself as underwhelming and unoriginal. With Paul Strohm and Frederick Cooper,[24] we urge that both context and global, as well as network and translation, are only enriched with cross-cultural and transnational comparisons in the medieval past, and in so doing, hope to be speaking on the behalf of other presenters at the conference as well. To those who ask about global politics before "global," "international," and even "national" were born, we retort: Has political theorizing ever been anything but global?

The opening salvo of the conference was explorations by Stefan Leder and Hans-Joachim Schmidt of conceptualizations of sovereignty and the common good in the Islamic and European contexts. Leder probes the concept of common interest in several Islamic mirrors, the logic with which it was bound to governance, the modes of its articulation, and the extent to which conflicting perceptions were mediated and negotiated. Common interest or good governance is analogized with the king's beautiful body in Giles of Rome's *De regimine principum,* as argued in Schmidt's essay. The king's beautiful body was further inflected, Schmidt finds, in Giles' insistence on beauty as a virtue, one that cemented the king's claim to legitimacy, as it served as evidence of his fitness for rule. The beautiful king was not simply his father's heir, but worthy of his office.

The question of context is taken up in essays by Charles F. Briggs and Matthias Haake. *De regimine principum*'s most common use, Briggs points out, was as a kind of school textbook of Aristotelian moral philosophy. While mirrors played an important role in shaping and popularizing moral and political discourse, paying attention to their immediate context – the university classroom and the mendicant and monastic schools – goes a long

23. Strohm 2010, 387.
24. Cooper 2013, 283–94.

way in explaining the subordination of politics to ethics in the mirrors under consideration in Brigg's essay. "Monocracy" is the immediate context of several literary texts written for sole rulers in Greco-Roman antiquity, anachronistically considered as mirrors for princes, according to Haake. In his estimation, probing deeper into the communicative functions of literary texts addressed to monocrats and the historical context of late antiquity helps to distinguish them from mirrors for princes proper.

Mirrors as palimpsests or a confluence of founts are the subject of contributions by Olga M. Davidson, Seyed Sadegh Haghighat, Johannes Niehoff-Panagiotidis, and Mohsen Zakeri. Haghighat and Zakeri explore Iranian themes and concepts in Islamic mirrors, while Davidson and Niehoff-Panagiotidis study the reception of Indian mirrors and advice literature in Islamic and Byzantine settings, respectively. What is to be made of the alien content of mirrors for princes, and are national origins reflected at all in individual borrowings? An anecdote about an Indian king in a Persian mirror dating from the eleventh century reflects and illuminates a multiplicity of histories, contexts, and traditions; it defies national or ethnic classification.

Staying with the question of classification, Hinrich Biesterfeldt, Isabel Toral-Niehoff, and Edwin P. Wieringa's contributions concern texts at the borders between mirrors for princes and encyclopedias. Biesterfeldt deals with a rather obscure, but all the more interesting text, Ibn al-Farīghūn's tenth-century *Jawāmiʿ al-ʿulūm*. Written in the form of tree diagrams (*tashjīr*), the text integrates its vision of the perfect ruler and his rule into a larger categorization of the arts and sciences. Toral-Niehoff shows that the tenth-century Andalusian Ibn ʿAbd Rabbih's authorial intention and political claim is best deciphered by a scrutiny of the classification scheme in effect in his *ʿIqd al-farīd*. The text's tight twining of good rule with divine protection may not appear original at first sight. In her close reading, however, a clearly pro-Umayyad Andalusian leaning is unveiled, which necessitates a close, if hidden relationship between context and content. Wieringa focuses on an early modern Malay specimen, Nūr al-Dīn al-Rānīrī's *Bustān al-salāṭīn,* written for Iskandar al-Thānī. Although the author praises his patron and his rule, he also makes indispensable his own position as adviser. The rule of scholars over princes is laid out in meticulous detail in Wieringa's essay to plot the use of mirrors for princes in Islamizing the Acehnese society, thus effecting social change, and at the same time, to question the conventional wisdom of a "peaceful" and "defanged" Islam shaped by Sufism and prevalent in Southeast Asia.

We thank the individual authors and the conference participants for the robust and engaging discussions occasioned by their contributions, and the Ilex Foundation – especially Christopher Dadian and Niloo Fotouhi – for their support of this publication.

Bibliography

Armitage, D. (2013), *Foundations of Modern International Thought*, Cambridge.

Bevir, M. (1999), *The Logic of the History of Ideas*, Cambridge.

Blaydes, L., J. Grimmer and A. McQueen (2013), "Mirrors for Princes and Sultans: Advice on the Medieval Christian and Islamic Worlds," *http://aalims.org/uploads/Mirrors%20Princeton.pdf* [3.7.2014].

Brett, A. and J. Tully (eds.) (2006), *Rethinking the Foundations of Modern Political Thought*, Cambridge.

Burke, P. (2002), "Context in Context," *Common Knowledge* 8: 152–77.

Cooper, F. (2013), "How Global Do We Want Our Intellectual History to Be?," in: S. Moyn and A. Sartori (eds.), *Approaches to Global Intellectual History*, New York, 283–94.

Dallmayr, F. (2004), "Beyond Monologue: For a Comparative Political Theory," *Perspectives on Politics* 2: 249–57.

Darling, L. (2013), "Mirrors for Princes in Europe and the Middle East: A Case for Historiographical Incommensurability," in: A. Classen (ed.), *East Meets West in the Middle Ages and Early Modern Times*, Berlin, 223–42.

Felski, R. (2011), "Context Stinks!," *New Literary History* 42: 573–91.

Gelvin, J. L. and N. Green (2014), "Introduction: Global Muslims in the Age of Steam and Print," in: J. L. Gelvin and N. Green (eds.), *Global Muslims in the Age of Steam and Print*, Berkeley, 1–23.

Gordon, P. (n. d.), "What Is Intellectual History? A Frankly Partisan Introduction to a Frequently Misunderstood Field," *http://history.fas.harvard.edu/people/faculty/documents/pgordon-whatisintellhist.pdf* [10.10.2011].

Grafton, A. (2006), "The History of Ideas: Precept and Practice, 1950–2000 and Beyond," *Journal of the History of Ideas* 62: 1–32.

Holsinger, B. (2011), "'Historical Context' in Historical Context: Surface, Depth, and the Making of the Text," *New Literary History* 42: 593–614.

Jay, M. (2011), "Historical Explanation and the Event: Reflections on the Limits of Contextualization," *New Literary History* 42: 557–71.

Jordan, S. R. with C. Nederman (2013), "The Logic of the History of Ideas and the Study of Comparative Political Theory," *Journal of the History of Ideas* 73: 627–41.

Kapila, S. and F. Devji (2013), "Introduction," in: S. Kapila and F. Devji (eds.), *Political Thought in Action: The Bhagavad Gita and Modern India*, Cambridge, iv–xv.

Kelley, D. R. (2005), "Forum: Intellectual History in a Global Age," *Journal of the History of Ideas* 66: 143–200.

March, A. F. (2009), "What is Comparative Political Theory?," *The Review of Politics* 71: 531–65.

Moyn, S. (2013), "On the Non-Globalization of Ideas," in: S. Moyn and A. Sartori (eds.), *Approaches to Global Intellectual History*, New York, 187–204.
Moyn, S. and A. Sartori (2013), "Approaches to Global Intellectual History," in: S. Moyn and A. Sartori (eds.), *Approaches to Global Intellectual History*, New York, 3–30.
Pocock, J. G. A. (2004), "Quentin Skinner, the history of politics and the politics of history," *Common Knowledge* 10: 532–50.
Printy, M. (2009), "Skinner and Pocock in Context: Early Modern Political Thought," *History and Theory* 48: 113–21.
Rüsen, J. (ed.) (2002), *Western Historical Thinking. An Intercultural Debate*, New York.
Sartori, A. (2010), "The Transfiguration of Duty in Aurobindo's Essay on the Gita," *Modern Intellectual History* 7: 319–34.
Skinner, Q. (1969), "Meaning and Understanding in the History of Ideas," *History and Theory* 8: 3–53.
Steinmetz, G. (2008), "Logics of History as a Framework for an Integrated Social Science," *Social Science History* 32: 535–54.
Strohm, P. (2010), "Historicity without Historicism," *postmedieval: a journal of medieval cultural studies* 1: 380–91.
Tucker, H. F. (2011), "Context?," *New Literary History* 42: vii–xii.
Wickham, C. (1985), "The Uniqueness of the East," *Journal of Peasant Studies* 12: 166–96.

Ibn Farīghūn's *Jawāmiʿ al-ʿulūm*:

Between Classification of Sciences and Mirror for Princes

Hinrich Biesterfeldt

IBN FARĪGHŪN IS A *homo unius libri*, and the little we know about him is hidden in the three extant manuscripts of his one book, *Jawāmiʿ al-ʿulūm*, "The Summaries, or Compendium, of the Sciences," a classification of all knowledge that may have been relevant to a court secretary of the fourth century Hijra.[1] The title pages of all three manuscripts tell us that the author was a student of the polymath Abū Zayd al-Balkhī (d. 322/934), known to contemporary scholarship mainly as an innovative geographer of the Islamic world and, as the bibliographies of Ibn al-Nadīm and Yāqūt tell us, himself an author of a classification of the sciences, *Aqsām al-ʿulūm* (not extant).[2] One manuscript bears the additional information that the dedicatee of *Jawāmiʿ* is Abū ʿAlī Aḥmad b. Muḥammad b. al-Muẓaffar, a Muḥtājid ruler (d. 344/955), governing Chaghāniyān, a province located on the right bank of the river Oxus in the basin of the Sorkhān river.[3] This scanty information places Ibn Farīghūn's *scripsit* in the middle of the fourth/tenth century and connects his scholarship with the Eastern Iranian intellectual tradition of al-Kindī (d. before 252/866), to which the author's teacher Abū Zayd belongs, as well as al-Kindī's student Aḥmad b. al-Ṭayyib al-Sarakhsī (died in prison 286/899) and Abū Zayd's student, the philosopher Abū l-Ḥasan al-ʿĀmirī (d. 381/992). The Muḥtājids served as vassals of the Sāmānids in the time of Ibn Farīghūn, and later, in the first decades of the 5th/11th century, probably as vassals of the Ghaznavids; after that, their name disappears from history. Abū ʿAlī Aḥmad, the recipient of *Jawāmiʿ*, is certainly the most important member of the Āl-i Muḥtāj: for fifteen years, under the Sāmānid amirs Naṣr b. Aḥmad (d. 331/943) and Nūḥ b. Naṣr (d. 343/954), he secured their domination over northern Iran, curbing the separatist forces of the local Daylamī and Kurd-

1. I wish to thank Professor Peter Adamson, Munich, for his valuable remarks on the penultimate version of this paper. On the manuscripts and editions of, and studies on, *Jawāmiʿ*, see Biesterfeldt 2012b.

2. See Biesterfeldt 2012a.

3. See Bosworth 1990.

ish rulers, extending Sāmānid authority to the West as far as Hamadān and Dīnawar, and even taking Rayy. His political and military vigor in fact led him to rebel against his dismissal by Nūḥ, after 331/943, upon charges of harsh and high-handed governorship over Khurāsān, and to try to install another Sāmānid prince on the throne of Bukhārā. Abū ʿAlī's political progress finally faltered; in the end he took refuge in Jibāl with the Būyids where he died, together with one of his sons, of the plague. The geographer Ibn Ḥawqal, writing in 367/988, praises Abū ʿAlī's chivalry (*uswāriyya*), but regrets his rebellion against his master.[4] While the political contents of Ibn Farīghūn's *Jawāmiʿ* may have appealed to Abū ʿAlī's sense of *riyāsa* and *siyāsa* (to quote Ibn Ḥawqal again), it is also noteworthy that the Muḥtājids were known as patrons of a number of significant Persian poets.[5]

Ibn Farīghūn's links with the Āl-i Muḥtāj cannot be further substantiated. His own name points to yet another minor Iranian dynasty, the Āl-i Farīghūn, which flourished in Gūzgān (Gūzgānān, or in Arabized form, Jūzjān, what is today in northern Afghanistan) from some time before the beginning of the 4th/10th century until the advent of the Ghaznavids in the early 5th/11th century and which played various political and military roles in the Sāmānid period.[6] One of the Farīghūnids, Abū l-Ḥārith Aḥmad, married his daughter to the Sāmānid ruler Nūḥ b. Manṣūr (r. 365–387/976–997). Abū l-Ḥārith, incidentally, is also the dedicatee of the anonymous Persian geographical work *Ḥudūd al-ʿālam*. As V. Minorsky has pointed out,[7] it is quite conceivable that our Ibn Farīghūn is "a scion of the ruling house, or of one of its lateral branches. It is hard to imagine a commoner calling himself Ibn Farīghūn at a time when the Banū Farīghūn were still ruling."[8]

In his article, Minorsky ventures an interesting hypothesis concerning the identity of the unknown author of *Ḥudūd al-ʿālam*, mentioned above, and Ibn Farīghūn, the author of *Jawāmiʿ al-ʿulūm*. Since both works belong to the same region, Gūzgān, and the same period (the composition of *Ḥudūd* was begun in 372/982), since both works display the tone of an author belong-

4. For the Muḥtājids and Abū ʿAlī's career, see Bosworth 1981 and Bosworth 1985b, references to Ibn Ḥawqal's *Ṣūrat al-arḍ* are given in the latter article, p. 765.

5. Bosworth 1985b, 766.

6. For a tentative genealogy of the Farīghūnids and an account of their role in the Sāmānid period, cf. Bosworth 1985a.

7. Minorsky 1964, 328.

8. Both "Farīʿūn" and "Furayʿūn" are unwarranted readings. The initial *ism* (given name) still awaits decipherment. MS Topkapı Sarayı 2768 has m-undotted hook-gh-b-y, MS Topkapı Sarayı 2675 has m-n-ʿ-n-y, and MS Escurial 950 has sh-ʿ-y-*alif mamdūda*. Readings such as "Shaʿyā," or "Mutaghabbī," or "Mubtaghā" (for the latter two, cf. Ritter 1950, 83) are most probably wrong. I agree with Minorsky's suggestion that perhaps "the scribes were embarrassed by some local Iranian appellation" (ibid.).

ing to the ruling class, not that "of a dependent commoner," and since both works refrain from elaborate prose (*Ḥudūd* consisting of maps accompanied by a brief description, *Jawāmiʿ* presenting its contents in the synoptic fashion of *tashjīr* – for which see below), their authors, according to Minorsky,[9] may well be the same person. The transition from the Arabic *Jawāmiʿ* to the Persian *Ḥudūd* might even "be a token of the new literary tendencies encouraged under the Sāmānids,"[10] and finally, the composition of *Ḥudūd* might be interpreted as a compensation for the omission of the discipline of geography in *Jawāmiʿ*. Minorsky himself admits that his arguments are "certainly indirect." In the first instance, there is no reference in the former text to the latter. Geography is not the only discipline that is missing from Ibn Farīghūn's work; this is probably due to the fact that geography – similar to historiography – has no established place in traditional classifications of the sciences. At a closer look, the sense for geographical *realia* and details that governs *Ḥudūd* stands in stark contrast to the systematic rigor of *Jawāmiʿ*. All in all, Minorsky's ingenious hypothesis still awaits corroboration from sources other than *Ḥudūd* and *Jawāmiʿ*.

Jawāmiʿ al-ʿulūm constitutes a fascinating and complex text. It is, with only very few exceptions, arranged in the so-called *tashjīr* format, the presentation of a given discipline or an aspect of Islamic statecraft as arboreal diagrams. This peculiar layout, documented from the third/ninth century onwards (and generally not widely attested), may have its roots in Greek scholarly literature of late antiquity. It was used primarily for Arabic textbooks on medicine and logic. *Tashjīr* is particularly conducive to a clear and systematic organization of encyclopaedic materials, and to making that content retrievable. It visualizes the hierarchy of knowledge and highlights the derivation of specific (the "branches") from general terms (the "trunks"), and foregrounds the interdependence of *all* fields of knowledge. A brief sketch of the contents of *Jawāmiʿ* will immediately show its peculiar blend of three major components: the Aristotelian system of the "philosophical" sciences, fields of Islamic scholarship, and the categories of statecraft and *Fürstenspiegel*:[11] Two fairly extensive blocks frame *Jawāmiʿ* – in the beginning, a chapter on Arabic grammar (mainly concerning the morphology of verbs, nouns, and particles), and in the end, a chapter on the occult sciences. Between these sections the sequence of subjects is roughly the following:

9. Minorsky 1964, 331–2.

10. For this development, see Fragner 1999 and Meisami 1999, 289–94.

11. For a closer description of the functions (and textual pitfalls) of *tashjīr* and more information on the contents of *Jawāmiʿ*, see Biesterfeldt 2012b; for analyses of selected chapters of *Jawāmiʿ*, see Biesterfeldt 1990 and 2008.

Professional skills of the court secretary (*kātib*, viz., *al-kharāj*, *al-jund*, *al-barīd*, *al-ḥākim*, "land tax, army, postal communication, judgeship," etc.), the rules of accounting, calligraphy and official correspondence that he has to observe, his ethical prerequisites for dealing with the ruler and his subjects - ethics of the ruler - politics and warfare - theology and religious duties - sources of knowledge, the parts of Aristotelian philosophy, and finally, forms and methods of scholarly transmission.

The subjects sketched here resonate clearly with salient features of mirrors for princes, insofar as they deal with the religious and moral foundations of political sovereignty.[12] However, they also touch on the practical infrastructure of the court and the chancery business (*inshā'*, "official correspondence," penmanship, etc.); on the other hand they transcend the mirror genre in classifying categories of theology, philosophy, and scholarship in general. In the following, I shall present and analyze three sections from *Jawāmi'* which are meant to illustrate its double function as a classification of the sciences and as a *Fürstenspiegel* which is characteristic of Ibn Farīghūn's work: history (*tārīkh*), virtues of the ruler, and various elements showing a politically "integrative" tendency of *Jawāmi'*. My references indicate the facsimile edition by F. Sezgin (hereafter "facsimile") and the (not altogether reliable) edition by al-Janābī (hereafter "edition").

History. On a double page (facsimile: 134–5/edition: 235–40), towards the end of the sequence of subjects which I have just sketched, the dominating catchword is "knowledge" (*'ilm*). It is divided into "linguistic expressions" (*alfāẓ*)[13] and, on the opposite page, "ideas" (*ma'ānī*), which, in strange asymmetry, in fact deal with the objects of historiography (*'ilm al-tārīkhāt*).[14] History comprises

> the mention of famous events which occurred in past times or over extensive periods, such as a ruinous deluge, a destructive earthquake, epidemics, or famines which annihilate nations; the names of famous rulers in the (various) regions, their number, days, and the length of their reigns, and the transfer (of rule) from one (house) to another; knowledge of the beginning of creation and its return (to its origins; that is, the events surrounding the End of Days); and the physical and intellectual conditions of previous ages. But this (knowledge)

12. Cf. the general remarks in Lambton 1971, 419.

13. I have dealt with this interesting exposition of various forms of communication in Biesterfeldt 2008.

14. Cf. Rosenthal 1968, 34–6 (translation), 539–40 (edition). I am making use of the translation by Meisami 1999, 8–9. The author of the Cairo edition misreads *tārīkhāt* as *nāranjāt*, linking it, p. 238, note 3, to *nayraj*, "deception"!

> may be contaminated by falsification because of remoteness in time. ... Only that should be accepted which is spoken of in books or in reliable accounts. [Further objects of historiography are:] accounts of the Prophet's birth, his mission, his battles and his circumstances up to the time of his death, which are useful for political matters and warfare against enemies; knowledge of the lives of the caliphs of Quraysh, their conquests, administration, the civil strife that took place between those contending for leadership from among the Khārijites (or: rebels) and from the time of the transfer of rule from the Umayyads to the Hāshimites, so that these may provide object lessons (*'ibar*) concerning the vicissitudes of time.

As still further objects of historiography Ibn Farīghūn enumerates the battle days (*al-ayyām*) of the Arabs, the history of the tribes which contains "sundry sayings and poems," the books and histories of Iranians, such as the *Testament* of Ardashīr Bābakān, the orations of Anūshirwān, and the *Kārnāmak* "which is useful for statecraft, forging political authority and of dealing with the grievances of the subjects" (*fī bāb al-siyāsa wa l-umūr al-sulṭāniyya wa l-qiyām bi-maẓālim al-ra'āyā*),[15] and finally the wise sayings of famous rulers and of persons of noble birth, scholars, secretaries, eloquent men, poets, and persons of outstanding virtues.

A parallel passage, *ādāb al-kuttāb* (facsimile: 56/edition: 107), adds to these works *Kalīla wa Dimna*, a collection of fables, repeats the necessary knowledge of historical dates, specifying the "three nations" (Persians, Byzantines, and Muslim Arabs), and addresses the linguistic and stylistic skills (*kalām*) necessary for the secretary of state.[16]

This collection of the objects of historiography, or of historical interest, is indicative of a deep conviction shared by professional historians contemporary with Ibn Farīghūn, such as al-Mas'ūdī (d. 345/956) and Miskawayh (d. 421/1030):[17] The advent of Islam is a central part of history. More specifically, history offers its students examples to be followed, and in particular provides the ruler with models to be re-enacted. History is not merely information on past times but a matter of moral requirement (and of aesthetic

15. For the Sasanian tradition of political advice, linked to Ardashīr, cf. de Fouchécour 1986, 84–100.

16. Cf. Rosenthal 1968, 52 (summary) with note 3, indicating similar passages in a twelfth-century *Fürstenspiegel*, *Īḍāḥ al-masālik wa tadbīr al-duwal wa l-mamālik*, and by other authors. "The absence of any reference to later dynasties and, above all, the absence of any theological elements as well as the comparatively minor position assigned to the history of Muḥammad and to that of scholars and cities would seem to be characteristic of the tenth century." (p. 36)

17. For respective quotations from *Murūj al-dhahab* and *Tajārib al-umam*, see Meisami 1999, 6–7.

edification). "[G]ood government is linked with the ruler's virtue, and the lessons of history are moral ones."[18] And the principal representative of the ruler, the *kātib*, and following him, every educated man, *adīb*, should have a command of historical knowledge to contribute to social gatherings.[19] A second characteristic of Ibn Farīghūn's passage is the fusion of Arabic, pre-Islamic and Islamic history and Sasanian (literary) tradition. Both elements, the ethical function of history and the combination of Arabic and Iranian traditions, are central features of the Islamic mirrors for princes of the classical period. The passage on history combines (a) the systematic exposition of the main elements of its subject matter to be known with (b) the way in which this knowledge should be applied – the aim of (a) might be called encyclopaedic, that of (b) is characteristic of the *Fürstenspiegel.*

The virtues of the ruler. A second area in which *Jawāmi'* is shaped by principal *Fürstenspiegel* concepts is the description of the ideal ruler and his secretaries. An elaborate page of *tashjīr* (facsimile: 78/edition: 144–5) shows the necessary virtues of the ruler (the headline is: *lā yakūnu l-maliku illā fāḍilan*, "the ruler is virtuous only if..."). I summarize: The *faḍīla* ("virtuousness") of the ruler is threefold –

> *bodily virtue* (strong chivalry, ability to wield the weapon – good appearance – or both);[20]
>
> *mental virtue*, "of perfect disposition, without superfluity or deficiency, or crookedness or blemish";
>
> - virtues of concupiscence (*shahwa*): courage (!) – chastity (*'iffa*) – contentedness (*qanā'a*);
> - virtues of aggression (*ghaḍab*): courage – endurance – calm/insight (*ḥilm*) – generosity – forgiveness – pardon – openhandedness (*raḥb al-dhirā'*) – discretion;
> - virtues of intellect (*tamyīz*): clearness of expression (*bayān*) – wisdom – common sense (*iṣābat ra'y*) – judiciousness (*ḥazm*) – sincerity

18. Meisami 1999, 7.

19. The famous Umayyad secretary 'Abd al-Ḥamīd (d. 132/750) advises his colleagues in his *Risāla* to first gain an understanding of religious matters, then of the Arabic language, of prose and poetry, and then of "both Arab and non-Arab political events, and ... the tales of (both groups) and the biographies describing them, as that will be helpful to you in your endeavours ..." (from the quotation given in Ibn Khaldūn's *Muqaddima*, 2:30–1).

20. This aspect is complemented in loving detail in a separate *tashjīr* on the same page, depicting the physique of the hero, branching out to such assets as light complexion (which indicates "purity of blood"), strong voice, etc., and losing itself in anatomical terminology. On the problem of the bodily appearance of the ruler, see Hans-Joachim Schmidt's contribution in the present volume.

(*ṣidq*) – ? *w-n-alif mamdūda* – mercy (*raḥma*) – shyness (*ḥayāʾ*) – high-mindedness (*ʿiẓam himma*) – reliability in contracts (*ḥusn ʿahd*) – humility (*tawāḍuʿ*);

virtue due to (innate) nobility and dignity (*wa faḍīla bi-sabab al-majd* [MSS *li-l-majd*] *wa l-sharaf*).

The last class of virtue is difficult to categorize. The delineation suggests that it is the counterpart of both the others. Perhaps what is meant is that physical and mental virtues are to be acquired and practiced and that only few privileged human beings – one might think of the ruler – are endowed with "original" virtue from their birth. A similar notion is discussed in Aristotle's *Eudemian Ethics* in chapter VIII (on the ethical relevance of Good Fortune, *eutychia*, and its impact on Good Actions, *eupragia*) where an alternative theory of virtue is introduced. Many people think, Aristotle says, "that [men performing good actions] are so *by nature*, and it is nature which puts certain qualities in them" (1247a10–11). It would be difficult, however, to trace the tradition of this notion and to point out the stage at which the additional aspect of "nobility and dignity" for the privileged bearers of this last class of virtue was introduced.[21]

The middle branch is of particular interest. The *faḍāʾil* of the ruler are grouped according to the three faculties of the soul, the "concupiscent," the "aggressive," and the "rational," which corresponds to the tripartite exposition of the human soul in Platonic ethics (*epithymētikos* 'concupiscent soul', *thymoeidēs* 'aggressive soul', *logistikos* 'rational soul'). It was widespread in Islamic ethical literature, conceivably through the medical and ethical writings of Galen of Pergamon (d. around 216 CE).[22] Among works on philosophical ethics proper that introduced Platonic psychology into Islamic ethics, Ps.-Aristotle's *On virtues and vices* might be singled out. This brief treatise was translated into Arabic twice, by Theodore Abū Qurra (d. around 205/820) and Abū l-Faraj Ibn al-Ṭayyib (d. 435/1043), and it starts out with naming the three faculties of the soul, associating the rational one with the virtue of wisdom (*ḥikma*), the aggressive one with the virtues of circumspection, calm and courage (*tathabbut, ḥilm, shajāʿa*), and the concupiscent one with "chastity and refraining from aiding the bodily pleasures" (*ʿiffa, al-imtināʿ min*

21. A parallel notion is vented by Socrates, at the very end of Plato's *Menon*, where he suggests that, resulting from an argument just discussed, virtue may arrive at someone by "divine allotment" (*theiai moirai*, 100b2). Ibn Farīghūn does not introduce the term *fiṭra*, "natural, innocent disposition, such as of newborns," here or elsewhere.

22. For the Platonic model, cf. Büttner 2006, for Galen's adaptation, cf. Tielemann 2003 and Schiefsky 2012.

musāʿadat al-shahawāt).[23] Ibn Farīghūn may be one of the first *Fürstenspiegel* authors to make use of the Platonic/Galenian system of virtues. The synopsis below shows common classifications of the ruler's virtues as they figure, from left to right, in *Jawāmiʿ*, Yaḥyā b. ʿAdī's (d. 363/974) *Tahdhīb al-akhlāq*, a standard text of Hellenistic ethics, and perhaps Ibn Farīghūn's source, and a *Fürstenspiegel* of the 7th/13th century, *Sulūk al-mālik fī tadbīr al-mamālik* by Ibn Abī l-Rabīʿ. Yaḥyā lists twenty virtues in all to which twenty vices correspond; almost all of them have their place in one of the three parts of the soul and are presented systematically.[24] Kings are not supposed to attain the highest degree of the theoretical way of life for themselves, but are called upon to appear to lead a virtuous life and to appoint the most qualified advisors for their political tasks.[25] It is in this context that Yaḥyā most clearly introduces concepts of the *Fürstenspiegel* into his ethics. The mirror for princes by Ibn Abī l-Rabīʿ, in its inventory of keywords and its penchant for enumeration and delineation, resembles Ibn Farīghūn's *Jawāmiʿ*;[26] its system of virtues, however, is far more formalized: It includes mention of the seat of the faculties of the soul within the human body and a classification of the virtues (and vices) according to ideal equilibrium (*iʿtidāl*), and excess and deficiency, of a given faculty.[27] All in all, a strikingly consistent system of virtues emerges, ethically defined by Yaḥyā and applied to a mirror for princes by Ibn Farīghūn and Ibn Abī l-Rabīʿ:[28]

23. I quote from Ibn al-Ṭayyib's version, Ps.-Aristotle, *Faḍīla*, 66, lines 10–14. The editor points out that Theodore's version was dedicated to Ṭāhir b. al-Ḥusayn (see below, with note 33) and that this may have contributed to his introducing Hellenistic ethical concepts into his *Fürstenspiegel* (Ps.-Aristotle, *Faḍīla*, 24).

24. Yaḥyā b. ʿAdī, *Tahdhīb al-akhlāq*, 84–7 (*al-tamām wa l-mulk*). Cf. Endress 2012, 323 and 324 (for the difference between the theoretical and the practical way of life).

25. Cf. Hatem 1985.

26. As already noted by Ritter 1950, 83, who dates the *Sulūk* as "perhaps rather old all the same" ("vielleicht doch ziemlich alt").

27. Cf. Ibn Abī l-Rabīʿ, *Sulūk al-mālik fī tadbīr al-mamālik*, 70–2. For the authorship and date of the *Sulūk*, see Plessner 1928, 30–5; cf. further al-Takrītī [2]1980 (not seen). The aspects of "equilibrium," *ziyāda* and *nuqṣān* obviously have their origin in Aristotelian ethics, probably by way of Miskawayh's *Tahdhīb al-akhlāq*.

28. The terminology of virtues is obviously open to interpretation. My English translations only aim at approximate meanings. Square brackets indicate my suggestion of editorial deletion, to be explained in the text.

Ibn Farīghūn	Yaḥyā b. ʿAdī	Ibn Abī l-Rabīʿ
quwwat shahwa 'faculty of concupiscence'	*al-quwwa al-shahwāniyya*	*al-quwwa al-shahwāniyya*
[*shajāʿa*] 'courage'	—	—
ʿiffa 'chastity'	*ʿiffa*	*ʿiffa*
qanāʿa 'contentedness'	*qanāʿa*	*qanāʿa*
quwwat ghaḍab 'faculty of aggressiveness'	*al-quwwa al-ghaḍabiyya*	*al-quwwa al-ghaḍabiyya*
shajāʿa 'courage'	*shajāʿa*	*shajāʿa*
ṣabr 'endurance'	*ṣabr*	*iḥtimāl al-kadd* (?) 'suffering of toil'
ḥilm 'calm, insight'	*ḥilm*	*ḥilm*
karam 'generosity'	—	*kibr al-nafs* (?) 'hubris, megalopsychia'
ṣafḥ 'forgiveness'	—	—
ʿafw 'pardon'	—	*ʿafw*
raḥb dhirāʿ 'openhandedness'	*sakhāʾ* (?) 'generosity'	—
[*kitmān al-sirr*] 'discretion'	—	—
quwwat tamyīz 'faculty of intellect'	*al-quwwa al-nāṭiqa* 'rational faculty'	*al-quwwa al-nāṭiqa*
bayān 'clearness of expression'	—	*nuṭq* 'enunciation'
ḥikma 'wisdom'	—	*ḥikma*
iṣābat raʾy 'common sense'	—	—
ḥazm 'judiciousness'	—	—
ṣidq 'sincerity'	*ṣidq al-lahja* 'sincerity of expression'[29]	*ṣidq*
wnʾ (?) (see below)	—	—
raḥma 'mercy'	*raḥma*	—
ḥayāʾ 'shyness'	—	—
ʿiẓam himma 'high-mindedness'	*ʿiẓam al-himma*	—
ḥusn ʿahd 'reliability in contracts'	*adāʾ al-amāna* 'performance of trustworthiness'	—
tawāḍuʿ 'humility'	*tawāḍuʿ*	—

29. *WKAS* II 1501–2 collects numerous examples for *ṣdq* with *lahja*, the first of which, *ṣādiq al-lahja*, translating Greek *to homilēsai orthōs* (Ps.-Aristotle, *Maqāla fī l-Faḍīla*, 65, line 22).

The conspicuous consistency of the three inventories is only slightly impaired by the fact that Yaḥyā's and more so Ibn Abī l-Rabī''s lists of terms are richer than Ibn Farīghūn's; besides, Yaḥyā's list[30] does not always correlate a given virtue to its part of the soul. Not all correspondences between the three lists are established. Ibn Farīghūn's *raḥb dhirā'*, tentatively equated with Yaḥyā's *sakhā'* (Greek *eleutheriotēs?*), is one such dubious case, Ibn Farīghūn's *karam* and Ibn Abī l-Rabī''s *kibr al-nafs* (*hubris, megalopsychia?*) is another. The *crux wn'* might be a garbled *wudd* ("friendship"); this appears in Yaḥyā's list, albeit without clear attribution to a part of the soul, and would fit the context of *raḥma* and *ḥayā'*.[31] The first occurrence of *shajā'a* under *quwwat shahwa* is obviously a dittography; *kitmān al-sirr* at the very end of *quwwat ghaḍab* should probably rather be attached to *quwwat tamyīz* (where Ibn Abī l-Rabī' and, not quite explicitly, Yaḥyā locate it). Not all the *faḍā'il* listed by Ibn Farīghūn constitute a plausible sequence. But what is important in this context is that the fusion of Hellenistic ethical concepts and Arabic and Iranian virtues which this passage displays seems to be characteristic of a branch of mirrors for princes which G. Richter calls "philosophische Fürstenspiegel,"[32] and which D. Gutas, quoting from Ṭāhir b. al-Ḥusayn's (d. 207/822) letter to his son 'Abd Allāh, describes as a constitutive element, used by Ibn Khaldūn (d. 808/1406), in his *Muqaddima*, to provide "a theoretical and analytical basis for [his inquiries into the origin and decay of civilizations] and to further a continuing appreciation of these writings as political documents, [an esteem] which was able to influence administrative politics."[33]

30. Yaḥyā b. 'Adī, *Tahdhīb al-akhlāq*, 69–75.

31. For *wudd* = *mawadda*, Greek *agapē*, cf. Walzer 1963, 227.

32. Richter 1932, 104–5. Writing on Miskawayh, he argues: "Finally, we are taught about the syncretistic tendencies [of Islamic *Fürstenspiegel*, H. B.] by the classical author on the system of Islamic ethics himself, Miskawayh, who has, beside his [*Tahdhīb al-*] *akhlāq*, published an exemplary extensive collection of wise sayings [Lebensweisheiten], culled from Persian, Greek, Arabic, or Indian traditions. ... From this, one can infer the high degree to which the Near Eastern ethical tradition – in particular its Persian sources – has modified the schooling in the ethical system of Greek practical philosophy." ("Über die synkretistischen Tendenzen belehrt uns schließlich der Klassiker islamisch-methodischer Ethik Miskawaihi selbst, der neben seinen aḫlāq beispielsweise auch ein großes Sammelwerk überlieferter Lebensweisheiten, aus persischen, griechischen, arabischen oder indischen Traditionen exzerpiert, herausgegeben hat. ... Man kann hieraus ersehen, wie stark wieder die vorderasiatische ethische Überlieferung, besonders soweit sie aus persischer Tradition herzuleiten ist, in ihrem Sinne auch die methodisch-ethische Schulung an der praktischen Philosophie der Griechen korrigiert hat.")

33. Gutas 1990, 358 (my translation), cf. also Richter 1932, 80–6. The entire letter of Ṭāhir, the general of the caliph al-Ma'mūn (r. 198–218/813–33), is quoted in Ibn Khaldūn's *Muqaddima*, 2: 140–56. Ibn Khaldūn reports in conclusion that "[a]l-Ma'mūn heard about it. When it had been read to him, he said: ... 'Ṭāhir did not omit any of the matters that concern this

Integrative elements. A third aspect concerns a politically "integrative" tendency of *Jawāmi'* which is a common objective of mirrors for princes. According to them, the ideal political rule is itself ruled by the principle of justice. The embodiment of justice is the ruler. According to Sasanian tradition, kingship "centres on the sultan divinely endowed with justice and knowledge and identifies his regime with justice, which is seen as the harmonious ordering of society."[34] The ideal ruler safeguards social hierarchy.[35] In Islamic history and its *Fürstenspiegel* concepts, classes changed, but the ideal of an integrative society remained. A later mirror for princes, *Baḥr al-fawā'id*, written in Persian, equals the subjects of the ruler to the family of God, "and whoever vexed them grieved God and would be called to account on the day of resurrection."[36] Ibn Farīghūn's *Jawāmi' al-'ulūm* displays a more abstract understanding of social coherence: Its most obvious manifestation is the frequent listing of members of the court in particular, and members of society in general. Each of both types of lists constitutes a unity which cannot function without any of its members. In systematizing the rules, *sharā'i'*, of *jihād*, the author discusses various legal problems concerning the status of the adversaries, types of treaties and regulation of the booty and resumes: "Concerning the legal situation (*al-ḥukm*) between the *dār al-Islām* and the *dār al-ḥarb*, nobody can assume [this responsibility] but a politically astute (*sā'is*) and excellent *imām* who deems his subjects as parts of his body and does not differentiate between remote and close ones." (facsimile: 75/ edition: 140, read *illā imām* instead of *al-imām*.) A variation and generalization of this popular idea expressing the organic structure of society appears at the beginning of a passage entitled *al-qawl* [*fī*] *l-'adl* 'justice': "This world is created, in regard of what divine wisdom has decreed for the position of everything in its place and for the affairs of people, in the best possible manner. The need for this world has the same weight as that for the other

world, the religion, administration, (the formation of) opinion, politics, the improvement of the realm and the subjects, the preservation of the government, obedience to the caliphs, and maintenance of the caliphate. He has dealt very well with all these matters, and has given directions (how to handle) them.'" (p. 156)

34. Lambton 1971, 419.

35. "Wahrung der Rangordnungen," in Richter 1932, 44, with note 2, referring to a model ascribed to Ardashīr: high nobility and the princes - theologians and the superintendants of the sacred fire - physicians, scribes, and astrologers - peasants, artisans, etc.

36. Lambton 1971, 430, with an interesting list of the ruler's duties to keep justice in society. On the work which "has some of the characteristics of an encyclopaedic work in the wide range of subjects it covers" (p. 426) and which advocates a "harmonious relationship of society in a divinely ordered system" (p. 442), see Lambton 1971, 426–36; de Fouchécour 1986, 263–75; for the anonymous author and the edition and the English translation of his work, cf. van Ess 2011, 1331–2.

world; both worlds are not contrary, but complementary, to each other, each implicating its counterpart." (facsimile: 126–7/edition: 226–7) One would assume that this passage – one of the very few parts of *Jawāmiʿ* not organized in *tashjīr*, but composed as a coherent prose text – goes on to discuss the relation between divine justice and the justice of the ruler, but what follows is a vigorous admonition of the "inhabitants of this world" to take care, everyone in his allotted place, of his own subsistence and not to put his trust in the compassion and help of his fellow beings. In this passage the concept of human society as an organism is subsumed under the concept of human life in "both worlds" which complement each other. Much as these general concepts are at work in *Jawāmiʿ* and however frequent the ranks of members of the court and of society are invoked,[37] the central symbol of social integration is, perhaps more than the ruler, the secretary, *al-kātib*. Ideally, he encompasses all the knowledge necessary for the welfare of the state, and he has a decisive position between the ruler and the ruled. Right after the introductory exposition of Arabic grammar, at the beginning of the section on the office of the secretary, *al-kitāba*, which is divided into writing proper (artfully defined as "clarity [*bayān*] manifesting in written form [*rasm*] what was latent") and accounting, the main responsibilities of the *kuttāb* are sketched. Their central position in society is phrased as follows: "There is no basis for the subjects (*al-raʿiyya*) but in kingship, and they are in need of secretaries who stand between them [and the king]. In the secretaries there is incorporated the education (*adab*) of the kings and the humility (*tawāḍuʿ*, cf. the list of *faḍāʾil* given above) of the subjects (*al-sūqa*)." (facsimile: 51/edition: 99, with atrocious misreadings) Following this statement, four prerequisites of the *kuttāb* are named: (moral, or religious) rectitude in their conduct of life (*taqwīm sīratihī wa madhhabihī*, which is elaborately subdivided), proper

37. The list of *kuttāb* has already been mentioned: *kātib al-kharāj, al-jund, al-barīd, al-ḥākim, al-ḍiyāʿ, kitābat al-khazn li-l-zīna* (MSS *li-l-zayn*) *wa l-ʿudda* (facsimile: 65–8/edition: 123–7; the last peculiar office, apparently a local specialty, is concerned with the administration of representative items such as jewellery, weapons, precious garments). Another list of court officials is assembled in facsimile: 89–90/edition: 166–71: *al-wazīr, al-ḥākim, ṣāʾin al-mamlaka, lisān al-malik, al-ḥājib, al-muḥtasib, ṣāḥib al-khabar, ṣāḥib khabar al-ʿummāl, al-rasūl, al-nadīm, al-ṭabīb* ("vizier, judge, protector of the kingdom, spokesman of the ruler, chamberlain, supervisor of the market trades, head of intelligence, head of intelligence of the governors of provinces, messenger, boon companion, physician"). For an example of a classification of society in general, cf. facsimile: 131/edition: 232–3: *al-nās arbaʿ ṭabaqāt: mulūk, ʿulamāʾ, ḥukamāʾ, ʿummār al-arḍ* ("mankind is divided in four strata: rulers, (religious) scholars, (secular) scholars/philosophers, cultivators of the earth") . The task of the kings is to follow the path of justice and beneficence, to safeguard political and religious order, and to defend their realm against enemies; the *ʿulamāʾ* are expected to cultivate the knowledge of God (*taʿarruf ilā Llāh*); the *ḥukamāʾ* are the guardians of the public welfare and givers of advice (*taqdīm al-naṣīḥa*); the "cultivators of the earth" take care of husbandry and commerce.

command of social intercourse with rulers, equals and followers, acquisition of knowledge (*ʿulūm*) and [its] instruments for the perfection of his craft, and its implementation (*ijrāʾ al-tadbīr fī stiʿmālihā*). This is the role of the secretary in a nutshell: Without him, both the ruler and the subjects are helpless; for the proper accomplishment of his duties he needs a unique combination of ethical, social, intellectual and practical skills.[38] As reflected in this passage, Ibn Farīghūn's work appears to cover a wide array of skills required for the maintenance of social stability and good rule in an era marked by intellectual vivacity in the face of political turbulence.

Thus it will have become clear, I hope, why I have situated *Jawāmiʿ al-ʿulūm* at the border "between classification of sciences and mirror for princes." Like its contemporary classifications of the sciences – echoed in al-Khwārazmī's *Mafātīḥ al-ʿulūm* (shortly after 367/977), al-Fārābī's (d. 339/950) venerable *Iḥṣāʾ al-ʿulūm*, Abū l-Ḥasan al-ʿĀmirī's improvised systematization of the philosophical and the religious sciences in his *al-Iʿlām bi-manāqib al-Islām*, to name but a few[39] – *Jawāmiʿ* strives to present a coherent system of knowledge, integrating and correlating the Islamic and "foreign" – mostly Hellenistic – fields of knowledge. They show "what is," and one might characterize their aim as *ontological. Jawāmiʿ* certainly follows this aim, if in a peculiarly abbreviative and sketchy manner. At the same time, they contain substantial parts which, as I have tried to show, deal with topics common to *Fürstenspiegel*. These parts – along with the chapters on religious principles and duties – reflect "what ought to be," and one might characterize their claim as *deontological.*

It is not easy to determine the actual purpose of *Jawāmiʿ*. Its scanty manuscript tradition and more importantly the fact that it is not referenced in later works and that the name of its author was completely forgotten, together suggest that the combination of "encyclopaedia" and *Fürstenspiegel* represents a dead end. For future research in the tradition of *Fürstenspiegel*, however, *Jawāmiʿ* constitutes a fascinating source.

38. In dwelling on the central position of the secretary, Ibn Farīghūn draws on a distinct literary tradition starting with al-Kindī; for him, see F. Rosenthal 1942; for Abū Zayd al-Balkhī, see Biesterfeldt 2012a, 162, nos. 96–104.

39. For these classifications of the sciences, see Biesterfeldt 2000.

Bibliography

[Ps.-Aristotle, *Maqāla fī l-Faḍīla*] Kellermann, M. (1965), *Ein pseudoaristotelischer Traktat über die Tugend ...*, PhD dissertation, Erlangen-Nürnberg.

Biesterfeldt, H. H. (1990), "Ibn Farīġūn's Chapter on Arabic Grammar in his Compendium of the Sciences," in: K. Versteegh and M. G. Carter (eds.),

Studies in the History of Arabic Grammar 2, Amsterdam, Philadelphia, 49–56.
—— (2000), "Medieval Arabic Encyclopedias of Science and Philosophy," in: S. Harvey (ed.), *The Medieval Hebrew Encyclopedias of Science and Philosophy* ..., Dordrecht, Boston, London, 77–98, repr. in: P. E. Pormann (ed.), *Islamic Medical and Scientific Tradition*, 4 vols., London, New York 2011, 1: 48–67.
—— (2008), "Ibn Farīghūn on Communication," in: P. Adamson (ed.), *In the Age of al-Fārābī. Arabic Philosophy in the Fourth/Tenth Century*, London, Turin, 265–76.
—— (2012a), "Abū Zaid al-Balḫī," in: U. Rudolph (ed.), *Philosophie in der islamischen Welt*, Band 1: 8.–10. Jahrhundert, Basel, 156–67, 244–6.
—— (2012b), "Ibn Farīġūn," in: U. Rudolph (ed.), *Philosophie in der islamischen Welt*, Band 1: 8.–10. Jahrhundert, Basel, 167–70, 246–7.
Bosworth, C. E. (1981), "The Rulers of Chaghāniyān in Early Islamic Times," *Iran* 19: 1–20.
—— (1985a), "Āl-e Farīġūn," *EIr* I: 756–8.
—— (1985b), "Āl-e Moḥtāj," *EIr* I: 764–6.
—— (1990), "Čāġānīān," *EIr* IV: 614–5.
Büttner, S. (2006), "The Tripartition of the Soul in Plato's *Republic*," in F.-G. Herrmann (ed.), *New Essays on Plato. Language and Thought in Fourth-Century Greek Philosophy*, Swansea, 75–93.
Dunlop, D. M. (1950–5), "The Ǧawāmiʿ al-ʿulūm of Ibn Farīġūn," in: ... *Zeki Velidi Togana Armağan* ..., Istanbul, 348–53.
Endress, G. (2012), "Yaḥyā b. ʿAdī," in U. Rudolph (ed.), *Philosophie in der islamischen Welt*, Band 1: 8.–10. Jahrhundert, Basel, 301–24, 355–9.
van Ess, J. (2011), *Der Eine und das Andere. Beobachtungen an islamischen häresiographischen Texten*, 2 vols., Berlin, New York.
de Fouchécour, Ch.-H. (1986), *Moralia. Les notions morales dans la littérature persane du 3e/9e au 7e/13e siècle*, Paris.
Fragner, B. G. (1999), *Die „Persophonie". Regionalität, Identität und Sprachkontakt in der Geschichte Asiens*, Berlin.
Gutas, D. (1990), "Ethische Schriften im Islam," in: W. Heinrichs (ed.), *Orientalisches Mittelalter*, Wiesbaden, 346–65.
Hatem, J. (1985), "Que le roi ne peut être parfait selon Yaḥyā ibn ʿAdī," *Annales de philosophie de l'Université Saint-Joseph* 6: 89–104.
Ibn Abī l-Rabīʿ, Aḥmad b. Muḥammad (1978), *Sulūk al-mālik fī tadbīr al-mamālik*, ed. Nājī al-Takrītī, Beirut, Paris.
Ibn Farīʿūn (1985), *Compendium of the Sciences. Jawāmiʿ al-ʿulūm*, Facsimile of ms 2768, Ahmet III Collection, Topkapı Sarayı Library, ed. F. Sezgin, Frankfurt am Main. [abbreviated in the text as "facsimile"]

Ibn Farī'ūn (1328/2007), *Kitāb Jawāmi' al-'ulūm*, ed. Q.K. al-Janābī, Cairo. [abbreviated in the text as "edition"]
Ibn Khaldūn (1958), *The Muqaddimah. An introduction to history*, tr. F. Rosenthal, 3 vols., New York.
Lambton, A.K.S. (1971), "Islamic Mirrors for Princes," in *La Persia nel medioevo: Atti del Convegno internazionale, Rome, 1970*, Rome, 419–42; repr. in A.K.S. Lambton., *Theory and Practice in Medieval Persian Government*, London 1980, nr. vi.
Meisami, J. Scott (1999), *Persian Historiography. To the End of the Twelfth Century*, Edinburgh.
Minorsky, V. (1962), "Ibn Farīghūn and the Ḥudūd al-'ālam," in: W.B. Henning and E. Yarshater (eds.), *A Locust's Leg. Studies in Honour of S.H. Taqizadeh*, London, 189–96. [I am quoting from the reprint in: Minorsky, V. (1964), *Iranica. Twenty articles*, Tehran, 327–32.]
Plessner, M. (1928), *Der* OIKONOMIKOC *des Neupythagoreers 'Bryson' und sein Einfluß auf die islamische Wissenschaft ...*, Heidelberg.
Richter, G. (1932), *Studien zur Geschichte der älteren arabischen Fürstenspiegel*, Leipzig.
Ritter, H. (1950), "Philologika XIII: Arabische Handschriften in Anatolien und İstanbul (Fortsetzung)," *Oriens* 3: 31–107.
Rosenthal, F. (1942), "Al-Kindī als Literat," *Orientalia* N.S. 11, 262–88; repr. in F. Rosenthal, *Muslim intellectual and social history. A collection of essays*, Aldershot 1990, no. VI.
Rosenthal, F. (1968), *A history of Muslim historiography*, Second revised edition, Leiden.
Schiefsky, M. (2012), "Galen and the Tripartite Soul," in: R. Barney, T. Brennan and Ch. Brittain (eds.), *Plato and the Divided Self*, Cambridge, 331–49.
al-Takrītī, N. (1980), *al-Falsafa al-siyāsiyya 'ind Ibn Abī l-Rabī' ma'a taḥqīq kitābihī* Sulūk al-mālik fī tadbīr al-mamālik, 2nd edition, Beirut. [not seen]
Tielemann, T. (2003), "Galen's Psychology," in: J. Barnes and J. Jouanna (eds.), *Entretiens sur l'antiquité classique: Galien*, Vandoeuvres, 131–69.
Walzer, R. (1963), "Some Aspects of Miskawaih's *Tahdhīb al-akhlāq*," in: *Studi orientalistici in onore di Giorgio Levi Della Vida*, 2 vols., Rome 1956, 603–21. [I am quoting from the reprint in: R. Walzer, *Greek into Arabic. Essays on Islamic Philosophy*, 2nd edition, Oxford 1963, 220–35.]
WKAS = Ullmann, M., *Wörterbuch der Klassischen Arabischen Sprache*, 2 vols. in 5 parts, Wiesbaden 1970–2009.
Yaḥyā b. 'Adī (1985), *Tahdhīb al-akhlāq*, ed. J. Ḥātim, Beirut.

Scholarly and Intellectual Authority in Late Medieval European Mirrors

Charles F. Briggs

IF THE STANDARD NARRATIVE of western political thought pays little heed to the European Middle Ages, it has especially ignored those books of moral and political instruction we call mirrors for princes or *Fürstenspiegel*. Even medievalists used to pay scant attention to them, preferring instead works of a clearly polemical nature, especially those produced in conflicts between Church and State, and those dedicated to the discussion of different types of constitution.[1] With a few notable exceptions, like Wilhelm Berges, medievalists characterized mirrors as jejune, derivative, and highly standardized didacticism, offering little in the way of creative or novel ideas.[2] This long period of neglect began to change in the 1970s, as scholars started reading mirrors in the light of the European reception of Aristotelian (and pseudo-Aristotelian) moral philosophical and political ideas. Certain especially influential mirrors, like the *De regno/De regimine principum* ("On Kingship/On the Rule of Princes") of Thomas Aquinas and Ptolemy of Lucca, the *De regimine principum* of Giles of Rome, and a work believed at the time to have been by Aristotle, but in fact of Hellenistic and Arabic origin, the *Secretum secretorum* ("The Secret of Secrets"), took their place alongside thirteenth- and fourteenth-century commentaries as representatives of this reception.[3] Early confidence in the transformative, modernizing impact of Aristotle's *Ethics* and *Politics* during the thirteenth-century has since given way to more nuanced views. One tendency has been to extend the reception of certain key Aristotelian political concepts back into the twelfth century;[4] a second approach has stressed how this reception was primarily marked by the appropriation and enlistment of Aristotelian ideas, whether to help legitimize medieval realities of government or to serve Christian ends;[5] a third has emphasized the importance of classical Roman political ideas, especially

1. Lagarde 1956–70; Ullman 1975.
2. Berges 1938.
3. Ptolemy of Lucca (d. 1327), *On the Government of Rulers*; Briggs 1999; Williams 2003.
4. Nederman 1997.
5. On governance, see Blythe 1992 and Reynolds 1997, 198, 321–2; on Christianity, see Lambertini 1995; Ubl 2000; Kempshall 1999.

in the city states of late thirteenth- and early fourteenth-century northern Italy.[6]

Meanwhile, several recent works have argued that the authors of some mirrors for princes sought to effect real political change by inserting pointed, though highly coded criticisms of contemporary rulers and political situations beneath the cover of their compositions' bland, generalized language.[7] One scholar has even made the case that Giles of Rome's *De regimine principum* advocates a pragmatic, situational ethics, and thereby constitutes a genuine break with the Augustinian Christian tradition and looks forward to Machiavelli's *Prince.*[8] Several recent studies have also argued that mirrors were instrumental in the growth of a more secular and self-consciously learned vernacular political culture during the course of the fourteenth century.[9]

This essay attempts to grapple with some observations and questions that have arisen from my own work on the late medieval European reception and influence of Aristotelian moral philosophical texts, and of Giles of Rome's *De regimine principum* in particular. The texts in question reflect the teaching methods used in the universities and the schools of the mendicant friars, and the translation of these texts to a lay audience also transferred certain aspects of that academic culture to this audience.[10] This can be seen quite clearly in the reception history of Giles of Rome's mirror, which although popular with its stated target audience of princes and nobles through the medium of vernacular translations, its largest readership by far was found, in fact, in the universities and schools of the mendicant orders. In other words, if *De regimine principum*'s ostensible purpose was to teach princes how to govern themselves, their households, and their realms, its most common use was as a kind of school textbook of Aristotelian moral philosophy.[11]

The four texts discussed below belong to a sub-species of the mirrors genre, one that uses as its framework the civic virtues, and most especially the four so-called "cardinal" virtues: namely prudence, justice, fortitude, and temperance. This set of virtues, which has Platonic and Stoic roots, appealed to aristocratic Romans like Cicero and Seneca, and found its way into the Latin Christian Middle Ages through their works and via Macrobius's *Commentary on the Dream of Scipio*, as well as some remarks of Saints Ambrose,

6. Skinner 1986.
7. Ferster 1996; Nederman 1998; Grassnick 2004; Hohlstein 2007.
8. Taranto 2004.
9. Krynen 1993, 167–239; Minnis 2005; Perret 2011.
10. Briggs 2003; Briggs 2010.
11. Briggs 1999, 91–107.

Jerome, and Augustine, and the *Formula vitae honestae*, a treatise on the four cardinal virtues by the sixth-century Spanish bishop, Martin of Braga (a work which throughout the Middle Ages was ascribed to Seneca).[12]

During the Carolingian period the cardinal virtues were appreciated as divinely given attributes of the Christian prince. Then, starting in the twelfth century, some scholarly clerics like John of Salisbury and the anonymous author (once thought to be William of Conches) of the *Moralium dogma philosophorum* ("Teachings of the Moral Philosophers") stressed the classical roots and political efficacy of the cardinal virtues, while others like Alan of Lille sought to enlist them, together with the three "theological" virtues of faith, hope, and charity in the war against the vices.[13] These two tendencies, the one primarily civic and this-worldly, and the other penitential and focused on an individual's salvation, were further developed in the thirteenth century, with the former strain being given voice in Brunetto Latini's *Tresor* (1260s) and the latter in the Dominican William Peraldus's *Summa de virtutibus* (1240s).[14] In the 1260s the Oxford and Paris educated Franciscan John of Wales combined both in his *Breviloquium de virtutibus* ("Glossary of the Virtues"), a collection of philosophical precepts and illustrative examples drawn largely from classical authorities and organized according to the four cardinal virtues. John compiled the *Breviloquium* to serve as both a kind of mirror of princes and to be a mine of material for preachers composing sermons.[15]

The translation of Aristotle's *Nicomachean Ethics*, *Politics*, and *Rhetoric* in the middle years of the thirteenth century at once complicated and encouraged the discourse of the virtues. First, while Aristotle lists prudence, justice, fortitude, and temperance as key virtues, they are only four of a larger inventory of twelve virtues, which also includes love of honor, magnanimity, liberality, magnificence, mildness, truth, affability, and sociability. Secondly, he taught that a virtuous character had to be learned through a process of habituation. Thirdly, he taught that virtuous acts resulted from rational judgments aimed at finding the mean between extremes. Fourthly, Aristotle stated that humans were political beings by nature and that the political life was good in itself, rather than being a consequence of primordial sin, as Augustine had taught.

The Dominicans Albert the Great and Thomas Aquinas were the first to try to incorporate Aristotle's teachings on moral philosophy into the preex-

12. Houser 2004, 6–39; Bejczy 2007.
13. Holmberg 1929; Bejczy 2007, 13.
14. Brunetto Latini (d. 1294), *Book of the Treasure*; Bejczy 2002.
15. Swanson 1988,

isting Christian, Augustinian, and Stoic frameworks.[16] The Augustinian friar Giles of Rome, who was himself a student of Aquinas at Paris during the late 1260s and early 1270s, then tried to deploy the new moral philosophy in his *De regimine principum*, which he composed between 1278 and 1280, and dedicated to the heir to the French throne, Philip the Fair.

These thirteenth-century developments are the essential background to a new kind of princely mirror that aimed to instruct rulers in moral philosophy through a treatment of the four cardinal virtues.[17] Like other later medieval European mirrors for princes they share the four characteristics of "vulgarisation, pedagogic basis, an overwhelming preoccupation with ethics, and Aristotelian theory."[18] These texts, however, have two other defining features. First, they fit their Christian message and Aristotelian moral philosophy into the Platonic/Stoic matrix of the cardinal virtues. Second, they have a certain liminal quality: that is, their purpose moves between the penitential one of preparing the individual soul for salvation and the political one of creating a well-ordered, just, and peaceful society. They are also liminal in the sense of not fitting comfortably within the standard narrative of the history of western political thought. In what follows I will treat four of these mirrors: Enrico da Rimini's *De quatuor virtutibus cardinalibus ad cives venetos* ("On the Four Cardinal Virtues to the Citizens of Venice," first decade of the 1300s); Engelbert of Admont's *Speculum virtutum* ("Mirror of the Virtues," composed between 1306 and 1313); Luca Mannelli's *Compendium moralis philosophiae* ("Compendium of Moral Philosophy," c. 1340); and Michael of Prague's *De quatuor virtutibus cardinalibus pro eruditione principum* ("On the Four Cardinal Virtues for the Instruction of Princes," 1387). After discussing each of the authors and their works, this essay will trace the fortunes of these texts and then return to the issue of why they do not fit well within the narrative of western political thought.

Enrico da Rimini was born, probably in Rimini, and probably in the middle of the thirteenth century. Other than the fact of his having been a member of the Order of Preachers, we know nothing about him until he was made prior of the Dominican convent of SS. Giovanni e Paolo in Venice in 1304. Other works ascribed to him are the *Tractatus de septem vitiis capitalibus* ("Treatise on the Seven Deadly Sins") and the *Liber de fide* ("Book Concerning the Faith"), and a collection of sermons. Although we don't know the details of his education, he no doubt was schooled in one or more of the schools, known as *studia*, of his order; and given that he was made prior of

16. Wieland 1982; Dunbabin 1982.

17. Houser 2004, 40–82.

18. Genet 1977, xiv.

the Venice convent, and that he demonstrates a sure grasp of philosophy, theology, and law, and makes confident use of ancient and medieval authorities in the *De quatuor virtutibus cardinalibus*, he likely spent time at one of the Dominicans' schools of advanced studies, known as *studia generalia*. Padua seems most likely, given Enrico's origins and later center of activities in its vicinity, though he may also have studied at the Dominican *studium generale* in Bologna or even Paris.[19] The initial target audience of his text was, according to the work's full title, the "citizens of Venice" (*cives venetos*), by which he likely meant the leading citizens of the Venetian Republic, namely those who served in the senate.[20] Enrico arranged his treatise in four books, each dedicated to one of the four cardinal virtues, starting with prudence, then discussing in turn justice, fortitude, and temperance. Throughout he deploys a battery of authorities, chief among them Aristotle, especially his *Ethics* and *Politics*, as well as the Bible, Aquinas's *Summa theologica*, Cicero, Seneca, Valerius Maximus, Macrobius, Augustine, and Ambrose. He also liberally peppers his text with stories taken from saints' lives and from classical and medieval history. The work evidently achieved some notoriety, as it survives in twenty-two manuscripts and in an incunable edition printed in Strasbourg between November 1472 and September 1475, whose editor, a certain Thomas Dorniberg of Memingen, "doctor of canon law and liberal arts" (*sacrorum canonum et artium liberalium doctor*), compiled and attached an alphabetical index of key terms, so that, as he tells us, those wishing to preach "sermons to laity or clergy" (*sermones ad populum sive ad clerum*), might easily find useful material in the text.[21]

We know much more about the next author, Engelbert of Admont. This Austrian Benedictine was born around 1250 and lived till 1331. Entering the monastery of Admont while still a boy, he made his way to Prague in 1271 to study at the cathedral school there. After three years in Prague, he traveled to Padua, where for five years he studied arts and medicine in the university and then, for four years applied himself to the course in theology in the city's Dominican *studium generale*. From there he returned to Austria, where he resided first at Salzburg (in the household of the archbishop and then as abbot of St Peter's) and then, from the mid-1290s, back at his home monastery of Admont, of which he was made abbot shortly before 1300.[22] Although he does not appear to have particularly distinguished himself as leader of his monastic community – some of the obedientiaries there described him

19. For Enrico da Rimini's biography, see Casagrande 1993.
20. Printed edition of Strasbourg 1472–75, fol. 11b.
21. Fol. 1.
22. Ubl 2000, 12–6.

as being "a lover of the speculative life, though useless in the active one" (*vite speculative amator, tamquam inutilis in activa*) – he did produce an impressive body of thirty-nine known philosophical, political, and theological writings.[23] Between 1297 and 1313 he wrote two mirrors for princes, the first entitled *De regimine principum* and the second, *Speculum virtutum*. This latter work Engelbert dedicated to the Habsburg dukes Albert II and Otto. Like Enrico da Rimini's *De quatuor virtutibus cardinalibus*, Engelbert's work had a modestly impressive circulation, as twenty-six medieval copies survive and we know of a further three lost copies.[24]

Heavily influenced by Giles of Rome's *De regimine principum*, and Giles's main sources (that is, Aristotle's *Ethics, Politics*, and *Rhetoric*) but also summoning an enormous battery of Roman classical, biblical, patristic, and medieval sources little used by Giles, the *Speculum virtutum* is divided into twelve parts. The first four of these introduce the reader to: 1) the purpose and ends of human life, namely human happiness; 2) the habits and character (both good and bad) of youths, old men, and men of middle age, of nobles, of commoners, and of the poor and powerless; 3) the passions; and 4) virtue and an overview of the different virtues, beginning with the four cardinal virtues (i.e. prudence, justice, fortitude, and temperance), and proceeding to the eight ancillary moral virtues (i.e. liberality, magnificence, magnanimity, love of honor, mildness, friendliness, truthfulness, and sociability). The final seven chapters go on to discuss the individual virtues in greater detail.

The next text, the *Compendium moralis philosophiae*, was written in the early 1340s by the Florentine Dominican Luca Mannelli, who dedicated it to Bruzio Visconti, poet, bibliophile, and bastard son of Luchino Visconti, *signore* of Milan and Pavia. Born between 1290 and 1296, Luca, a member of the merchant-banker family of the Mannelli, entered Florence's Dominican convent of Santa Maria Novella sometime before 1316, was prior of the convent of San Domenico in Pistoia by 1331, and had returned to his home convent by 1333. His educational formation is unknown, though one can assume he followed the normal course of studies in one or more of the Dominican *studia* of the Roman province. Thanks, it seems, to his ties to his confrere, Angelo Acciaiuoli, bishop of Florence, Luca made his way to Avignon in 1344, where he took up residence for some years at the papal *curia*. There he seems to have proved quite serviceable to Pope Clement VI, who named him almost immediately bishop of Zituni in Greece, then, in 1347 bishop of Osimo. He governed both dioceses via vicars, while he stayed in Avignon and compiled his two other major works a, *Tabulatio et expositio Sen-*

23. Ubl 2000, 15.
24. Engelbert of Admont (d. 1331), *Speculum virtutum*, 24–62.

ecae ("Index and Commentary on Seneca") done at the request of Clement VI, and the *Expositio Valerii Maximi, Factorum ac dictorum memorabilium libri IX* ("Commentary on Valerius Maximus's 'Nine Books of Memorable Deeds and Sayings'"). He ended his days in 1362 as bishop of Fano.[25]

The original Latin text of Luca's *Compendium moralis philosophiae* survives uniquely in the manuscript he presented to Lord Bruzio, now Bibliothèque nationale de France ms. lat. 6467, but originally kept in the Biblioteca Visconteo-Sforzesca in Pavia.[26] Its opening leaf boasts a lovely illuminated border, probably executed by the noted artist Andrea da Bologna, which represents at the foot of the page an enthroned Bruzio, holding a sword in his right hand and an open book in his left, with his feet resting on a horned devil, labeled *Superbia*. Standing to the left of Bruzio are representations of Saints Thomas Aquinas, Ambrose, and Augustine, and to his right, Valerius Maximus, Seneca, and Aristotle. At the top of the page is a medallion labeled "Milan," and to either side are twelve other medallions each representing Lombard towns in the Visconti orbit. Friar Luca himself appears in the initial, holding a copy of his *Compendium*. Three copies of an Italian translation are also extant; it seems likely that this translation is contemporary to the Latin original, and that it was done by Luca himself.[27] It is the only one of the four texts discussed here that was translated into the vernacular. One of these copies, dating from around 1400, refers (in the Latin colophon) to Luca as "venerable man and doctor" (*per venerabilem virum et doctorem*), which suggests the possibility of his having completed advanced university study, though this is our only evidence for this.

The *Compendium* begins with a dedicatory prologue to Bruzio that explains which sources Luca will be principally drawing from: namely, Aristotle's *Ethics*, Cicero's *De officiis* and *Tusculan Disputations*, and the prima and secunda secundae of Aquinas's *Summa theologica*. In the text itself, however, he also borrows from the Bible, Augustine, Ambrose, Jerome, and Origen, Seneca, Macrobius, Vergil, Juvenal, Valerius Maximus, Sallust, Quintilian, Isidore of Seville, and Boethius. Quoting Cicero, *Tusculan Disputations*, II.v.13, Luca informs his dedicatee that moral philosophy cultivates the soul, pulling out the vices by the roots and making it fit for the sowing of seeds which bear the richest fruit when fully grown.[28] The work itself is divided into three

25. Kaeppelli 1948, 238–44; Kaeppeli, 1970–93, 3:89–90; Cinelli 2007.

26. Kaeppeli 1948, 244; Pellegrin 1969, 27.

27. These are Florence, Biblioteca Nazionale, MS Pal. lat. 581 and MS Pal. lat. 649, and Rome, Biblioteca Apostolica Vaticana, MS Barb. lat. 4031: Kaeppeli 1948, 247.

28. BnF ms. lat. 6467, fols. 1–1v: "Cultura autem animi est philosophia. Hec extrahit vitia radicitus et preparat animos ad satus accipiendos eosque mandat his et ut ita dicam seritque ut culti fructus uberimos ferant."

treatises, the first explains the basic elements of moral philosophy, namely the Aristotelian concepts of *habitus* and the mean, as well as the passions and the virtues; the second is dedicated to a discussion of the four cardinal virtues; and the third to an examination of friendship.

The fourth and final text was written in 1387 by Michael, prior of the Charterhouse just outside Prague. Because the Hussites destroyed his priory in 1419, we have no records of his early life or education, but we do know that he was prior there by 1356, that he also served as Visitor of the Carthusians' High-German province and as prior of the Charterhouse at Gyrio in Austria, where he died in 1401. Michael's other known writings, besides the *De quatuor virtutibus cardinalibus pro eruditione principum*, are a *Dialogus de custodia virginitatis* ("Dialogue on Guarding One's Virginity") and a consolatory letter to one of his fellow Carthusian priors, John of Aggsbach, entitled *Remediarium abiecti prioris* ("Remedy for a Despondent Prior").[29]

As for the *De quatuor virtutibus cardinalibus*, whose alternative title in all five surviving manuscripts is given as *De regimine principum*, Michael wrote it in the form of a dialogue between himself and his dedicatee, Rupert II of Wittelsbach, duke of Bavaria. After a dedicatory prologue to Duke Rupert, in which Michael credits as his chief inspirations for writing his work Aquinas's *De regno* and Giles of Rome's *De regimine principum*, the dialogue proceeds through four books, each devoted to one of the four cardinal virtues, beginning with prudence, then temperance, then justice, then fortitude. Besides Aquinas and Giles, Michael makes use of Augustine, Jerome, Ambrose, John Chrysostom, Aristotle, Cicero, Seneca, Martin of Braga, Valerius Maximus, Vegetius, and Macrobius. He also quotes copiously from the Bible. As I mentioned earlier, five copies of the text survive, all in central European libraries, except for the one in the Vatican library, which itself was taken from the library of the counts Palatine during the Thirty Years' War.[30]

These authors and their works share several similarities. First, all four authors were members of religious orders. Enrico and Luca were both Dominicans, Engelbert a Benedictine, and Michael a Carthusian. Moreover, Engelbert studied theology for four years in the Dominican *studium* at Padua. Thus the three earliest authors share a common, Dominican, and indeed, Italian, educational formation. It so happens that the Dominicans distinguished themselves for the enthusiastic and thorough-going fashion in which they incorporated Aristotelian moral philosophy into their system of education. Italian Dominicans added to this an avid interest in Roman moral philosophy. We see these elements in Ptolemy of Lucca's *De regimine*

29. Storey 1972, 1–19; Witkowski 2007, 23–35.
30. Storey 1972, 104–8.

principum and Remigio de' Girolami of Florence's *De bono communi* ("On the Common Good") both composed c. 1300.[31] From 1307 to 1316 Remigio was, moreover, the master of students in Florence's Dominican *studium* (during the time when Luca Mannelli would have been starting his vocation in the order there).[32] Other Dominicans who compiled texts on moral philosophy as part of their teaching duties in the schools of their order were Conrad of Ascoli and Guido Vernani, who taught at Bologna in the first and second decades of the fourteenth century, Galvagno della Fiamma at Milan in the 1320s, Bartolomeo da San Concordio, who taught in several of the Tuscan *studia* during the 1320s and 1330s, and Miliano da Spoleto at Arezzo, in the 1330s.[33] The Dominican commitment to teaching moral philosophy was codified in a decision of the general chapter in 1314, which stipulated the teaching of moral philosophy in all its provincial and general *studia*.[34] In fact, it seems to have been in direct response to this demand that Bartolomeo da San Concordio composed his own *Compendium moralis philosophiae*, which combines an abridgment of Giles of Rome's *De regimine principum* with copious additions drawn from classical, patristic, and biblical sources.[35]

The point of Dominican education was to produce effective preachers, teachers, and confessors. To do so, the Dominicans became experts at a kind of pedagogy of *haute vulgarisation* that bridged the gap between theory and practice and that illustrated theological doctrine and philosophical principles with concrete examples drawn from biblical, Aristotelian, classical, patristic, and medieval authorities. This technique is clearly visible throughout the works of all three of our Dominican-schooled authors. Enrico and Engelbert were especially good at this, never letting an opportunity slip by when a good illustrative story was called for. No wonder, then, Thomas Dorniberg's recommendation in the 1470s that Enrico's work should be used principally as a source of material for sermons; and no wonder also that several of the surviving manuscripts of Engelbert's *Speculum* also contain preaching texts, and that a copy, now lost, is described as follows: "Sermon on the passion of Christ, and several sermons on the compassion of the Blessed Virgin, and Engelbert on the virtues" (*Item sermo de passione Christi et plures sermones de conpassione beate virginis et Engelbertus de virtutibus*).[36]

31. On Ptolemy of Lucca, see Davis 1984, 254–89 and Ptolemy of Lucca, *On the Government of Rulers*, 21–41, 293–4. On Remigio de' Girolami, see Davis 1984, 157–63, 198–223.

32. Mulchahey 2005, 147–55.

33. Briggs 2005, 183–5.

34. Mulchahey 1998, 333–6.

35. Briggs 2005.

36. In 1477, Heinrich Jäck, a graduate of the University of Vienna and preacher in Biberbach, gave this manuscript to the hospital of Augustinian Canons in Biberbach: Engelbert of Admont, *Speculum virtutum*, 62.

Dominican education was, however, only one expression of a broader educational culture associated with the clergy and with the universities. This helps explain why so many of the surviving manuscripts are products of this environment. If we focus on the 26 surviving and three recorded lost manuscripts of Engelbert of Admont, all of which have been fully and expertly catalogued and described by Karl Ubl, we find that virtually all have connections either to universities and university graduates, or to ecclesiastical foundations and the religious orders. Indeed none clearly demonstrates princely or noble ownership or patronage, although one (Vienna, Österreichische Nationalbibl. MS 2435) can be shown to have been in the possession of Vienna's Hofbibliothek since 1576. Moreover, only one, now in Hamburg's Staats- und Universitätsbibliothek (MS msc. philos. 170), can be tied to a non-university-educated lay owner during the medieval period: Hinrich Hoyer, mayor of Hamburg, who may have procured this manuscript during his visit to the Council of Constance in 1417.[37] The suspicion that these manuscripts belonged to a learned, clerical milieu is enhanced by their contents. When, as is often the case, Engelbert's *Speculum* is combined with other works, these accompanying texts are ones normally used either to help compose sermons or to teach and study moral philosophy. Two manuscripts will serve by way of example. Accompanying the *Speculum virtutum* in Hereford, Cathedral Library MS O.6.ii, a book which belonged to John Otteley, a fellow of Clare Hall, Cambridge in the 1460s, are a brief extract from Aristotle's *Politics* and John of Wales's *Breviloquium* and *Communiloquium* (a collection of extracts for preachers).[38] In a manuscript now in Stuttgart (Württembergische Landesbibl. Cod. theol. fol. 190B) the *Speculum virtutum* is followed by Francesco Zabarella's *Tractatus de sententia excommunicationis* ("Treatise concerning the Sentence of Excommunication"), a collection of miracles and parables from the Gospels (*Miracula, parabola etc. salvatoris quae leguntur in evangeliis*), Henry of Langenstein's *De proprietate* ("On Ownership") and another work ascribed to him entitled *Forma vivendi quam Christus religiosis tradidit* ("Manner of Living which Christ Handed Down to the Religious Orders") which is perhaps by Henry of Langenstein, the *Quaestio de mysterio incarnationis* ("Question concering the Mystery of the Incarnation") of Nicholas of Lyra, a series of exhortations for a virtuous life (*Exhortationes ad virtutem*), an *Opusculum tripartitum de praeceptis, de confessione et de scientia mortis* ("Tract in Three Parts on the Ten Commandments, on Confession, and on Dying Well") of Jean Gerson, Henry of Langenstein's *De confessione*, and a collection of extracts from Augustine, Bernard of Clairvaux, the Lives of the

37. Engelbert of Admont, *Speculum virtutum*, 38–9.
38. Engelbert of Admont, *Speculum virtutum*, 39–40.

Fathers, Bede, Valerius Maximus, Hostiensis, Vincent of Beauvais, Seneca, and Jerome. This book had belonged to the Benedictines of Zwiefalten.[39]

The surviving manuscripts of the other three works seem to confirm the evidence from the Engelbert manuscripts.[40] A copy of Enrico's *De quatuor virtutibus cardinalibus*, now in Bamberg (Staatl. Bibl. MS Theol. 50), belonged in the fifteenth century to the Carmelites there, while another, now in Tübingen (Universitätsbibl. MS Mc 334), was copied at Heidelberg in the 1440s by Dr. Melchior Wittich, who then gave it to the Dominicans of Esslingen. The former manuscript also contained a *Tractatus de passione domini* ("Treatise on Our Lord's Passion") and the latter a commentary on Martin of Braga's *Formula vitae honestae*. A collection of extracts from Enrico's mirror (in Munich, Bayerische Staatsbibl. clm 3603) also contains several works of Cicero, the pseudo-Ciceronian *Ad Herennium*, and a "dyalogus moralis [inter Concupiscentiam et Senecam]," written in 1467 by a student named Heinrich Gorlicz. The two manuscripts of Michael of Prague's mirror that betray signs of ownership also show signs of clerical/scholarly ownership and use. The first, now in Munich (Bayerische Staatsbibl. clm 11478), combines Michael's text with John Buridan's commentaries on Aristotle's *Ethics* and ps-Aristotle's *Economics*, as well as Jean Gerson's *De duplici statu in Dei ecclesia curatorum et privilegiatorum* ("On the Two-fold Status in the Church of God of Curates and Exempt Clergy"); it belonged to Rudolf Volkhart of Heringen, who was a graduate in arts and medicine from the University of Vienna, and a canon of Regensburg. The second, now in Prague (Cathedral Libr. G 12 [1003]), belonged, from 1419, to one Magister Johannes Herttenberger. The only exception to this rule is Luca's *Compendium*, whose Latin original survives uniquely in the copy he presented to Bruzio Visconti. That there is no evidence of the Latin text having circulated further may be due to Luca having left his convent for the papal *curia* in Avignon shortly after completing it, and thus never employing it as a teaching text. Although the ownership of the three extant copies of the Italian translation remains undetermined, it seems likely, given their language, that they circulated among the laity, and thus may have reached Luca's ostensible target audience of princely and aristocratic readers.

Luca's translation efforts remind us that our four authors overtly directed their treatises toward princely and aristocratic readers. It also suggests that at least part of their goal was their stated purpose to teach these readers the political and salvific benefits of practicing the civic virtues. But the

39. Engelbert of Admont, *Speculum virtutum*, 53–5.

40. I have not yet been able to consult all the catalogue descriptions of these manuscripts.

content, form, and fortunes of these mirrors also strongly suggest that because these texts so strongly reflected and expressed their authors' own educational backgrounds and aims they could not help but be destined for the very classrooms in which their authors had been taught. Engelbert, we know, began compiling Admont, Stiftsbibl. MS 608, a notebook of copious extracts from classical and Aristotelian moral philosophical texts, not long after returning to Austria from his studies in Padua.[41] That he later used this notebook as the source for both his mirrors for princes does not negate the essentially *scholarly* predilections of an abbot who was described by some of his fellow monks as a "lover of the speculative life, though useless in the active one." A now-lost copy of Engelbert's notebook made its way to the Dominicans of Vienna, while one of the two other surviving copies belonged to one Friedrich von Berching, lector in the Dominican convent of Eichstätt. As for the other surviving copy (Oxford, Bodleian Libr. Canon class. lat. 271), it shows signs of having originated in a scholarly milieu.[42]

Michael of Prague wrote his mirror for Duke Rupert II of Bavaria, but the preoccupations of Carthusian education and spirituality shine through in his decisions to present his lessons in the form of a dialogue, which was a well-established monastic pedagogical genre, and to avoid discussing the art of warfare, even though this topic is taken up by his principal sources, Thomas Aquinas and Giles of Rome: "for those men had written . . . and approved many things for kings which more often pagan kings have been accustomed to observe rather than Christian ones." Michael, for his part, says that the practicalities of warfare have little bearing on the spiritual wellbeing of a Christian prince, and that he intends rather to confine his teaching to "those matters which are incumbent upon Christian princes either to do or not do in such a way that if they do in the opposite manner they will diminish their own dignity and commit sin."[43] One cannot help

41. Ubl 2000, 22.

42. This is a paper manuscript copied in the first third of the fifteenth century by a single scribe, probably from northern Italy, in a current hand. It has no decoration other than flourishes in red ink. In addition to the material from Engelbert's notebook it contains Guido della Colonna's *Historia Troiana*, several items connected with the legend of Alexander the Great, a brief extract from Robert the Monk's *Gesta Dei per Francos*, and some texts related to the life and miracles of St. Jerome. The connection between the manuscripts of Engelbert's notebook is discussed in Fowler 1977.

43. Storey 1972, 113–4: "Isti [Thomas Aquinas and Giles of Rome] enim secundum moralem racionem solempnissime scripserunt multaque probaverunt regibus conpetere que sepius reges pagani magis quam cristiani solent observare, ut scilicet qualiter sit fundanda civitas, qualiter disponendus exercitus ad bellum, quomodo instruenda acies, quomodo civitas oppugnanda, si magis in bello conveniat hostes ferire punctim vel cesim, multaque similia, de quibus hic nichil dicetur quia ista eciam quinque, si non taliter fierent, principem peccati reum non facerent.

but think that Rupert himself was very much interested in such mundane affairs as waging war. The reception history of Giles of Rome's *De regimine principum*, whose final part is on warfare, clearly shows such an interest on the part of its princely and noble readers.[44] Michael's decision to avoid such matters may help to explain why his work had far greater attraction for men like himself than like Duke Rupert.

The mirrors of Enrico da Rimini, Engelbert of Admont, Luca Mannelli, and Michael of Prague do not satisfy our current expectations of what makes a political text "political." In part this is because, like other later medieval mirrors, they privilege the ethical over the political, seeing personal character and relationships as being more important to the common weal than constitutional, structural, or process-related issues. But it also results from the fact that although part of these mirrors' purpose is to teach rulers how to govern more effectively, the pedagogical preoccupations of each author were nonetheless determined more by the current demands of their own clerical milieux. These texts exude the air of university classroom and the mendicant and monastic schools. No wonder they were better suited to the needs of preachers, pastors, and university masters than to their stated audience of princes and aristocrats.

Despite this, these mirrors betray their authors' confidence in the practical value of their bookish brand of learning. And if those in positions of political power did not necessarily read all the works of instruction penned by such *érudits*, they nonetheless got the message that these men and their knowledge could at times be useful. After all, there is copious evidence that the commonplace of the civic virtues did come to play an increasingly important role in late medieval society as a kind of shorthand and matrix for visualizing, thinking about, and talking about social, political, and eternal life.[45] Yet whereas the mirrors discussed here and others like them played a role in shaping and popularizing this moral and political discourse, the paths by which they did so were neither simple nor straightforward. They admonish us to remain open-minded toward what "politics" meant in different times and places, and to consider carefully the social and cultural contexts in which these political texts were generated and circulated.

Hic autem dicitur de hiis que principibus cristianis taliter facienda vel non facienda incumbunt, quod si aliter facerent, et sue dignitati derogarent et ut sepe peccatum incurrerent."

44. Briggs 1999, 63–6.

45. Briggs (forthcoming).

Bibliography

Bejczy, I. P. (2002), "A Genealogy of Morals: The Cardinal Virtues in Medieval Discourse," *Medieval Sermon Studies*, alt. no. 46: 95–6.

—— (2007), "The Concept of Political Virtue in the Thirteenth Century," in: I. P. Bejczy and C. J. Nederman (eds.), *Princely Virtues in the Middle Ages, 1200–1500*, Turnhout, 9–32.

Berges, W. (1938), *Die Fürstenspiegel des hohen und späten Mittelalters*, Leipzig.

Briggs, C. F. (1999), *Giles of Rome's "De regimine principum": Reading and Writing Politics at Court and University, c. 1275–c. 1525*, Cambridge.

—— (2003), "Teaching Philosophy at School and Court: Vulgarization and Translation," in: F. Somerset and N. Watson (eds.), *The Vulgar Tongue: Medieval and Postmedieval Vernacularity*, University Park, 99–111.

—— (2005), "Moral Philosophy and Dominican Education: Bartolomeo da San Concordio's *Compendium moralis philosophiae*," in: R. B. Begley and J. W. Koterski (eds.), *Medieval Education*, New York, 182–96.

—— (2010), "Knowledge and Royal Power in the Later Middle Ages: From Philosopher-Imam, to Clerkly King, to Renaissance Prince," in: S. J. Ridyard (ed.), *Power in the Middle Ages: Forms, Uses, Limitations*, Sewanee, 81–97.

—— (forthcoming), "Moral Philosophy and Wisdom Literature," in: R. Copeland (ed.), *The Oxford History of Classical Reception in English Literature*, vol. 1, Oxford.

Casagrande, C. (1993), "Enrico da Rimini," in: *Dizionario Biografico degli Italiani*, vol. 42, Rome, 756–7.

Cinelli, L. (2007), "Mannelli, Luca," in: *Dizionario Biografico degli Italiani*, vol. 69, Rome, 81–4.

Davis, C. T. (1984), *Dante's Italy and Other Essays*, Philadelphia.

Dunbabin, J. (1982), "The Reception and Interpretation of Aristotle's *Politics*," in: N. Kretzmann, A. Kenny and J. Pinborg (eds.), *The Cambridge History of Later Medieval Philosophy*, Cambridge, 723–37.

Engelbert of Admont (2004), *Die Schriften des Alexander von Roes und des Engelbert von Admont, Teil 2: Engelbert von Admont, "Speculum virtutum,"* ed. K. Ubl, Hanover.

Ferster, J. (1996), *Fictions of Advice: The Literature and Politics of Counsel in Late Medieval England*, Philadelphia.

Fowler, G. B. (1977), "Manuscript 608 and Engelbert of Admont (c. 1250–1331)," *Archives d'histoire doctrinale et littéraire du Moyen Age* 44: 149–242.

Genet, J.-P. (ed.) (1977), *Four English Political Tracts of the Later Middle Ages*, London.

Grassnick, U. (2004), *Ratgeber des Königs: Fürstenspiegel und Herrscherideal im spätmittelalterlichen England*, Cologne.
Hohlstein, M. (2007), "*Clemens princeps: Clementia* as a Princely Virtue in Michael of Prague's *De regimine principum*," in: I. P. Bejczy and C. J. Nederman (eds.), *Princely Virtues in the Middle Ages, 1200–1500*, Turnhout, 201–17.
Holmberg, J. (ed.) (1929), *Das "Moralium dogma philosophorum" des Guillaume de Conches: lateinisch, altfranzösisch und mittelniederfränkisch*, Uppsala.
Houser, R. E. (2004), *The Cardinal Virtues: Aquinas, Albert, and Philip the Chancellor*, Toronto.
Kaeppeli, T. (1948), "Luca Mannelli († 1362) e la sua *Tabulatio et expositio Senecae*," *Archivum Fratrum Praedicatorum* 18: 237–64.
—— (1970–93), *Scriptores Ordinis Praedicatorum Medii Aevi*, 4 vols., Rome.
Kempshall, M. S. (1999), *The Common Good in Late Medieval Political Thought*, Oxford.
Krynen, J. (1993), *L'empire du roi: idées et croyances politiques en France, XIIIe-XVe siècle*, Paris.
Lagarde, G. de (1956–70), *La naissance de l'esprit laïque au déclin du Moyen Age*, 3rd ed., 6 vols. in 5, Louvain.
Lambertini, R. (1995), "The Prince in the Mirror of Philosophy: Uses of Aristotle in Giles of Rome's *De regimine principum*," in: B. C. Bazán, E. Andújar and L. G. Sbrocchi (eds.), *Moral and Political Philosophies in the Middle Ages*, vol. 3, Ottawa, 1522–34.
Latini, Brunetto (1993), *Brunetto Latini, The Book of The Treasure (Li Livres dou Tresor)*, tr. P. Barrette and S. Baldwin, New York and London.
Minnis, A. J. (2005), "'I speke of folk in seculer estaat': Vernacularity and Secularity in the Age of Chaucer," *Studies in the Age of Chaucer* 27: 25–58.
Mulchahey, M. M. (1998), *"First the Bow is Bent in Study": Dominican Education before 1350*, Toronto.
—— (2005), "Education in Dante's Florence Revisited: Remigio de' Girolami and the Schools of Santa Maria Novella," in: R. B. Begley and J. W. Koterski (eds.), *Medieval Education*, New York, 143–81.
Nederman, C. J. (1997), *Medieval Aristotelianism and Its Limits*, Aldershot.
—— (1998), "The Mirror Crack'd: The *Speculum Principum* as Political and Social Criticism in the Late Middle Ages," *The European Legacy* 3: 18–38.
Pellegrin, E. (1969), *La bibliothèque des Visconti et Sforza, Ducs de Milan*, Supplement, Florence.
Perret, N.-L. (2011), *Les traductions françaises du "De regimine principum" de Gilles de Rome: parcours matériel, culturel et intellectuel d'un discours sur l'éducation*, Leiden.

Ptolemy of Lucca (1997), *On the Government of Rulers/De regimine principum, Ptolemy of Lucca, with Portions Attributed to Thomas Aquinas*, tr. J. M. Blythe, Philadelphia.

Reynolds, S. (1997), *Kingdoms and Communities in Western Europe 900–1300*, 2nd ed., Oxford.

Skinner, Q. (1986), "Ambrogio Lorenzetti: The Artist as Political Philosopher," *Proceedings of the British Academy* 72: 1–56.

Storey, W. G. (1972), *The "De quatuor virtutibus cardinalibus pro eruditione principum" of Michael the Carthusian of Prague: A Critical Text and Study*, Salzburg.

Swanson, J. (1988), *John of Wales: A Study of the Works and Ideas of a Thirteenth-Century Friar*, Cambridge.

Taranto, D. (2004), "Egidio Romano e il *De regimine principum*: mutazioni concettuali dei paradigma degli specula," *Il pensiero politico* 37: 360–86.

Ubl, K. (2000), *Engelbert von Admont: Ein Gelehrter im Spannungsfeld von Aristotelismus und christlicher Überlieferung*, Vienna.

Ullman, W. (1975), *Law and Politics in the Middle Ages: An Introduction to the Sources of Medieval Political Ideas*, Cambridge.

Wieland, G. (1982), "The Reception and Interpretation of Aristotle's *Ethics*," in: N. Kretzmann, A. Kenny and J. Pinborg (eds.), *The Cambridge History of Later Medieval Philosophy*, Cambridge, 657–72.

Williams, S. J. (2003), *The "Secret of Secrets": The Scholarly Career of a Pseudo-Aristotelian Text in the Latin Middle Ages*, Ann Arbor.

Witkowski, R. (2007), "Michael of Prague and His Three Treatises," in: R. Bindel (ed.), *35 années de recherche et de spiritualité*, Salzburg, 23–44.

Aetiologies of the *Kalīla wa Dimna* as a Mirror for Princes

Olga M. Davidson

IT IS WELL KNOWN THAT THE STORIES contained in the multiform text known in Arabic as the *Kalīla wa Dimna* were used for purposes of education in statecraft. The literary form of such education is commonly known by its medieval Latin designation as *speculum principum* or "mirror for princes." In the case of the *Kalīla wa Dimna*, the genesis of the stories told in this multiform text is explained in statements that are attached as introductions or prefaces or even appendices to the main body of stories. These statements, which can sometimes include stories in their own right, are what I call *aetiologies*, or, more precisely, *aetiological narratives*. As for the actual stories of the *Kalīla wa Dimna*, most of them are *animal fables*. In the essay that I present here, I argue that the aetiological narratives of this multiform text of animal fables, the *Kalīla wa Dimna*, are designed to explain not only the genesis of these fables but also their use as a mirror for princes. I will also argue that these aetiological narratives are multiform in their own right, just as the fables themselves are multiform.

Such multiformity is typical of oral traditions, which require ongoing adjustment to the *reception* of whatever has been composed. In his study of the oral traditions that shaped the poetry attributed to Homer and Hesiod, Gregory Nagy has defined reception thus:

> I use the term *reception* ... not in the narrow sense that applies in studies of literature, where this term conventionally refers to whatever happens after a given piece of literature is composed for *transmission* to the public. A broader sense of the term is needed when we are dealing with literary traditions that stem from oral traditions.... How, then, are we to understand the phenomenon of *reception* in oral traditions? The answer has to do with the *transmission* of *composition* by way of *performance*. In any oral tradition, ... the process of composition is linked to the process of performance, and any given composition can be recomposed each time it is performed. The performer who recomposes the composition in performance may be the same performer who composed it earlier, or it may be a

> new performer, even a succession of new performers. The point is, such *recomposition-in-performance* is the essence of *transmission in oral traditions.*[1]
>
> This kind of *transmission* is the key to a broader understanding of *reception.* Unlike what happens in literature, where reception by the public happens only *after* a piece of literature is transmitted, reception in oral traditions happens *during* as well as *after* transmission. That is because the process of composition in oral traditions allows for recomposition on each new occasion of performance for a public that sees and hears the performer. In oral traditions, there is an organic link between reception and performance, since no performance can succeed without a successful reception by the public that sees and hears the performer or performers.[2]

I add here to Nagy's formulation another dimension of such reception: in the case of fables, which are used for education in statecraft, the reception depends on the patron. After all, the intended patrons and audience of fables are rulers of state, and it is their statecraft that the fables are intended to shape.

A Brief Introduction to the Animal Fable as a Traditional Form of Discourse

Animal fables are stories about talking animals, whose words can be quoted directly. The telling of such stories, which do not exclude humans interacting with animals, is a very old and traditional form of discourse that is found all over the world in a wide variety of unrelated cultures. Clearly, such fables originate from oral traditions. And, just as clearly, the many different forms of animal fables cannot be traced back to any single original form.

Still, in some cases, traditions of this kind of storytelling as attested in different cultures can in fact be traced back in time to a common – not necessarily an original – source. Such is the case with animal fables attested in the earliest surviving phases of ancient Greek and ancient Indic traditions, which can be traced back to the common linguistic heritage of Greek and Indic as Indo-European languages.[3] The ancient Greek tradition of telling fables featuring talking animals is attested already in the Hesiodic *Works and Days*, which contains the embedded fable of *The Hawk and the Nightingale*

1. Nagy 2009, 282.
2. Nagy 2009, 283.
3. Nagy 2011, §§121–4.

(verses 202–12) and in the iambic poetry attributed to Archilochus, which contains the embedded fable of *The Fox and the Eagle* (fragment 174 ed. West). The eventual textualization of the poetic traditions attributed to Hesiod and Archilochus can be dated to the sixth century BCE, or even earlier.

Correspondingly, the ancient Indic tradition of telling fables featuring talking animals is prominently attested in the Buddhist texts known as the *Jātaka Tales*, composed in the Pāli language, and in such "Hindu" texts as the *Pañcatantra* and the *Hitopadeśa*, both composed in Sanskrit. The textualization of the *Jātaka Tales* is dated around the fifth century BCE, while the dating for the *Pañcatantra* and the *Hitopadeśa* is later. With due allowances for the fact that the dating of Sanskrit texts is notoriously slippery, I note that the textualization of the *Pañcatantra* is conventionally estimated at around the third century BCE, while the *Hitopadeśa* as we know it was produced as a text in the twelfth century CE.

In other cases, the animal fables of one culture are borrowed from corresponding fables in another culture. One such case is the *Kalīla wa Dimna*, which is the Arabic name for a collection of fables borrowed from earlier fables composed in Middle Persian, which in turn were borrowed – at least in part – from still earlier fables composed in Sanskrit.

A Sketch of the Structure of the *Kalīla wa Dimna*

Before we consider the textual traditions that culminated in the collection of fables that we know as the *Kalīla wa Dimna*, I offer here a sketch of the structure of this collection. The fables of the *Kalīla wa Dimna* are divided into a sequence of (usually) ten main stories, which contain sub-stories, which in turn can even contain sub-sub-stories. The ten main stories are the following:

- The first five of the ten main stories are *The Lion and the Ox*, *The Ring-Dove and her Companions*, *The Owls and the Crows*, *The Ape and the Tortoise*, and *The Ascetic and the Weasel*. These stories were borrowed from the five main fables of the *Pañcatantra*, which I have already mentioned earlier.
- The sixth, seventh, and eighth of the ten main stories are *The Mouse and the Cat*, *The King and the Bird*, and *The Lion and the Jackal*. These stories were borrowed from fables found in Book XII of the *Mahābhārata*, which is the main epic of Indic civilization.
- The ninth is *The King and his Eight Dreams*, borrowed from an unattested Sanskrit source.

- The tenth is *The King of the Mice and his Ministers*, an external source for which cannot be determined.

Besides the main body of fables organized along the lines of the ten main stories, the *Kalīla wa Dimna* also features a set of statements that introduce this main body of stories. These introductory statements sometimes include stories in their own right. These are the *aetiological narratives* alluded to earlier.

A Sketch of the Textual Traditions of the *Kalīla wa Dimna*

Here is an inventory of the attested texts of the *Kalīla wa Dimna*. This inventory tracks a corresponding inventory presented in a monograph by François de Blois.[4]

(1) At the core of the textual tradition of the *Kalīla wa Dimna* is a wide variety of texts written in Arabic. If we follow the aetiological narratives attached to these texts, we find that the fables of the *Kalīla wa Dimna* originated only indirectly from Sanskrit prototypes. There was an intermediate stage, in the form of a text written in Middle Persian. This Middle Persian text, which is not attested, was attributed by the aetiological narratives to a physician named Burzūya, who lived in the era of the Sasanian king Khusruw I (Kisrā in the Arabic script) Anūshirwān, emperor of the Persian Empire from 531 to 579 CE. This Middle Persian text, as posited by the aetiological narratives, was later translated into Arabic by a Persian savant named ʻAbd Allāh ibn al-Muqaffaʻ, the date of whose death is conventionally set at 757 CE. The oldest of the texts stemming from the Arabic translation of Ibn al-Muqaffaʻ is dated to 1221 CE, called by de Blois the "ʻAzzām manuscript," while the second oldest is dated to 1338 CE, called the "Shaykhū manuscript." Finally, I must mention two poetic versions of *Kalīla wa Dimna*: one by Ābān al-Lāḥiqī (d. around 815 CE), which survives in only a few quotations, and another by Ibn al-Habbārīya (d. 1115 or 1116 CE).[5]

(2) The oldest attested text of the *Kalīla wa Dimna*, however, is a version composed not in Arabic. It is the *Qalīlag w Damnag*, composed in Syriac. This "older Syriac" version, as it is called, is dated to the

4. de Blois 1990.
5. de Blois 1990, 5.

sixth century CE.[6] As de Blois argues, this "older Syriac" text was a "translation" (for the problematic usage of the term "translation" see below) from the same Middle Persian text that became the prototype for all the Arabic versions of the *Kalīla wa Dimna*.[7] This older Syriac version was composed by a savant named Bōḏ – according to a 14th-century Nestorian Christian named 'ḇeḏ Īshō', who notes that Bōḏ also composed other treatises, including *Discourses on the Faith*, *Against the Manichaeans*, and *Against the Marcionites*. The religions of both the Manichaeans and the Marcionites are strongly dualistic, and this observation is relevant in what I will argue later about the Persian savant Ibn al-Muqaffa', who is credited with the Arabic translation of the *Kalīla wa Dimna*. The narrator, the 14th-century Nestorian Christian named 'ḇeḏ Īshō', reports about Bōḏ: "And he [Bōḏ] interpreted the book of Qalīlag w Ḏamnag from the Indian."[8] Bōḏ was active around the year 570 CE.[9] The expression used by 'ḇeḏ Īshō', *pashsheq men hendwāyā* 'interpreted from the Indian', is discounted by de Blois, who claims that the Syriac text was not "translated" from the Sanskrit but from Middle Persian.[10] He cites as his authority the work of earlier orientalists who show occurrences of Middle Persian words in the Syriac text. Even the name Bōḏ is evidently Iranian, morphologically parallel to Avestan *baoδah-*, meaning "wise."[11] No doubt there was Middle Persian mediation. But I must point out an empirical fact that stands in the way of assuming, as does de Blois, that Bōḏ simply "translated" a Middle Persian text. That empirical fact is this: the older Syriac version aetiologizes itself as an interpretation stemming from the Indic tradition of fables, not from a Middle Persian translation. And the claims made in aetiological narratives about a tradition, whether these claims are true or not, can be used as evidence for reconstructing the actual reception of that tradition, as we will see later.

As de Blois notes, there are medieval "translations" – again he uses that word – some of which are roughly contemporaneous with the oldest Arabic manuscripts, and so de Blois considers them fair game "in reconstructing

6. de Blois 1990, 2.

7. de Blois 1990, 1. Only later (12, n. 1), does de Blois inform the reader that this Syriac *Qalīlag w Damnag* was composed in verse.

8. de Blois 1990, 2 cites the edition of Giuseppe Simone Assemani (Rome 1725) 219–20.

9. Assemani 1725, 219, n. 2, via de Blois 1990, 2, n. 9.

10. de Blois 1990, 2.

11. For the Avestan form, see Bartholomae 1904, col. 919. I agree with de Blois (de Blois 1990, 3) when he writes: "*c.f.* [*sic*] *budhaḥ*, 'wise'."

ibn al-Muqaffaʿ's text."[12] So even though de Blois cannot even reconstruct that text on the basis of existing Arabic manuscripts, he still treats stemmatologically these versions in non-Arabic languages – when these non-Arabic versions all claim various authors of their own. Here is the inventory of de Blois, which can be added to the first and the second sets of texts I have already listed:

> (3) There is a Syriac version, dated to the 10th or 11th century, independent of the older Syriac version of the 6th century. This later version, "translated" from the Arabic, is described by de Blois as "rather free."[13] He adds: "The translator has padded the text considerably and introduced numerous quotations from the Bible."[14] I highlight here the use of the word "padding," to which I will return later.
>
> (4) There is a Greek "translation" (as de Blois calls it), entitled *Stephanites kai Ichnelates*, by Symeon Seth, dating from the latter part of the 11th century.
>
> (5) There are also New Persian "translations" (again, as de Blois calls them): [15]
>
> (5a) The oldest known example of a New Persian version was commissioned by the Samanid vizier Abū l-Maʿālī Balʿamī (d. between 992 and 997 CE), and the story of that commissioning is told in the *Shāhnāma* of Firdawsī (d. 1019 or 1025 CE). This version, as de Blois argues, "was apparently the basis for the Persian versification by the celebrated poet Rōdakī [born 858 CE and died somewhere around 941], of which scattered verses survived."[16] I draw attention to the term "versification" used by de Blois, which for him is a mechanical process.[17]
>
> (5b) A Persian prose "translation" (as de Blois calls it) by Abū l-Maʿālī Naṣr Allāh, dated to the 12th century.

12. de Blois 1990, 5.
13. de Blois 1990, 5.
14. de Blois 1990, 5.
15. de Blois 1990, 5. All the remaining quotations in this list are from the same page of de Blois.
16. de Blois 1990, 5.
17. Davidson 2013b [2000], 46. See also Davidson 2013a [2006], 38, 45.

(5c) There is another Persian version, composed "in a straightforward prose style" by Muḥammad ibn 'Abd Allāh al-Bukhārī, and also dated to the 12th century. This "translation," as de Blois calls it, "is evidently quite independent of Abū al-Ma'ālī's."[18]

(5d and 5e) There are also two other Persian versions, both based on the version of Abū l-Ma'ālī, and dated to the 16th century.

(6) There is an older version of a Hebrew "translation," as de Blois calls it, which is dated to the first part of the 12th century. A Latin version by John of Capua, which is "translated" from the Hebrew, is dated to the 13th century.

(7) There are a number of Renaissance-era "translations," as de Blois calls them, of John's Latin version into various European languages.

(8) There is also a newer version of a Hebrew "translation," as de Blois calls it, dated to the 12th century, and "made directly from the Arabic."

(9) Finally, there is a Spanish "translation," as de Blois calls it, "made directly from the Arabic" and dated to the 13th century. In view of the frequent word-for-word correspondences in this case, I agree that this version may be described as a "translation" in the contemporary sense of the word.

A Rethinking of the Concepts of "borrowing" and "translation" as Applied to the Fables of the *Kalīla wa Dimna*

In my brief introduction to the animal fable as a traditional form of discourse, I had said that fables of the *Kalīla wa Dimna* were borrowed from earlier fables composed in Middle Persian, which in turn were borrowed – at least in part – from still earlier fables composed in Sanskrit. In my inventory of the attested texts of the *Kalīla wa Dimna*, I noted that de Blois describes these texts as "translations" from earlier fables composed in Middle Persian, which in turn were "translated" – at least in part – from still earlier fables composed in Sanskrit. But what is exactly meant by "borrowing" and "translation"?

18. de Blois 1990, 6. All the remaining quotations in this list come from this same page of de Blois and from the next page.

A fable such as *The Sage and the Mouse Maiden*, which is a sub-story of the fable of the Owls and the Crows as we see it attested in the *Pañcatantra*, could not have been simply "borrowed" and "translated" by the Middle Persian traditions of animal fables and then further "borrowed" and "translated" in, say, the multiple Arabic traditions of the *Kalīla wa Dimna*. That is because the Sanskrit *Pañcatantra* and such later collections as the Arabic *Kalīla wa Dimna* are significantly different from each other in form.[19] Furthermore, there are multiple Arabic traditions of the *Kalīla wa Dimna*, not a singular Arabic tradition. Even further, we cannot be sure whether these multiple Arabic traditions were ultimately derived from the *Pañcatantra* as we know it. As we are about to see, there must have existed other Indic versions of the *Pañcatantra*.

The *Pañcatantra* was composed in a form of discourse known as *prosimetrum*, where some parts of the discourse are in poetry while other parts are in prose. And the parts that are composed in poetry are not necessarily insertions of poetic "quotations" from other poetry. Rather, the discourse is flexible in its capacity to switch from prose to poetry. As Nagy points out, "Indic narratives of fables regularly show a mixture of poetry and prose, with the parts composed as poetry tending toward older and higher levels of discourse while the parts composed as prose tend toward newer and lower levels."[20] Further, "in a typical Indic fable, the part composed in poetry tends to be the moral of the story, while the part composed in prose is the story itself."[21]

When the register of poetry in the *Pañcatantra* indicates a more elevated form of discourse, it can refer to a custom – as in the fable of the Mouse Maiden, where two passages of poetry refer to norms concerning marriage between members of different castes.[22] Not one of the corresponding versions of this fable in the *Kalīla wa Dimna* transmits the content of the second verse, but some of the versions do transmit the content of the first, which says that parents who do not marry off their daughter before she menstruates may be considered *śūdra*-s. But the transmission of this content in the *Kalīla wa Dimna* is in prose. And any reference to the workings of a caste system is omitted in all versions of the *Kalīla wa Dimna*. That omission renders a literal-minded "translation" unlikely. And, more interestingly and

19. de Blois 1990, 8 notes that in the "older Syriac" version, the Sage is called a *dēnīg*, which is a Middle Persian word; then, in the Arabic versions, the Sage is *nāsik*. But in fragments 299 and 300 of Rōdaki, which show poeticized versions of the fable of the Ring-Dove, the word is *dīnī* (de Blois 1990, 8 n. 2).

20. Nagy 2011, §122, following Witzel 1997, especially 388.

21. Nagy 2011, §122, following Hanson and Kiparsky 1997, 37.

22. *Pañcatantra* (ed. Edgerton 1924, 1:341–2; 2:381); via de Blois 1990, 7, n. 3.

importantly, the content of the poetry can be transmitted, even if the form is changed to prose.

As de Blois concedes, "all descendants of the Middle Persian version" contain a passage that is missing in the *Pañcatantra*: it is a quoted dialogue between the Sage and the Mouse Maiden who has by now been transformed into a young girl in his care and whom he must marry off.[23] Only in this dialogue, as we find it attested in the *Kalīla wa Dimna*, the Sage gives the girl the option of choosing a husband. In the version of the *Pañcatantra* as we have it, by contrast, the Sage simply decides by himself to marry off the girl to the Sun. So now de Blois is forced to invoke the opinion of earlier orientalists who have conceded that "the Near Eastern versions [of the *Kalīla wa Dimna*] reflect here a different and perhaps older recension of the Sanskrit text than that represented by the existing texts of the *Pañcatantra*."[24]

But there are easier ways to account for a detail that is missing in the extant versions of the *Pañcatantra*. The story of the Mouse Maiden is attested in a wide variety of Indic oral traditions,[25] narrated all over India as also in the textual traditions of the earliest collections, namely, the *Jātaka Tales*, the *Pañcatantra*, and the *Kathāsaritsāgara*.[26]

De Blois ignores the evidence of oral traditions. For him, variations in the texts of the *Kalīla wa Dimna* are merely the result of vicissitudes in the textual transmission. For example, if he finds a longer version of a detail in a fable contained in the *Kalīla wa Dimna*, he resorts to treating such a longer version as "a good illustration of the translator's fondness for padding the text."[27]

The presence of variation in the texts of the Arabic *Kalīla wa Dimna* does not mean that the differences we find are arbitrary. They are organic. For example, an analysis of the various different versions of *The Sage and the Mouse Maiden* as we find this fable attested in the textual traditions of the Arabic *Kalīla wa Dimna* shows that the variations are not merely textual: they are also performative. That is, the multiformity of the textual traditions of the Arabic *Kalīla wa Dimna* is the result of multiformity in the actual performance of such fables as *The Sage and the Mouse Maiden* for real audiences. And such acts of performance need to be explained in terms of the oral traditions at work in the telling of fables.

23. de Blois 1990, 9.

24. de Blois 1990, 9.

25. It is known to folklorists as the Aarne-Thompson Tale-Type 2031C, "The man who seeks the greatest being as a husband for his daughter."

26. Ramanujan 1997, 245.

27. de Blois 1990, 10.

On Multiformity in the Textual Tradition of the *Kalīla wa Dimna*

The contention of this study is that multiformity, even in textual traditions, is a clear sign of an earlier multiformity in oral traditions. Many of the textual differences in the inventory of attested texts of the *Kalīla wa Dimna* may be explained in terms of such multiformity:

- In the case of the Greek version (number 4 in the inventory), de Blois remarks: "Where the later Syriac version stretches the text, the Greek version reduces it to a bare minimum."[28] From the standpoint of oral traditions, such variation can be described in terms of *expansion* and *contraction.*
- In the case of the Persian prose version attributed to Abū l-Ma'ālī (number 5b), here is de Blois' description: "The translator has stuffed it with quotations from Arabic and Persian poems, from the Qur'an and Ḥadīth, and so on, all of which sounds rather quaint in the mouths of animals in the jungles of India."[29] But if this work by Abū l-Ma'ālī is merely a "translation" and if Abū l-Ma'ālī is merely a "translator," then how may its reception be explained? The animal fable, as a literary form, is not unique to "the jungles of India." They are found in a wide range of cultures. Furthermore, for de Blois, recomposition in the context of reception is seen as "padding": "In order to fit these quotations into the book, the translator has padded the prose text, too, to a considerable extent."[30] What de Blois has in mind is a passive "translator," incapable of creative recomposition. A comparative perspective, however, allows for the accommodation of such "quotations," conceded already by de Blois in the case of the *Pañcatantra.* But he does not see that such expansion in the context of "quotations" is a common feature of animal fables in general. And he does not take into account the discourse of the *Pañcatantra* as a form of *prosimetrum.*
- In the case of the newer Hebrew prose version (number 8), de Blois believes it to be "much freer than the older [Hebrew] one," and "spiced with innumerable quotations from the Bible."[31] I note simply that such

28. de Blois 1990, 5.
29. de Blois 1990, 5.
30. de Blois 1990, 5.
31. de Blois 1990, 6.

"spicing" is analogous to the elevations of register in the discourse of *prosimetrum*.

De Blois, however, accounts for all signs of multiformity in the textual tradition of the *Kalīla wa Dimna* in terms of scribal activity:

> A comparison of the various [Arabic] manuscripts reveals at once such a degree of discrepancy that one must often wonder whether they are really copies of one and the same book. It appears that the Arabic *Kalīla wa Dimna* has to a large degree become a victim of its own popularity.[32]

The divergences among the manuscripts of the *Kalīla wa Dimna* as described throughout the monograph of de Blois reinforce this initial impression. The text's popularity, rather than an indication of positive reception and frequent performance, is for de Blois, an occasion for further scribal innovation:

> For one thing, the frequent reading of the book insured that all the old copies were rapidly worn out and had to be replaced. For another, editors and copyists felt free to alter the text, to add new stories and rewrite old ones, to combine material from various manuscripts, and so on, in a way which would have been unthinkable in the case of a "serious" work, say on theology.[33]

In his formulation, the popularity of a text is a matter of its reading rather than listening. Further, could "wear and tear" extend to serious works – equally "popular" – in say, theology, for example? Should we not think that they too suffered from lots and lots of wear and tear at the hands of lots and lots of readers?

The first explanation offered by de Blois for the instability of the textual tradition of the Arabic *Kalīla wa Dimna* does not stand up to scrutiny. De Blois proceeds to offer a second explanation, namely that "editors and copyists felt free to alter the text, to add new stories and rewrite old ones, to combine material from various manuscripts, and so on, in a way which would have been unthinkable in the case of a 'serious' work."[34] In contrast to works on serious subjects, such as theology, the "*Kalīla wa Dimna* was generally (if not always) considered to be a "popular work, a piece of entertainment, which one did not need to approach so respectfully."[35]

32. de Blois 1990, 3.
33. de Blois 1990, 3.
34. de Blois 1990, 3.
35. de Blois 1990, 3.

In de Blois's usage, both terms – "serious" and "popular" – are confined to writing and reading. What is missing in this narrow usage is the idea that fables were meant for performance before audiences and that the tellers of the fables had to adjust to their audiences. By contrast, a discourse on, say, theology could be notionally non-adjustable.

Whereas some things, like scripture, are notionally unchanging, other things, like fables, are meant to change, applied in different ways in different situations. In the case of the Greek *Fables of Aesop*, for example, the earlier forms show no explicit formulation of any moral to the story. Only the later forms spell out the moral: "and the moral of the story is." And we can see a comparable kind of non-explicitness in the Sanskrit *Pañcatantra* as well. The moral has to be read from the contextualization. This kind of activity is brought to life in Book XII of the *Mahābhārata*, where the contextualization of performance is dramatized by the fact that the narratives of animal fables are embedded in a narrative that shows how and why the fables are performed by the character of Bhiṣma to the character of Yudhiṣṭhira.

The need to adjust the content of fables to every new situation is illustrated in the quotations from *Kalīla wa Dimna* in the *'Uyūn al-akhbār* by Ibn Qutayba (d. 889 CE) and the *Kitāb al-'Iqd al-farīd* by Ibn 'Abd Rabbih (d. 940 CE). As de Blois notes, following the opinions of previous orientalists, "the passages in Ibn Qutaybah do not seem always to be literal quotations: often one finds instead a free paraphrase of ibn al-Muqaffa''s text."[36]

Multiform Aetiologies for the Multiform Text of the *Kalīla wa Dimna*

I have already described as multiform not only the received text of the *Kalīla wa Dimna*, which is attested in many different versions, but also the aetiological narratives that were attached to this text, which are also attested in many different versions.

I concentrate here on two versions of the story of the acquisition of the *Kalīla wa Dimna*. These and other versions can be found in the multiple introductions to the multiple texts of the *Kalīla wa Dimna*. In one version, a physician named Burzūya is sent to India by King Khusruw on a quest to find a wondrous plant that heals mortality and confers immortality. He finds instead the book of fables that becomes ultimately the *Kalīla wa Dimna*. In another version, the mythological aspects of the quest are shaded over: Burzūya goes to India to find medicinal herbs but brings back the book of

36. de Blois 1990, 4.

fables instead. In both versions, Burzūya "translates" the book from the language of the Indians into his own language, which is of course Middle Persian. The mythological version of the aetiology of the *Kalīla wa Dimna* is deemed to be "spurious" by de Blois, and the demythologized one is supposedly historical.[37] The latter is followed by a first-person statement, as if spoken by Burzūya, where the physician talks about himself and about his world view. De Blois suggests that this statement, which is missing in the older Syriac version, is the centerpiece of the "autobiography" of Burzūya. For de Blois this first-person account is the historical core of the genesis of the *Kalīla wa Dimna* as we know it:

> Then, I thought about medicine and realised that a physician cannot give his patient a remedy which would heal his illness to such a degree that he would never again suffer from it, or from any other illness. Seeing that there is no guarantee against the same disease, or an even more serious one, recurring, I came to the conclusion that knowledge of the hereafter is the only thing which brings permanent salvation from all diseases. Thus, I came to hold medicine in contempt and to long for religious knowledge. But when I had come to this conclusion, I felt uncertainty concerning religion. I found nothing in my books of medical learning which could show me which religion was the true one. I found that there are many religions and creeds and that the followers of these creeds differ one from the other. Some inherited their religion from their ancestors, others, adopted it on account of fear and coercion, yet others hoped by means of it to acquire worldly goods, pleasures, and prestige. But every one of them claims that his religion is the true and correct one and that whoever contradicts him lives in error and deception. Concerning the creator and what he created, the beginning and the end of the world, and other questions they have violently different opinions, but every one of them despises, opposes, and attacks the others. I decided to frequent the scholars and leaders in every religious faction and to examine what they teach and stipulate in the hope that perhaps I could learn to distinguish truth from falsehood and attach myself confidently to the truth without having to accept on the authority of others something that I could not know or understand by myself. I pursued this plan, investigated and studied. But I discovered that all of these people merely repeat what was handed down to them. Each one praises his own religion and curses the religion of those who disagree with him. It became

37. His most succinct formulation can be found in de Blois 1998, 423.

> clear to me that their conclusions are based on illusions and that their speech is not motivated by a sense of fairness. In not one of them did I find that degree of honesty and rightmindedness which would induce rational persons to accept their words and be satisfied with them.[38]

Rather than a dramatization of Burzūya as a speaker who levels the playing field before telling the fables of the book of *Kalīla wa Dimna*, de Blois sees in this first-person statement the historical core of the "autobiography" of Burzūya. To him, this passage is "rejecting all established religions." A more nuanced interpretation, however, yields a speaker who is simply resisting the zero-sum attitude of dualist religions such as Manichaeanism. It is fruitful to recall here the Syriac figure Bōḏ, to whom the older Syriac version of the *Kalīla wa Dimna* was attributed. Bōḏ also composed works in this vein, including *Discourses on the Faith*, *Against the Manichaeans*, and *Against the Marcionites*.

A Western European Parallel to the Mythological Version of the Aetiology of the *Kalīla wa Dimna*

The mythological narrative about a quest for a plant that confers immortality – a quest that results in the finding of a book instead of immortality pure and simple – is a common motif in a wide variety of folktale traditions. In Western European traditions, the best-known parallel is the narrative about the quest for the Holy Grail, attested in countless versions, the most extensive and comprehensive of which is a massive text written in Old French and dating to the early thirteenth century, commonly designated by English-speaking experts as the *Vulgate Cycle* or the *Arthurian Vulgate* – and by French-speaking experts as *la vulgate arthurienne en prose*. I will refer to it here simply as the *Vulgate Cycle*, following the nomenclature originating from the title given to the text edited by Heinrich Oskar Sommer – an edition dating back to the early twentieth century.[39]

The narrative of this *Vulgate Cycle*, a text extending to roughly four thousand quarto pages (the three attested manuscripts are London, British Library, Add. MS 10292, 10293, and 10294), is remarkably cohesive in its central purpose, which is, to represent the grail as essential for life not because of its contents *per se* but because it contains a wealth of stories about King Arthur, his knights and beyond – without fidelity to a single ideology, politi-

38. de Blois 1990, 26.
39. Sommer 1908–16.

cal view or religious outlook. The cohesiveness is in the very container itself, which is the master narrative, not in what the container contains, that is, in the content.[40]

In both the European narrative about the finding of the Grail and the Near Eastern narrative about the finding of the *Kalīla wa Dimna* – especially in the Arabic versions – the narrators' life story and worldview are expressed in the first person. Moreover, in the European instance, the primary narrators have ostensibly composed their texts in Latin, and only the secondary narrators compose in French. In the Near Eastern instance, too, an original alien language is envisaged.

In a separate project, I intend to study in further detail the parallelisms between the narrative strategies in the stories of the *Vulgate Cycle* and in the stories about the finding of the *Kalīla wa Dimna*. For now, however, it will suffice to highlight the fact that the first-person narratives that we see in stories about the finding of the *Kalīla wa Dimna* are hardly unusual from the standpoint of comparative folklore studies. And, there is no justification for simply assuming that such first-person narratives are necessarily "historical." Rather, the origin narratives of the *Kalīla wa Dimna* were designed to explain not only its genesis, but also its multiform reception in the many different societies that were affected by this collection of fables – and that in turn affected the content of these fables.

40. For a comprehensive discussion, see Leupin 1982.

Bibliography

Bartholomae, C. (1904), *Altiranisches Wörterbuch*, Strasbourg.

De Blois, F. (1990), *Burzōy's Voyage to India and the Origin of the Book of* Kalīlah wa Dimnah, London.

—— (1998), "Kalīla wa Dimna," in: J. S. Meisami and Paul Starkey (eds.), *Encyclopedia of Arabic Literature*, 2 vols., London, II: 423–25.

Davidson, O. M. (2001),"Some Iranian Poetic Tropes as Reflected in the 'Life of Ferdowsi' Traditions," in: M. G. Schmidt and W. Bisang (eds.), *Philologica et Linguistica: Festschrift für Helmut Humbach*, Trier, Supplement 1–12.

—— (2002), "Haft K̲vān," *EIr* XI: 516–9.

—— (2005), "Persian/Iranian Epic," in: J. M. Foley (ed.), *A Companion to Ancient Epic*, Malden, 264–76.

—— (2008), Review of Yamamoto 2003. *Orientalistische Literaturzeitung* 103.3: 305–316. Recast in Davidson 2013b:99–112.

—— (2013a), *Poet and Hero in the Persian Book of Kings*, 3rd ed., Cambridge MA (2nd ed. Costa Mesa CA 2006; 1st ed. Ithaca NY 1994).

—— (2013b), *Comparative Literature and Classical Persian Poetics*, 2nd ed., Cambridge MA (1st ed. Costa Mesa CA 2000).

—— (forthcoming), "Parallel Heroic Themes in the Medieval Irish *Cattle Raid of Cooley* and the Medieval Persian *Book of Kings*."

Edgerton, F. (1924), *The Pañcatantra Reconstructed*, 2 vols., New Haven.

Ferdowsi (1960–71), *Shāhnāma*, ed. Y. E. Bertels et al., 9 vols., Moscow.

Hanson, K. and P. Kiparsky (1997), "The Nature of Verse and its Consequences for the Mixed Form," in: J. Harris and K. Reichl (eds.), *Prosimetrum: Crosscultural Perspectives on Narrative in Prose and Verse*, Cambridge and Rochester NY, 17–44.

Harris, J. and K. Reichl (eds.) (1997), *Prosimetrum: Crosscultural Perspectives on Narrative in Prose and Verse*, Cambridge and Rochester NY.

Leupin, A. (1982), *Le Graal et la littérature: Étude sur la vulgate arthurienne en prose*, Paris.

Nagy, G. (1996), *Poetry as Performance: Homer and Beyond*, Cambridge.

—— (2009), "Hesiod and the Ancient Biographical Traditions," in: F. Montanari, A. Rengakos and C. Tsagalis (eds.), *Brill's Companion to Hesiod*, Leiden, 271–311.

—— (2011), "Diachrony and the Case of Aesop," *Classics @* 9 (http://chs.harvard.edu/wa/pageR?tn=ArticleWrapper&bdc=12&mn=4024, last viewed 10/21/2013).

Ramanujan, A. K. (1997), *A Flowering Tree and Other Oral Tales from India*, ed. and with preface by S. Blackburn and A. Dundes, Berkeley.

Sommer, H.-O. (1908–16), *The Vulgate Versian of the Arthurian Romances*, 7 vols., Washington DC.

Witzel, M. (1997), "Saramā and the Paṇis: Origins of Prosimetric Exchange in Archaic India," in: J. Harris and K. Reichl (eds.), *Prosimetrum: Crosscultural Perspectives on Narrative in Prose and Verse*, Cambridge and Rochester NY, 387–409.

Ziolkowski, J. (1993), *Talking animals: medieval Latin beast poetry, 750–1150*, Philadelphia.

Writing to a Ruler, Speaking to a Ruler, Negotiating the Figure of the Ruler

Thoughts on "Monocratological" Texts and their Contexts in Greco-Roman Antiquity*

Matthias Haake

"Ehrwürdige Exzellenz, nein,
Hochverehrter Herr Staatspräsident, nein,
Allgewaltiger Lenker der Geschicke Ihres mustergültigen Landes!"
D. Grünbein, "Lieber Schurke. Ein Brief an die Tyrannen dieser Welt," *Der Spiegel* no. 18, 2010 (3.5.2010), 144–7, here 144.

"The most part of dedications are charged with flattery; ..."
A. Behn, *Oroonoko*. Edited with an Introduction and Notes by J. Todd, London 2003, 1.

I. Mirrors for Princes – a Universal Phenomenon?[1]

The prevalence of mirrors for princes across cultural, political, religious, and historical divides is a commonplace among students of pre-modern political thought – and many modern scholars assume that mirrors for princes are a more or less universal phenomenon in monocratically formed politi-

* The following contribution is a revised version of my paper given at Berlin. It is neither possible nor intended to treat exhaustively the wide field "Mirrors for Princes in Antiquity?" in this article; the aim is rather limited to the presentation of some basic considerations. References are therefore restricted to a justifiable minimum. For valuable comments on my paper I would like to thank the participants of the Berlin conference. Finally, I am very much indebted to Marie Drauschke (Münster), Ann-Cathrin Harders (Bielefeld) and Anna Linnemann (Münster) for their support during the preparation of my paper as well as of the present article.

1. Anton 2004, 15 as well as Anton 2006, 11 has rightly alluded to a fuzziness of the term "Fürstenspiegel" by differentiating between "Fürstenspiegel" in a narrower sense (concerning princes) and in a wider sense (concerning kings); this terminological fuzziness is also true with regard to the notional equivalents of the word "Fürstenspiegel" like mirror for princes etc. in other modern languages.

cal communities throughout pre-modern history.[2] However, the occurrence of specimens of mirrors for princes in non-monocratical (communicative) contexts has been assumed as well.[3] As such, an appropriate starting point is Pierre Hadot's famous and – at least but not merely in the field of classics – almost canonical lemma *Fürstenspiegel*, as spelt out in the *Reallexikon für Antike und Christentum*.[4] In this entry, Hadot deals with numerous texts encompassing a large span of time and a wide geographical horizon;[5] this range may be delineated by the following examples: at the one end are texts written in the late third millennium BCE, namely the Sumerian *Cylinder Inscriptions* of the ruler Gudea of Lagash[6] and the Middle Egyptian *Instruction for King Merikare*;[7] and on the other end are those written in the ninth century, that is to say Smaragdus of Saint-Mihiel's *Via Regia*[8] or Hincmar of Reims's *On the Person and the Office of the King*.[9] The latest text Hadot refers to in his lemma is the dubious pseudo-Plutarchean *Institutio Traiani* first mentioned by John of Salisbury in his *Policraticus* which was finally redacted in 1159 CE and which was dedicated to Thomas Becket, then Lord Chancellor of the English king Henry II.[10]

However, that Hadot's lemma is limited to mirrors for princes from an-

2. The term "monocracy" means "the government of a sovereign (or quasi sovereign) social group by a single man, whatever the name given to him who exercises the power: chief, king, emperor, monarch, prince, president..."; for this definition see Gilissen 1970, 20 in the context of his wider attempt to define and characterize the concept of monocracy (Gilissen 1970, 19–29). For a short introduction to different types of monocracies and the respective terminology see Gilissen 1970, 35–46. Due to the historical development of the meaning of the word monarchy it is difficult and partially inadequate to use this *prima facie* obvious term for all types of political orders of "sole rulership"; see Luraghi 2013b, 11. On the Greek word "monarch" see Luraghi 2013a, 131–2.

3. See for example Eder 1995 and Schulte 2001, esp. 13, 35–41 and 170–83.

4. A history of the carrier of the "mirror for princes-concept" in historical and literary studies as well as in other disciplines is a true desideratum.

5. Hadot 1972. For an elaborated, but widely neglected criticism of Hadot's "mirror for princes-approach" see Eder 1995, esp. 156–8. However, Eder's own approach is far less convincing than his qualified criticism.

6. Hadot 1972, 562. Regarding the *Cylinder Inscriptions* of Gudea one might refer to Suter 2000, 71–159.

7. Hadot 1972, 558–60. On the *Instruction for King Merikare* see for example Quack 1992, esp. 89–137; see furthermore the short remarks of Baines 1995, 20–1 and Lichtheim 1996, 247–8.

8. Hadot 1972, 622. On Smaragdus of Saint-Mihiel's *Via Regia* see Anton 1968, 132–79 and the comprehensive approach by Eberhardt 1977, esp. 86–266, 335–45, 361–91 and 491–688.

9. Hadot 1972, 623. Hincmar of Reims's *On the Person and the Office of the King* is subject of the remarks by Anton 1968, 281–355.

10. Hadot 1972, 623–4. Regarding the pseudo-Plutarchean *Institutio Traiani*, controversially discussed in modern scholarship, one might refer among others to Kerner 1988 as well as Kerner 1992; still worth reading is Liebeschütz 1943, 34–9. On John of Salisbury's *Policraticus* in general see Berges 1938, 131–43.

cient Egypt, the ancient Near East, ancient Israel, Greco-Roman antiquity and the medieval and Byzantine worlds up to the ninth century is not due to any objective consideration but to the chronological framework of the *Reallexikon für Antike und Christentum*.[11] While Hadot was unable to amplify his delineations on mirrors for princes until the late middle ages or early modern times, other scholars have done so. They agree on the existence of mirrors for princes from antiquity to the early modern period,[12] or even from the late third millennium BCE until the twentieth century.[13] In this regard, the influential study by Lester K. Born published in 1933 deserves attention. Skeptical of the very origins of mirrors for princes he wrote: "Just how far back into antiquity the roots of this *genre*, the *speculum principis* reach, is not yet completely proven. But that there is a continuous tradition from the time of Isocrates who addressed the first such treatise we know of in classical times to Nicocles the King of Cyprus down to the twentieth century is beyond question, ..."[14] For a twentieth-century specimen, Born mentioned the article *Prinzenerziehung* of the Austrian Generalmajor (i.e. major general) Auspitz published in 1904.[15]

11. See Hadot 1972, 556.

12. See for example Rabeler 2007, 328–32.

13. See among others Blum 1981, 5–23; Singer 1983 and Philipp and Stammen 1996. For collections of mirrors for princes from the Early and High Middle Ages as well as from the Early modern period see Anton 2006 as well as Mühleisen, Stammen and Philipp 1997; a list of "Western European" mirrors for princes starting with John of Salisbury's *Policraticus* and ending in the late fourteenth century was compiled by Berges 1938, 291–356 and from 1400 until the twentieth century continued by Singer 1981, 51–167. Blum 1981, 30–56 offers an overview on Byzantine mirrors for princes and on pp. 56–8 a very short survey of writings which are similar to the character of mirrors for princes; for some narrow remarks on Slavic mirrors for princes see Blum 1981, 23–39 and Hannick 1989, 1056–7. On Scandinavian as well as Irish and Welsh mirrors for princes see Bagge 1989 and Richter 1989 respectively. See Berger 1989 for mirrors for princes in Romance languages. For Arabic and Persian mirrors for princes see the considerations by Leder 1999, 21–45 and see his list of Arabic and Persian mirrors for princes on pp. 46–50; one might also refer to the very short remarks of Richter-Bernburg 1989 and Tietze 1989 on Arabic, Islamic and Ottoman mirrors for princes as well as to Dakhlia 2002, Ould Cheikh 2003, Aigle 2007 and de Fouchécour 2009, 357–454.

14. Born 1933, 583.

15. Born 1933, 584; see also Singer 1981, 167. The article in question is Auspitz 1904. The first name of Auspitz, not mentioned in the context of his article, is Leopold; on Leopold Auspitz see Schnedl–Bubenicek 1985, 70–1 and Broucek and Peball 2000, 390. In this context one could consequently refer also to a rather unknown and somewhat more recent but by all means highly interesting text by the German Classical philologist Hans von Arnim: At the University of Frankfurt he delivered a speech titled *Ein altgriechisches Königsideal* on January 27th, 1916; see Arnim 1916. When von Arnim delivered this speech on the occasion of the birthday of the German Emperor Wilhelm II during the Great War, it was – at least in Germany – one of the very last occasions to write a mirror for princes. Due to his social status as professor (of Greek philology) and also due to his then pioneering work on Dio Chrysostom and his analysis

II. Greco-Roman Antiquity – a World Full of Mirrors for Princes?

According to Hadot's lemma, Greco-Roman antiquity was indeed a world full of mirrors for princes – from the very beginning in the early archaic period of Greek history in the eighth century BCE until the transformation of the late Antique world into the Medieval and Byzantine worlds respectively in the sixth and seventh centuries CE, divided into a western Mediterranean and an eastern Mediterranean sphere. Hadot included a broad spectrum of texts under the label "Fürstenspiegel:" the Homeric epics[16] and Pindar's odes for victorious tyrants at the Panhellenic Games;[17] various Attic tragedies;[18] Isocrates' "Cypriotic" writings *To Nicocles, Nicocles or the Cyprians* and the *Euagoras*;[19] Xenophontic texts such as the dialogue *Hiero*, the *Cyropaedia* or the encomiastic *Agesilaus*;[20] Platonic dialogues such as the *Republic* or the *Statesman*;[21] Hellenistic inscriptions and papyri;[22] the so-called *Letter of Aristeas*;[23] imperial texts such as Augustus' *Res Gestae*[24] or Marcus Aurelius's *Meditations*[25] and some of Julian's speeches and his other writings;[26] Sene-

of Dio's four speeches *On Kingship* (Arnim 1898, esp. 398–435), often considered as mirrors for princes in modern scholarship (see, e.g., Hadot 1972, 597–600 and Schulte 2001, 208–18), von Arnim might have seemed to be simply predestinated to make such a speech at the University of Frankfurt. On von Arnim see Berner 2012.

16. Hadot 1972, 569–70; on "Homeric kings and kingship" see now the considerations by Luraghi 2013a, 132–5.

17. Hadot 1972, 572–3; on Pindar's "tyrannic" victory odes, see Mann 1998, 248–68 and 274–81; see also Mann 2013.

18. Hadot 1972, 573–4. On the representation of kings in Attic tragedy see for example Alföldi 1955, 25–55; Lanza 1977, esp. 3–159 and Flaig 1998, 63–86.

19. Hadot 1972, 574–6; on Isocrates' "Cypriotic" writings see Eucken 1983, 213–69.

20. Hadot 1972, 576–8. On Xenophon's *Hiero* see most recently Schorn 2008 and Leppin 2010; Gray 2011, 246–90 is the most up-to-date approach to the *Cyropaedia*; the *Agesilaus* has been treated among others by Pontier 2010 and Gray 2011, 30–2.

21. Hadot 1972, 578–80; on Plato's concept of the philosopher-king in the *Republic* see Reeve 1988, esp. 191–5 and Flaig 1994, 37–43; on the philosopher-king in the late Platonic dialogues see Schofield 1998.

22. Hadot 1972, 585–6. Hadot's explanations rest upon an approach comparable to Schubart 1937a and Schubart 1937b; for a criticism of Schubart's attempt see Gehrke 1982, 248 as well as Gehrke 2013, 74 respectively.

23. Hadot 1972, 587–9; on the *Letter of Aristeas* see now Hunter 2011.

24. Hadot 1972, 586–7. On Augustus' *Res Gestae* see most recently Witschel 2008 and Cooley 2009, 1–55.

25. Hadot 1972, 600–1. On Marcus Aurelius' *Meditations* see for example Pernot 2003 who is as well of the opinion that this text is a mirror for princes; see now also amongst others Reydams-Schils 2012.

26. Hadot 1972, 604–5. On Julian's two panegyric orations on Constantius II see now

ca's *On Clemency*;[27] the four orations *On Kingship* by Dio Chrysostom,[28] those speeches of Themistius addressing the emperors Constantius II, Jovian, Valens and Theodosius,[29] the "Julianic" speeches of Libanius,[30] Synesius of Cyrene's oration *On Kingship*;[31] Pliny the Younger's *Panegyric*[32] and the other Latin Panegyrics;[33] very different texts by Christian authors such as Eusebius of Caesarea's so-called *Tricennial Oration* and *Life of Constantine*,[34] *On the Death of Theodosius* by Ambrose of Milan,[35] and finally, a passage from *Of the City of God* by Augustine of Hippo.[36]

But what are the characteristics of mirrors for princes? According to Hadot the essential feature of mirrors is "... the fact that the literary genre of advice for princes has – from earliest antiquity on – always followed the same rules and conventions even though it appears in various forms and descriptions: that is as eulogium or execration, an unconnected sequence of sentences or a didactic and systematic treatise, biography or utopia."[37] It is self-evident that such a definition is both broad and unspecific – and perhaps this aspect is one of the secrets to the success of Hadot's approach. Its basic element, that is the idea of mirrors for princes as "advice for rulers," comprises, by and large, the scholarly *communis opinio* in the field of classical studies.[38] Thus the term mirrors for princes – and its equivalents in other

---

Tougher 2012 and Drake 2012 respectively; Julian's *Letter to Themistius the Philosopher* as well as his satirical text *The Beard-Hater*, both more or less relevant in the present context, were recently reconsidered by Watt 2012 and Baker-Brian 2012. On Julian's *Caesars* see Baldwyn 1978.

27. Hadot 1972, 594–5; for an introductory essay on Seneca's *On Clemency* see recently Braund 2009.

28. Hadot 1972, 597–600; on the much discussed orations *On Kingship* by Dio Chrysostom see for example Moles 1990.

29. Hadot 1972, 603–4. For introductory remarks in terms of the relevant orations by Themistius one might refer to Leppin and Portmann 1998.

30. Hadot 1972, 606; on the "Julianic" speeches of Libanius see more recently for example Scholl 1994.

31. Hadot 1972, 606–7; see also for example Brandt 2003.

32. Hadot 1972, 609–10; from the vast number of publications regarding Pliny's *Panegyric* one might refer for example to Ronning 2007, 24–136 und Roche 2011.

33. Hadot 1972, 608–9; on these eleven texts see for example Nixon and Saylor Rodgers 1994, 1–35 and Lopetegui 2013.

34. Hadot 1972, 614–5. On Eusebius' *Life of Constantine* see Cameron and Hall 1999; Drijvers 2004; and Thelamon 2007; on his *Tricennial Oration* see Drake 1976, 3–79 and also Wienand 2012, 421–37.

35. Hadot 1972, 617–8; on Ambrose's *On the Death of Theodosius* see for example Biermann 1995, 49–50, 103–19, 143–50 and 178–91.

36. Hadot 1972, 618. On this passage in the fifth book of Augustine's *Of the City of God* one might refer to O'Daly 1999, 99 and Weithman 2001, 246.

37. See Hadot 1972, 556 (translation Anna Linnemann).

38. Instructive in this context are the admittedly cautious, but in the end affirmative re-

European languages as *speculum regis*, *Fürstenspiegel* or *miroir au prince* – is frequently used in scholarly texts, not seldom almost programmatically, but often in a rather uncritical way.[39] Even if one is willing to admit the existence of mirrors for princes in classical antiquity, it remains true that theoretical approaches and attempts to conceptualize them are a rather rare phenomenon in the field of Classics.[40]

But is it appropriate to refer to mirrors for princes of Greco-Roman antiquity as such, applying the term *avant la lettre*? This question merits further elaboration, especially since neither the term nor Hadot's approach have been uniformly accepted by classicists and ancient historians.[41]

III. Mirrors for Princes – Terminology and Definitions

Mirror for princes, as a term, is not attested in texts from antiquity.[42] In Europe, the very first occurrence of the combination of "mirror" and "prince / king" (more precisely *speculum* and *rex* respectively) is attested in the Latin title of a work by Godfrey of Viterbo in 1183: the unfinished *Speculum regum* dedicated, but not assigned to the later German emperor Henry VI.[43] Another early evidence for the combination of the words "mirror" and "prince/ king" in a title, strictly speaking the second one, is the Norwegian *Konungs-Skuggsiá* (i.e. *The King's Mirror*) written by an unknown author and dating to the mid-thirteenth century.[44] Even later, namely to the fourteenth century, date the first instances of titles such as *Le Mireoirs as Princes* of Watriquet de Couvain and *Speculum regis Edmundi II* attributed to Simon Islip.[45]

marks by Zimmermann 1998, 321–2 n. 169 which can be considered to some extent as paradigmatic with regard to the handling of Hadot's definition by many Classical scholars.

39. See e.g. Adam 1970; Irmscher 1978; Mazza 1980; Charles-Saget 1986; Squilloni 1990; Eder 1995; Schulte 2001; Demandt 2002; Brandt 2003; Pernot 2003; Drijvers 2004; Gray 2011; and Körner 2011.

40. But see for instance Eder 1995, 156 and especially Schulte 2001, 9–10 and 13–8.

41. See for example Kaerst 1898; Hahm 2000, esp. 458 n. 5; Virgilio 2003, 47–85; Sidebottom 2006; and Eckstein 2009, 253–5. The same is true for most of Oswyn Murray's extensive and essential work on Greek monarchical theory; see for example the more or less explicit statement of Murray 2007, 15. However, cf. otherwise the isolated statement of Murray 1998, 262. Against the use of the term mirror for princes with reference to texts from Greco-Roman antiquity see explicitly Haake 2003, 84 as well as Haake 2013, 166–7 and also Haake 2012, 67–8.

42. See for example Hadot 1972, 556.

43. On Godfrey of Viterbo's *Speculum regum* see Dorninger 1997, esp. 60–5 and Anton 2006, 24–6. See, however, the worthwhile remarks of Jónsson 2006, 156. For the combination of "Fürst" and "Spiegel" in German see Singer 1981, 22–4 and also Haake 2003, 104–5 n. 9.

44. On this text see Bagge 1987 and the important explanations by Jónsson 1987, esp. 391–5 and 400–7.

45. See Jónsson 1987, 405–6 with n. 27 as well as Jónsson 2006, 156 with n. 10; on the works referred to see Berges 1938, 342–3 nos. 32–3.

Against this background it is necessary to ask for the reasons and the reasoning for applying the term mirrors for princes to earlier medieval texts and, even more important regarding the present topic, to texts written in Greco-Roman antiquity. Or, put differently: Do mirrors for princes exist *avant la lettre*? In the end, all this leads to the cardinal question: What is a mirror for princes? Yet, as simple this question might at first glance seem to be, as difficult is it to find a satisfying answer.[46]

Medievalists use the term mirror for princes generally in a rather diffused way,[47] while conceding that it is impossible to define mirrors for princes according to the literary criteria of a genre in the narrow sense.[48] According to Hans Hubert Anton:

> A mirror for princes is a text written with a paraenetic intention, which either addresses a king, prince or regent as a person each or a (fictitious) official as representative of a social group. It is meant to be composed either as independent work or as cohered part in a wider context. The paraenesis can express itself through direct admonitions concerning the ruler's ethics and administration as well as through considerations on political and social theoretical contexts related to the addressee. It can refer to the person and office of the ruler, and – in a wider sense – to the given comprehensive political and ecclesiastic orders. The texts' specific place is between "is" and "ought"; it is the discussion of political ethics they have in common with the ... theoretical works.[49]

In its fundamentals this definition does not differ significantly from other approaches to delineating the parameters of medieval mirrors for princes as a genre. Otto Eberhardt has offered the following classification:

> A mirror for princes is a conclusive work which discusses – with the purpose of a basic transfer of knowledge or exhortation – the proper behavior of a ruler as exhaustively as possible with regard to his special position; often, a personal relationship to the ruler underlies these works.[50]

Or, Ulrike Graßnick has suggested:

46. See for example the considerations of Graßnick 2004, 41–4.
47. As rightly emphasized by Anton 2006, 3.
48. See again but in some way unsatisfactorily Anton 2006, 3. See for example the delineations by Peil 1986, 54–5 and 89–92.
49. See Anton 2004, 15 (translation Anna Linnemann) or, identically, Anton 2006, 3–4.
50. See Eberhardt 1977, 280 (translation Anna Linnemann).

> Late medieval mirrors for princes serve above all for the consulting and education of rulers. They are texts of pragmatic writtenness, which make explicit and implicit use of the mirror metaphor in terms of both content and concept. Hence, the implications and approaches of the two concepts "pragmatic writtenness" and "mirror metaphor" are essential characteristics of the genre. Mirrors for princes can be written in different forms, either in verse or in prose, as a pragmatic individual text or integrated into a narrative-fictional context. They all have in common, however, the aim to convey models of sovereign behavior in the form of writtenness.[51]

The above three definitions have the following in common: a predominant focus on content, especially on the figure of the (good) ruler;[52] a preoccupation with function, that is the provision of advice to a ruler; and third, at least to a large extent, the omitting of many aspects developed in the field of literary studies relative to the determination of literary genres *strictu sensu*. The second aspect is often deduced from the first one and the third one results more or less consequently from the two former ones, so that nearly any text that concerns rulers and governance is considered by some modern scholars as a mirror for princes. The "mirror" quality, however, is generally considered less important and frequently ignored.[53]

Einar Már Jónsson formulated a rather outlier definition for medieval mirrors for princes: "A Fürstenspiegel is a treatise written for a prince - and generally dedicated to him in some way - whose main purpose is to describe the ideal prince, his behavior, his role and position in the world."[54] Although at first glance this may appear as rather similar to the previous definitions, there is an important difference insofar as the literary genre is concerned. Whereas the other definitions operate with the concept of genre despite acknowledging its rather fluid boundaries, Jónsson denies the very applicability of genre as a classification for the study of mirrors for princes:

> If one defines "literary genre" on the basis of formal and at the same time programmatic criteria that hint at a particular choice of

51. See Graßnick 2004, 332–3 (translation Anna Linnemann). For a definition of the concept of "pragmatic writtenness" as applied by Graßnick see Keller and Worstbrock 1988, 389. For a first attempt of Graßnick to define mirror for princes see Graßnick 2004, 44.

52. It is worth referring in this context to Le Goff 1996, 402–31.

53. On the word "mirror" in book titles from the medieval and early modern periods see Lehmann 1953, esp. 27–45; Bradley 1954; Grabes 1973, 245–87; Roth 1995; Jónsson 1995, 157–212; Connoche-Bourgne 2003; and Pomel 2003.

54. See Jónsson 1987, 394 (translation Anna Linnemann) as well as again Jónsson 2006, 159 who defines four classes of medieval mirrors for princes against the background of his quoted delineations; see Jónsson 2006, 160–2.

> topics and a particular attitude towards them, such as the typical titles "sum," "maxims," "mirror," etc., it is clear that the "mirrors for princes" do not form a literary genre. If one defines it from a more historical perspective, as a group of literary works whose authors were inspired by the same models, influenced each other mutually and followed the same rules, one is also obliged to say that the "mirrors for princes" do not form a literary genre. If, finally, a purely material criterion is adopted and one defines a literary genre as a group of writings that speaks about the same subject, such as the historical works, then the "mirrors for princes" can hardly be defined as a homogeneous literary genre. At any rate, the "Fürstenspiegel" are not a literary genre in the same way as, for example, the works entitled *Speculum* or *Summa*.[55]

The above *tour d'horizon* is hardly a comprehensive survey of mirrors for princes insofar as definition, classification and nomenclature are concerned. Rather, the more limited objective is to illustrate the relative vagueness and inhomogeneity of mirrors for princes as a concept in medieval studies and to point to the subsequently requisite criteria for the application and the applicability of this concept to texts from Greco-Roman antiquity.

IV. Traveling Concept – On the Use and Abuse of the Term Mirrors for Princes for Texts from Greco-Roman Antiquity

Walter Eder once has argued:

> When defined not only by the formal criterion (prose-encomium) and content related criterion (praise of a ruler), but also by the criterion of the advice's practicability, the subject of a mirror for princes ... can be defined as the presentation of political-ethical aims, which ought to be strived for and achieved in practical life, by using the example of the ideal rulers' education and behavior.[56]

And Lucio Bertelli has observed that the " 'Fürstenspiegel' is a literary genre that [occurred] in different forms – treatise, panegyric, biography. ..."[57] Both depictions, the one by the ancient historian and the one by the classicist respectively, seem to be to a large extent congruent with the previously

55. Jónsson 2006, 164 (translation Anna Linnemann).
56. Eder 1995, 159 (translation Anna Linnemann).
57. See Bertelli 2002, 54 (translation Anna Linnemann).

mentioned definitions of mirrors for princes developed in the field of medieval studies. Yet, contrary to what one might deduce from this analogy, the applicability of the "mirrors for princes-concept" to texts from Greco-Roman antiquity is far from being solved. From a medievalist's point of view, Anton has argued that only few mirrors for princes existed in antiquity;[58] as exception to the rule he referred – besides some Late Antique Greek texts – to Seneca's *On Clemency* and Pliny's *Panegyric*.[59] Graßnick, however, is of the opinion that in Ancient Greece and Rome a considerable number of mirrors for princes were written even if many of these texts are *strictu sensu*, and according to her own definition, no mirror for princes, but contain only elements of this genre.[60] But what do those classicists who uphold the position that there were mirrors for princes in antiquity have to say? Ryan K. Balot, for example, seems to be of the opinion that the dedicatory letter of the pseudo-Aristotelian *Rhetoric to Alexander* is more or less the very first example of the yet to flourish genre of mirrors for princes.[61] In Vivienne J. Gray's view, however, mirrors for princes predate Xenophon's *Cyropaedia*,[62] whereas according to Wilfrid Parsons, a passage from Augustine's *Of the City of God* can be considered the first mirror for princes.[63] Walter Eder in a sophisticated contribution on the role of mirrors for princes in the Athenian democracy of the fourth century BCE, posits that texts written by Isocrates and Xenophon, dealing with monarchical rule and addressed to contemporaneous rulers should not be understood as being intended to give advice to the explicit addressees, but to strengthen the aristocratic element in the Athenian democracy by fostering the creation of political awareness and the education of Athenian aristocrats through the medium of figurative speech.[64]

This more or less random but representative sample of inconsistent statements by medieval as well as classical scholars concerning mirrors for princes in Greco-Roman antiquity resembles the "Babylonian confusion of tongues" and calls for clarity, albeit a challenging task. The two main reasons for this situation are quite obvious: on the one hand, on a scholarly level, the fluidity that characterizes the mirror for princes as a concept, and on the other hand, on the plane of common knowledge, the prevalence of

58. See Anton 2004, 17 as well as Anton 2006, 9 who refers to Hadot 1972 as exponent of the common view in terms of the existence of mirrors for princes in antiquity.

59. See again Anton 2004, 17 as well as Anton 2006, 9.

60. See Graßnick 2004, 52.

61. See Balot 2006, 269.

62. See Gray 2011, 5 n. 1.

63. See Parsons 1942, 129.

64. See Eder 1995, esp. 155.

a hardly defined but nevertheless broadly recognizable consensus on the approximate meaning of the term.[65] Thus, it is perhaps not so surprising to find little scholarly interest in the question of genre as it pertains to mirrors for princes in antiquity as a whole.

One rare exception is J. Manuel Schulte's monograph which is, according to the author, the only book-length study of mirrors for princes in Greco-Roman antiquity.[66] However, apart from its merits in bringing together and discussing a wide range of texts from Greco-Roman antiquity on the subject of good governance, Schulte's work suffers from a not altogether compelling conceptual foundation.[67] His decision to adopt Niklas Luhmann's schema of the mirror in ethics – as delineated in *Die Gesellschaft der Gesellschaft*[68] – is perhaps not as effective as Schulte has assumed, since it requires more or less an *ipso facto* recognition of the existence of mirrors in antiquity. Equally problematic is his consideration of Niccolò Machiavelli's *Il Principe* – described by Quentin Skinner as "a contribution to the *genre* of advice-books for princes which at the same time revolutionized the *genre* itself"[69] – as the ideal-typical model for a veritable mirror for princes, since Schulte then proceeds to characterize mirrors for princes written in Greco-Roman antiquity on the basis of a typology crafted from a fifteenth century text.[70] Furthermore, Schulte's conceptualization rests primarily on content, ignoring aspects of form as well as audience, another serious drawback.[71] Finally, one might doubt the utility of applying the term mirror for princes to texts from Greco-Roman antiquity, since such a move would necessarily imply the existence of a very particular genre across historical, political, social, and literary divides.[72]

Bearing in mind the conceptual vagueness of mirrors for princes and considering also that the only text from Greco-Roman antiquity which is widely accepted as a mirror for princes, namely Seneca's *On Clemency*[73] – wherein the mirror is an explicit metaphor – is a unique document, then

65. This can be shown by referring to Hohl 1958, 151 and Kerkhecker 2002, 135.

66. Schulte 2001, 66.

67. On Schulte 2001 see Weber 2003.

68. Luhmann 1997, esp. 915; for Schulte's appropriation of Luhmann see Schulte 2001, esp. 9 and 260–1.

69. See Skinner 1978, 118.

70. See Schulte 2001, 15–6. On Machiavelli's *Il Principe* see for example Skinner 1978, 113–38 and Chabod 2006; Gilbert 1939 is still worth reading.

71. See Schulte 2001, 16–8.

72. See Schulte 2001, 16–8 and 250–61.

73. For this common sensical approach see Braund 2009, 17. On the respective introductory passage in Seneca's *On Clemency* see Braund 2009, 153–5; in this context see also Haake 2003, 106–7 n. 12.

the applicability of mirror for princes to texts from that period, methodologically as well as heuristically, is brought under question. The present author's unease in aggregating a number of Greek and Latin texts – broadly pertaining to the question of good rule – into a common typology derives in the first instance from the absence of evident benefits to such an approach and in the second from the absence of such unifying terminology in antique texts themselves. As delineated above, classifying Greco-Roman texts written in antiquity as mirrors for princes bespeaks an obsessive focus on content at the expense of other textual respects, such as structural and situational contexts and that of form.[74]

However, studying political thought in terms of timeless, universal concepts[75] has been effectively challenged by the so-called Cambridge School, on the one hand,[76] and historical pragmatics, an approach developed in the field of literary studies, on the other.[77] What if any are the ramifications of such considerations for an analysis of texts from Greco-Roman antiquity whose subject is the good ruler, conventionally referred to as mirrors for princes?

V. Reflecting on the Monocrat and Considering the Practice of Monocratical Rule in Greco-Roman Antiquity – Texts and Contexts

Among the important implications of the methodological delineations presented above is the exhortation to take seriously the generic aspect of pre-modern texts.[78] To do so, the five constitutive determinants of genre must be heeded:[79] first, the author is seen not as an individual but as a member of a specific social group with a characteristic social role, and second, the addressee is regarded in the same manner too. Both author and addressee constitute the explicit frame of the communicative situation of each text.

74. But see for example the thought provoking, if not entirely convincing, study by Eder 1995.

75. For critical remarks on such an approach by the present author see Haake 2003, 107–8 n. 14.

76. In this context Skinner 1969, on which see Major 2005, is fundamental; see also the more programmatic explanations by Skinner 1978, IX–XIV. For an analysis of mirrors for princes Skinner's approach has been applied for example by Tilmans 1991 on some Renaissance mirrors for princes written in the Netherlands.

77. Gumbrecht 1977 is one of the key texts for this approach. On historical pragmatics see recently Jucker and Taavitsainen 2010.

78. As example one may refer in this context to the article of Stammen 1990 on mirrors for princes from the early modern period.

79. See Raible 1980.

Third, the form of the text in question has to be considered and, fourth, its actual content; fifth and finally, it is essential to discuss the problem of the implied audience of the texts, applying the same categories as used for the author and the addressee.[80]

The application of this model to texts from Greco-Roman antiquity dealing with monocrats and monocratical ruling may be productively demonstrated by reference to a particular group of Hellenistic texts, the treatises *On Kingship,* whose earliest specimen was in all probability written by Aristotle and addressed to his former pupil Alexander the Great,[81] and which are often but inapplicably classified as mirrors for princes in modern research.[82] Their authors are invariably philosophers writing in their social role as intellectuals;[83] the addressees are without exception Hellenistic kings; from the essential perspective of form, they are self-contained prose texts; their content consists not of monarchical theory or concrete and situational instructions for a king but of a delineation of the figure of the good ruler along well-established *topoi* as opposite to the tyrant; and finally, the implied audience is the world of the Hellenistic cities.[84]

Three further aspects regarding the treatises *On Kingship* are important.[85] First, the philosophers who authored such texts were members of different philosophical schools; thus, writing *On Kingship* had nothing to do with the affiliation to a specific philosophical school. Second, there are no substantial differences between the various specimens of these treatises on a contentual level despite the fact that their authors belonged to different philosophical schools. Third, the kings to whom treatises *On Kingship* were addressed were members of different dynasties – a clear model as to the practice of addressing these texts cannot be deduced.

It is now possible to contextualize the texts in question in their respective situational framework that is their socio-political, cultural, intellectual and historical contexts.[86] To concretize this general statement by referring again to Hellenistic treatises *On Kingship*: most of these texts were written

80. This passage is a more or less literal adoption from Haake 2013, 167.

81. See Haake 2013, 168.

82. See Haake 2003, 84 as well as Haake 2013, 166–7.

83. On the concept and social role of the intellectual see Haake 2003, 97–100.

84. The preceding explanations are a very short summary of Haake 2003, 88–91 as well as of Haake 2013, 174–8. On Roman imperial and late antique treatises *On Kingship* see Haake 2012, 70–2 and 77–81.

85. For the following delineations see again more detailed Haake 2003, 88–90 as well as Haake 2013, 174–7; see also Haake 2012, 69–70.

86. Haake 2008, esp. 284–5 has demonstrated that statements considered undoubtedly as antimonarchical in a Greek context have a completely different meaning, despite their Greek language and form, when proclaimed in a different political and cultural context.

in the early Hellenistic period when the world of the Greek cities was in general not directly ruled by kings but usually at least strongly dominated by them. This situation was for both – the cities as well as the kings – a difficult one since "[e]xcept in the retrospective imagination of historians and philosophers, no Greek *polis* [*i.e.* city] had yet been ruled by a legitimate monarch."[87]

The Greek cities had to deal with the Hellenistic kings and *vice versa* and this situation resulted in the development of new forms of communication. The most prominent element among these new forms of communication between cities and kings, a configuration of power completely alien to the traditional framework of Greek cities, is the civic ruler cult. By means of the civic ruler cult, the king's superior position in terms of power was conceptualized by ascribing to him a superhuman status and it was concurrently possible to place the king beyond the institutional order of the city but within its universe; and finally: granting a civic ruler cult had always a prospective message, since it expressed in a more or less implicit manner the city's expectations as regards the future behavior of the king.[88] On a highly symbolic level, the treatises *On Kingship* are, like the civic ruler cult, part of the communication between cities and kings in the Hellenistic period. Resting upon the semantics of the communicative web covering these treatises and shaped especially by the social configurations of the king, the philosopher and the Hellenistic city, their function may be characterized briefly in the following way: While the writings of the philosophers were to some extent part of the inner-philosophical competition, receiving them enabled the Hellenistic kings to present themselves as good rulers – free from tyrannical blemishes – in front of the audience of the world of the Hellenistic cities.[89]

It is obvious that this interpretation of the Hellenistic treatises *On Kingship* could not have been achieved on the basis of the "mirror for princes approach" with its strong content-focused perspective and its generally accepted underlying paraenetic intention of these texts. Of course, it is an important task to analyze the delineations regarding the (good) king and the practice of good rule in the Hellenistic texts considered as mirrors for princes in modern research within the context of the Greek history of ideas of monarchical thought.[90] But such an interest should be restricted to the

87. Luraghi 2013a, 131.

88. On the Hellenistic ruler cult Habicht 1970 is fundamental; see also Price 1984, 23–52 and Chaniotis 2003 as well as Haake 2003, 93; Haake 2011, 118–9 n. 42; and Haake 2013, 181.

89. See *en detail* Haake 2003, 91–5 as well as Haake 2013, 178–84.

90. See for example Murray's "The Idea of the Shepherd King from Cyrus to Charlemagne" (Murray 1990). On pre-Hellenistic reflections on monarchy see for example Bertelli 2002, 17–

respect of content and subsequently focus on questions regarding the development and reception of monarchical ideas. If, however, the claim extends to topics concerning intention and function, then the mirror for princes approach should be discarded in view of its homogenizing tendency. Rather it can be deduced that it is necessary to differentiate the texts often characterized as mirrors for princes according to their generic features – outlined above – that are constitutive of genre. Of central importance to any understanding of the meaning of a text is its original and intended communicative context which determines its semantics – an aspect which is not always taken sufficiently into account by the "mirrors for princes-approach."

To return to Hadot's lemma *Fürstenspiegel*, it may now be stated that his approach neglects some important aspects. Among them, the following may be highlighted: the question whether a ruler commissioned a text and whether there were other vectors linking the author to the ruler, and further, whether the text is addressed to the ruler of a realm where the author also lived. The same is true in terms of what one might call performative elements of the text in question:[91] Was it presented in front of an addressed ruler in the form of a speech as was Pliny's *Panegyric*, for example? Or, was the text addressed and sent to a king such as the Hellenistic treatises *On Kingship*? Or, did an author negotiate questions regarding the figure of the sole ruler and his practice of rule in a philosophical text such as Plato's *Statesman*?

There remains a final aspect in the interpretation of monocrats and monocratical rule in Greco-Roman antiquity which has escaped scholarly attention, and this regards the structural context in which these texts are embedded, one that is characterized by the presence of strong antimonarchical discourses.[92] This circumstance is linked to the fact that "the monocracies in classical antiquity had not ... *primarily* shaped the historical orders, but had, in a way, secondarily, placed themselves in basically differently oriented normative systems or – using another image – had covered the primary orders secondarily."[93]

It is self-evident that monocrats in Greco-Roman antiquity found themselves in a weak position, having to demonstrate their rule-worthiness in a milieu marked with entrenched disdain for monocratical rule of any kind.

43; Haake 2003, 85–8; as well as Haake 2013, 169–73; and Luraghi 2013a, 132–44. On Hellenistic reflections on monarchy see Walbank 1984, 75–81; Hahm 2000, 458–64; and Eckstein 2009, 247–55.

91. Against this see the approach of Schulte 2001.
92. On this topic see the contributions in Börm (forthcoming).
93. See Gotter 2008, 185 (translation Anna Linnemann).

VI. On "Monocratological" Texts in Greco-Roman Antiquity – Some Final Remarks

Reflections on the monocrat, whether in the shape of the archaic tyrant, the Hellenistic king, or the Roman emperor, are found in Greek and Latin literature from the eighth century BCE to the sixth and seventh century CE. The political language of monocracy in Greco-Roman antiquity is found in numerous and disparate texts, from all literary genres – thus embodying different functions and variegated intentions. Nevertheless, none should be considered as mirror for princes.

Finally, the utility of a descriptive neologism, that comprises texts of varied character without denying those differences, one that refers primarily to content but does not bear on generic or functional respects of these texts and does not imply any cogent further link between them is apparent. One such possibility is offered in the term "monocratological texts,"[94] to refer to texts reflecting the available stock of knowledge about monocratical rule in antiquity, resting upon either historical experiences or imagined conceptions. Whether a text dealing with the figure of a monocrat and monocratic rule in a general or in a specific way; authored by a poet, historian or philosopher; written in poetry or prose; addressed to a monocrat or not; presented as speech in front of a ruler or sent to him in the form of an epistle; formulated for a specific occasion or not; enjoys a more theoretical or a rather descriptive character. The term monocratological text enables us to combine literary products of widely variegated characteristics, without determining the function(s) or meaning(s) of any one of them, while pointing to the only respect shared by all of them, that of content, namely the monocrat and the practice of monocratical rule.

94. The term "monocratological" is coined according to the word "nomological" (or "nomologisch" in German respectively) used by Weber 1904, 53 and 66. For its application to antiquity see for example Meier 1988, 43–9.

Bibliography

Adam, T. (1970), *Clementia Principis. Der Einfluß hellenistischer Fürstenspiegel auf den Versuch einer rechtlichen Fundierung des Principats durch Seneca*, Stuttgart.

Aigle, D. (2007), "La conception du pouvoir dans l'islam. Miroirs des princes persans et théorie sunnite (XIe – XIV siècle)," *Perspectives médiévales* 31: 17–44.

Alföldi, A. (1955), "Gewaltherrscher und Theaterkönig. Die Auseinandersetzung einer attischen Ideenprägung mit persischen Repräsentationsformen im politischen Denken und in der Kunst bis zur Schwelle des Mittelalters," in: K. Weitzmann (ed.), *Late Classical and Medieval Studies in Honor of Albert Mathias Friend, Jr.*, Princeton, 15–55.
Anton, H. H. (1968), *Fürstenspiegel und Herrscherethos in der Karolingerzeit*, Bonn.
—— (2004), "Fürstenspiegel (Königspiegel) des frühen und hohen Mittelalters. Ein Editionsprojekt an der Universität Trier," *Jahrbuch für historische Forschung in der Bundesrepublik Deutschland 2003*, 15–32.
—— (2006), *Fürstenspiegel des Frühen und Hohen Mittelalters. Ausgewählt, übersetzt und kommentiert*, Darmstadt.
von Arnim, H. (1898), *Leben und Werke des Dio von Prusa. Mit einer Einleitung: Sophistik, Rhetorik, Philosophie in ihrem Kampf um die Jugendbildung*, Berlin.
—— (1916), *Ein altgriechisches Königsideal. Rede zur Kaisergeburtstagsfeier am 27. Januar 1916*, Frankfurt.
Auspitz, Generalmajor (sic) (1904), "Prinzenerziehung," *Deutsche Revue* 29.3: 68–74.
Bagge, S. (1987), *The Political Thought of The King's Mirror*, Odense.
—— (1989), "Fürstenspiegel: B. Volkssprachliche Literaturen – IV. Skandinavische Literaturen," in: *Lexikon des Mittelalters* IV: 1052–3.
Baines, J. (1995), "Kingship, Definition of Culture, and Legitimation," in: D. O'Connor and D. P. Silverman (eds.), *Ancient Egyptian Kingship*, Leiden, 3–47.
Baker-Brian, N. (2012), "The Politics of Virtue in Julian's *Misopogon*," in: J. Baker-Brian and S. Tougher (eds.), *Emperor and Author: The Writings of Julian the Apostate*, Swansea, 263–80.
Baldwyn, B. (1978), "The *Caesares* of Julian," *Klio* 60: 449–66.
Balot, R. K. (2006), *Greek Political Thought*, Malden, MA.
Berger, G. (1989), "Fürstenspiegel: B. Volkssprachliche Literaturen – I. Romanische Literaturen," in: *Lexikon des Mittelalters* IV: 1049–50.
Berges, W. (1938), *Die Fürstenspiegel des hohen und späten Mittelalters*, Stuttgart.
Berner, H.-U. (2012), "Arnim, Hans von," in: *Der Neue Pauly Supplemente VI: Geschichte der Altertumswissenschaften. Biographisches Lexikon*, 34–5.
Bertelli, L. (2002), "*Perì Basileias*: i trattati sulla regalità dal IV secolo a.C. agli apocrifi pitagorici," in: P. Bettiolo and G. Filoramo (eds.), *Il dio mortale. Teologie politiche tra antico e contemporaneo*, Brescia, 17–61.
Biermann, M. (1995), *Die Leichenreden des Ambrosius von Mailand. Rhetorik, Predigt, Politik*, Stuttgart.

Blum, W. (1981), "Einleitung," in: *Byzantinische Fürstenspiegel. Agapetos, Theophylakt von Ochrid, Thomas Magister*, tr. W. Blum, Stuttgart, 1–58.

Börm, H. (ed.) (forthcoming), *Antimonarchical Discourses in the Ancient World*, Stuttgart.

Born, L. K. (1933), "The *specula principis* of the Carolingian Renaissance," *Revue belge de philologie et d'histoire* 12: 583–612.

Bradley, R. (1954), "Backgrounds of the Title *Speculum* in Medieval Literature," *Speculum* 29: 100–15.

Brandt, H. (2003), "Die Rede περὶ βασιλείας des Synesios von Kyrene – ein ungewöhnlicher Fürstenspiegel," in: F. Chausson and É. Wolff (eds.), *Consuetudinis Amor. Fragments d'Histoire romaine (IIe–VIe siècles) offerts à Jean-Pierre Callu*, Rome, 57–70.

Braund, S. (2009), "Introduction," in: Seneca, *De Clementia*, ed., tr. and comm. S. Braund, Oxford, 1–91.

Broucek, P. and K. Peball (2000), *Geschichte der österreichischen Militärhistoriographie*, Cologne.

Cameron, A. and S. G. Hall (1999), "Introduction," in: *Eusebius of Caesarea, Life of Constantine*, intr., tr. and comm. A. Cameron and S. G. Hall, Oxford, 1–53.

Chabod, F. (2006), "Introduzione," in: *Niccoló Macchiavelli, Il Principe*, ed. and comm. G. Inglese, Turin, V–XLV.

Chaniotis, A. (2003), "The Divinity of Hellenistic Rulers," in: A. Erskine (ed.), *A Companion to the Hellenistic World*, Oxford, 431–45.

Charles-Saget, A. (1986), "Un miroir-au-prince au Ier siècle après J.C.: Dion Chrysostome, *Sur la royauté*, I," in: B. Cassin (ed.), *Le plaisir de parler. Études de sophistique compaerée*, Paris, 111–29.

Connoche-Bourgne, C. (2003), "*Miroir* ou *Image* ... Le choix d'un titre pour un texte didactique," in: F. Pomel (ed.), *Miroirs et jeux de miroirs dans la littérature médiéval*, Rennes, 29–38.

Cooley, A. E. (2009), *Res Gestae Divi Augusti. Text, Translation, and Commentary*, Cambridge.

Dakhlia, J. (2002), "Les Miroirs des princes islamiques: une modernité sourde?," *Annales* 57: 1191–206.

Demandt, A. (2002), "Der Fürstenspiegel des Agapet," *Mediterraneo antico* 5: 573–84.

Dorninger, M. E. (1997), *Gottfried von Viterbo. Ein Autor in der Umgebung der frühen Staufer*, Stuttgart.

Drake, H. A. (1976), *In Praise of Constantine. A Historical Study and New Translation of Eusebius' Tricennial Orations*, Berkeley.

—— (2012), "'But I digress ...': Rhetoric and Propaganda in Julian's Second

Oration to Constantius," in: J. Baker-Brian and S. Tougher (eds.), *Emperor and Author: The Writings of Julian the Apostate*, Swansea, 35–46.
Drijvers, J. W. (2004), "Eusebius' *Vita Constantini* als vorstenspiegel," *Lampas* 37: 161–4.
Eberhardt, O. (1977), *Via Regia. Der Fürstenspiegel Smaragds von St. Mihiel und sein literarische Gattung*, Munich.
Eckstein, A. M. (2009), "Hellenistic Monarchy in Theory and Practice," in: R. K. Balot (ed.), *A Companion to Roman Political Thought*, Malden, MA, 247–65.
Eder, W. (1995), "Monarchie und Demokratie im 4. Jahrhundert v. Chr.: Die Rolle des Fürstenspiegels in der athenischen Demokratie," in: W. Eder (ed.), *Die athenische Demokratie im 4. Jahrhundert v. Chr. Vollendung oder Verfall einer Verfassungsform? Akten eines Symposiums, 3.–7. August 1992, Bellagio*, Stuttgart, 153–73.
Eucken, C. (1983), *Isokrates. Seine Positionen in der Auseinandersetzung mit den zeitgenössischen Philosophen*, Berlin.
Flaig, E. (1994), "Weisheit und Befehl. Platons "*Politeia*" und das Ende der Politik," *Saeculum* 45: 34–70.
—— (1998), *Ödipus. Tragischer Vatermord im klassischen Athen*, Munich.
de Fouchécour, C.-H. (2009), *Le sage et le prince en Iran médiéval. Morale et politique dans les textes littéraires persans Xe–XIIIe siècles*, 2nd edition, Paris. (First edition Paris 1986.)
Gehrke, H.-J. (1982), "Der siegreiche König. Überlegungen zur Hellenistischen Monarchie," *Archiv für Kulturgeschichte* 64: 247–77.
—— (2013), "The Victorious King: Reflections on the Hellenistic Monarchy," in: N. Luraghi (ed.), *The Splendors and Miseries of Ruling Alone. Encounters with Monarchy from Archaic Greece to the Hellenistic Mediterranean*, Stuttgart, 73–98.
Gilbert, F. (1939), "The Humanist Concept of the Prince and *The Prince* of Machiavelli," *Journal of Modern History* 11: 449–83.
Gilissen, J. (1970), "Essai d'étude comparative de la monocratie dans le passé," in: *La monocratie*, 2 vols., Brussels, 1: 5–135.
Gotter, U. (2008), "Die Nemesis des Allgemein-Gültigen. Max Weber's Charisma-Konzept und die antiken Monarchien," in: P. Rychterová, S. Seit and R. Veit (eds.), *Das Charisma. Funktionen und symbolische Repräsentationen*, Berlin, 173–86.
Grabes, H. (1973), *Speculum, Mirror und Looking-Glass. Kontinuität und Originalität der Spiegelmetapher in den Buchtiteln des Mittelalters und der englischen Literatur des 13. bis 17. Jahrhunderts*, Tübingen.
Graßnick, U. (2004), *Ratgeber des Königs. Fürstenspiegel und Herrscherideal im spätmittelalterlichen England*, Cologne.

Gray, V.J. (2011), *Xenophon's Mirror of Princes. Reading the Reflections*, Oxford.
Gumbrecht, H.-U. (1977), "Historische Textpragmatik als Grundlagenwissenschaft der Geschichtsschreibung," *Lendemains* 6: 125–35.
Haake, M. (2003), "Warum und zu welchem Ende schreibt man *peri basileias*? Überlegungen zum historischen Kontext einer literarischen Gattung im Hellenismus," in: K. Piepenbrink (ed.), *Philosophie und Lebenswelt in der Antike*, Darmstadt, 83–138.
—— (2008), "Die patchwork-Repräsentation eines lykischen Dynasten: Apollonios, Sohn des Hellaphilos, und das Grab vom Asartaş Tepesi," in: E. Winter (ed.), *Vom Euphrat bis zum Bosporos - Kleinasien in der Antike. Festschrift für Elmar Schwertheim zum 65. Geburtstag*, Bonn, 277–96.
—— (2011), "Antigonos II. Gonatas und der Nemesistempel von Rhamnous. Zur Semantik kultischer Ehren für einen hellenistischen König an einem athenischen ‚lieu de mémoire'," in: M. Haake and M. Jung (eds.), *Griechische Heiligtümer als Erinnerungsorte - von der Archaik bis in den Hellenismus. Erträge einer internationalen Tagung in Münster, 20.–21. Januar 2006*, Stuttgart 2011, 109–27.
—— (2012), "Zwischen Alexander dem Großen und Arcadius, von Anaxarchos von Abdera zu Synesios von Kyrene. Die Gattung Über das Königtum im Kontext antiker Alleinherrschaften – eine Skizze," in: L. Del Corso and P. Pecere (eds.), *Il libro filosofico. Dall'antichità al XXI secolo - Philosophy and the Books. From Antiquity to the XXIth Century*, Turnhout, 65–82.
—— (2013), "Writing down the King. The Communicative Function of Treatises On Kinship in the Hellenistic Period," in: N. Luraghi (ed.), *The Splendors and Miseries of Ruling Alone. Encounters with Monarchy from Archaic Greece to the Hellenistic Mediterranean*, Stuttgart, 165–206.
Habicht, C. (1970), *Gottmenschentum und griechische Städte*, 2nd edition, Munich. (First edition Munich 1956.)
Hadot, P. (1972), "Fürstenspiegel," in: *Reallexikon für Antike und Christentum* VIII: 555–632.
Hahm, D. E. (2000), "Kings and Constitutions: Hellenistic Theories," in: C. Rowe and M. Schofield (eds.), *The Cambridge History of Greek and Roman Political Thought*, Cambridge, 457–76.
Hannick, C. (1989), "Fürstenspiegel: C. Byzantinischer Bereich und slavische Literaturen – II. Slavische Literaturen," in: *Lexikon des Mittelalters* IV: 1056–7.
Hohl, E. (1958), "Über das Problem der Historia Augusta," *Wiener Studien* 71: 132–52.
Hunter, R. (2011), "The Letter of Aristeas," in: A. Erskine and L. Llewellyn-Jones (eds.), *Creating a Hellenistic World*, Swansea, 47–60.

Irmscher, J. (1978), "Das Bild des Untertanen im Fürstenspiegel des Agapetos," *Klio* 60: 507–9.
Jónsson, E. M. (1987), "La situation du *Speculum regale* dans la littérature occidental," *Études Germaniques* 42: 391–408.
—— (1995), *Le miroir. Naissance d'un genre littéraire*, Paris.
—— (2006), "Les 'miroirs aux princes' sont-ils un genre littéraire?," *Médiévales* 51: 153–66.
Jucker, A. and I. Taavitsainen (eds.) (2010), *Historical Pragmatics*, Berlin.
Kaerst, J. (1898), *Studien zur Entwicklung und theoretischen Begründung der Monarchie im Altertum*, Munich.
Keller, H. and F. J. Worstbrock (1988), "Träger, Felder, Formen pragmatischer Schriftlichkeit im Mittelalter. Der neue Sonderforschungsbereich 231 an der Westfälischen Wilhelms-Universität Münster," *Frühmittelalterliche Studien* 22: 388–409.
Kerkhecker, A. (2002), "*Privato officio, non publico*. Literaturwissenschaftliche Überlegungen zu Ciceros 'Pro Marcello'," in: J. P. Schwindt (ed.), *Klassische Philologie* inter disciplinas. *Aktuelle Konzepte zu Gegenstand und Methode eines Grundlagenfaches*, Heidelberg, 93–149.
Kerner, M. (1988), "Die Institutio Traiani – spätantike Lehrschrift oder hochmittelalterliche Fiktion?," in: *Fälschungen im Mittelalter. Internationaler Kongreß der Monumenta Germaniae Historica München, 16.–19. September 1986*, 6 vols., Hanover, 1: 715–38.
—— (1992), "Die Institutio Traiani und Johannes von Salisbury, ein mittelalterlicher Autor und sein Text," in: H. Kloft and M. Kerner (eds.), *Die Institutio Traiani. Ein pseudo-plutarchischer Text im Mittelalter: Text – Kommentar – Zeitgenössischer Hintergrund*, Stuttgart, 93–124.
Körner, C. (2011), "Das Verständnis von Herrschaft in der anonymen Rede Εἰς βασιλέα (Ps.-Aelius Aristides): Ein Fürstenspiegel," *Klio* 93: 173–92.
Lanza, D. (1977), *Il tiranno e il suo pubblico*, Turin.
Le Goff, J. (1996), *Saint Louis*, Paris.
Leder, S. (1999), "Aspekte arabischer und persischer Fürstenspiegel. Legitimation, Fürstenethik, politische Vernunft," in: A. De Benedictis (ed.), *Specula principum*, Frankfurt, 21–50.
Lehmann, P. (1953), *Mittelalterliche Büchertitel II*, Munich.
Leppin, H. (2010), "Xenophons *Hieron*. Überlegungen zur Geschichte des monarchischen Denken im klassischen Athen," in: B. Linke, M. Meier and M. Strothmann (eds.), *Zwischen Monarchie und Republik. Gesellschaftliche Stabilisierungsleistungen und politisches Transformationspotential in den antiken Stadtstaaten*, Stuttgart, 77–89.
Leppin, H. and W. Portmann (1998), "Einleitung," in: *Themistios: Staatsreden*, tr. H. Leppin and W. Portmann, Stuttgart, 1–26.

Lichtheim, M. (1996), "Didactic Literature," in: A. Loprieno (ed.), *Ancient Egyptian Literature: History and Forms*, Leiden, 243–62.
Liebeschütz, H. (1943), "John of Salisbury and Pseudo-Plutarch," *Journal of the Warburg and Courtauld Institutes* 6: 33–9.
Lopetegui, G. (2013). "The *Panegyrici Latini*: Rhetoric in the Service of Imperial Ideology," in: A.J. Quiroga Puertas (ed.), *The Purpose of Rhetoric in Late Antiquity. From Performance to Exegesis*, Tübingen, 189–207.
Luhmann, N. (1997), *Die Gesellschaft der Gesellschaft*, Frankfurt.
Luraghi, N. (2013a), "One-Man Government. The Greeks and Monarchy," in: H. Beck (ed.), *A Companion to Ancient Greek Government*, Malden, MA, 131–45.
—— (2013b), "Ruling Alone: Monarchy in Greek Politics and Thought," in: N. Luraghi (ed.), *The Splendors and Miseries of Ruling Alone. Encounters with Monarchy from Archaic Greece to the Hellenistic Mediterranean*, Stuttgart, 11–24.
Major, R. (2005), "The Cambridge School and Leo Strauss: Texts and Contexts of American Political Science," *Political Research Quarterly* 58: 477–85.
Mann, C. (1998), *Athlet und Polis im archaischen und frühklassischen Griechenland*, Göttingen.
—— (2013), "The Victorious Tyrant: Hieron of Syracuse in the Epinicia of Pindar and Bacchylides," in: N. Luraghi (ed.), *The Splendors and Miseries of Ruling Alone. Encounters with Monarchy from Archaic Greece to the Hellenistic Mediterranean*, Stuttgart, 25–48.
Mazza, M. (1980), "L'intellettuale come ideologo: Flavio Filostrato ed uno 'speculum principis' del III secolo d.C.," in: *Il comportamento dell'intellettuale nella società antica*, Genoa, 33–66.
Meier, C. (1988), *Die politische Kunst der griechischen Tragödie*, Munich.
Moles, J. (1990), "The Kingship Orations of Dio Chrysostom," *Papers of the Leeds Latin Seminar* 6: 297–375.
Mühleisen, H.O., T. Stammen and M. Philipp (1997), *Fürstenspiegel der Frühen Neuzeit*, Frankfurt.
Murray, O. (1990), "The Idea of the Shepherd King from Cyrus to Charlemagne," in: P. Godman and O. Murray (eds.), *Latin Poetry and the Classical Tradition. Essays in Medieval and Renaissance Literature*, Oxford, 1–14.
—— (1998), "Modello biografico e modello di regalità," in: S. Settis (ed.), *I Greci. Storia - Cultura - Arte - Società. 2: Una storia greca. III. Trasformazioni*, Turin, 249–69.
—— (2007), "Philosophy and Monarchy in the Hellenistic World," in: T. Rajak et al. (eds.), *Jewish Perspectives on Hellenistic Rulers*, Berkeley, 13–28.
Nixon, C.E.V. and B. Saylor Rodgers (1994), "General Introduction," in: *In*

Praise of Later Roman Emperors: The Panegyrici Latini, Introduction, Translation and Historical Commentary with the Latin text of R. A. B. Mynors, Berkeley, 1–37.
O'Daly, G. (1999), *Augustine's* City of God. *A Reader's Guide*, Oxford.
Ould Cheikh, A. W. (2003), "La science au(x) miroir(s) du prince. Savoir et pouvoir dans l'espace arabo-musulman d'hier et d'aujourd'hui," *Revue des mondes musulmans et de la méditerranée* 101–2: 129–55.
Parsons, W. (1942), "The Mediaeval Theory of the Tyrant," *The Review of Politics* 4: 129–43.
Peil, D. (1986), "Emblematische Fürstenspiegel im 17. und 18. Jahrhundert: Saavedra – Le Moyene – Wilhelm," *Frühmittelalterliche Studien* 20: 54–92.
Pernot, L. (2003), "Miroir d'un Prince par lui-même: les *Pensées* de Marc Aurèle," in: I. Cogitore and F. Goyet (eds.), *L'Éloge du Prince. De l'Antiquité au temps des Lumières*, Grenoble, 91–104.
Philipp, M. and T. Stammen (1996), "Fürstenspiegel," in: *Historisches Wörterbuch der Rhetorik* III: 495–507.
Pomel, F. (2003), "Réflexions sur le miroir," in: F. Pomel (ed.), *Miroirs et jeux de miroirs dans la littérature médiévale*, Rennes, 17–26.
Pontier, P. (2010), "L'*Agésilas* de Xénophon: comment on réécrit l'histoire," in: M.-R. Guelfucci (ed.), *Action politique et écriture de l'histoire II. Le narrateur homme d'action. Actes du colloque, Besançon, 16 au 18 octobre 2008*, Trois-Rivières, 359–83.
Price, S. R. F. (1984), *Rituals and Power. The Roman Imperial Cult in Asia Minor*, Cambridge.
Quack, J. F. (1992), *Studien zur Lehre für Merikare*, Wiesbaden.
Rabeler, S. (2007), "Fürstenspiegel," in: W. Paravicini (ed.), *Höfe und Residenzen im spätmittelalterlichen Reich: Hof und Schrift*, Ostfildern, 329–46.
Raible, W. (1980), "Was sind Gattungen? Eine Antwort aus semiotischer und textlinguistischer Sicht," *Poetica* 12: 320–49.
Reeve, C. D. C. (1988), *Philosopher-Kings. The Argument of Plato's* Republic, Princeton.
Reydams-Schils, G. (2012), "Social Ethics and Politics," in: M. van Ackeren (ed.), *A Companion to Marcus Aurelius*, Malden, MA, 437–52.
Richter, M. (1989), "Fürstenspiegel: B. Volkssprachliche Literaturen – V. Irische und walisische Literatur," in: *Lexikon des Mittelalters* IV: 1053.
Richter-Bernburg, L. (1989), "Fürstenspiegel: D. Arabisch-islamisch-osmanischer Bereich – I. Arabisch-islamischer Bereich," in: *Lexikon des Mittelalters* IV: 1058.
Roche, P. (2011), "Pliny's Thanksgiving: An Introduction to the *Panegyricus*," in: P. Roche (ed.), *Pliny's Praise. The* Panegyricus *in the Roman World*, Oxford, 1–28.

Ronning, C. (2007), *Herrscherpanegyrik unter Trajan und Konstantin. Studien zur symbolischen Kommunikation in der römischen Kaiserzeit*, Tübingen.

Roth, G. (1995), "Spiegelliteratur," in: *Lexikon des Mittelalters* VII: 2101–2.

Schnedl-Bubenicek, H. (1985), "Wissenschaftlerin auf Umwegen. Christiane Touaillbon, geb. Auspitz (1878–1928) – Versuch einer Annäherung," in: R. G. Ardelt, W. J. A. Huber and A. Staudinger (eds.), *Unterdrückung und Emanzipation. Festschrift für Erika Weinzierl zum 60. Geburtstag*, Vienna, 69–81.

Schofield, M. (1998), "The Disappearing Philosopher-King," in: *Boston Area Colloquium in Ancient Philosophy* XIII, Leiden, 213–41.

Scholl, R. (1994), *Historische Beiträge zu den julianischen Reden des Libanios*, Stuttgart.

Schorn, S. (2008), "Die Vorstellung des xenophontischen Sokrates von Herrschaft und das Erziehungsprogramm des *Hieron*," in: L. Rossetti and A. Stavru (eds.), *Socratica 2005. Studi sulla letteratura socratica antica presentati alle Giornate di studio di Senigallia*, Bari, 177–203.

Schubart, W. (1937a), "Das hellenistische Königsideal nach Inschriften und Papyri," *Archiv für Papyrusforschung* 12: 1–26.

—— (1937b), "Das Königsbild des Hellenismus," *Die Antike* 13: 272–88.

Schulte, J. M. (2001), *Speculum Regis. Studien zur Fürstenspiegel-Literatur in der griechisch-römischen Antike*, Münster.

Sidebottom, H. (2006), "Dio Chrysostom and the Development of *On Kingship* Literature," in: D. Spencer and E. Theodorakopoulos (eds.), *Advice and its Rhetoric in Greece and Rome*, Bari, 117–57.

Singer, B. (1981), *Die Fürstenspiegel in Deutschland im Zeitalter des Humanismus und der Reformation. Bibliographische Grundlagen und ausgewählte Interpretationen: Jakob Wimpfeling, Wolfgang Seidel, Johann Sturm, Urban Rieger*, Munich.

—— (1983), "Fürstenspiegel," in: *Theologische Realenzyklopädie* XI: 707–11.

Skinner, Q. (1969), "Meaning and Understanding in the History of Ideas," *History and Theory* 8: 3–53.

—— (1978), *The Foundations of Modern Political Thought. Volume One: The Renaissance*, Cambridge.

Squilloni, A. (1990), "Il profilo del capo politico nel pensiero del IV secolo: lo *speculum principis*," *Il Pensiero politico* 23: 201–18.

Stammen, T. (1990), " Fürstenspiegel als literarische Gattung politischer Theorie im zeitgenössischen Kontext – ein Versuch," in: H.-O. Mühleisen and T. Stammen (eds.), *Politische Tugendlehre und Regierungskunst. Studien zum Fürstenspiegel der Frühen Neuzeit*, Tübingen, 255–85.

Suter, C. E. (2000), *Gudea's Temple Building. The Representation of an Early Mesopotamian Ruler in Text and Image*, Groningen.

Thelamon, F. (2007), "Constantin: 'l'empereur à Dieu' selon Eusèbe de Césarée dans la *Vita Constantini*," in: F. Lachaud and L. Scordia (eds.), *Le Prince au miroir de la littérature politique de l'Antiquité aux Lumières*, Rouen, 31–43.
Tietze, A. (1989), "Fürstenspiegel: D. Arabisch-islamisch-osmanischer Bereich – II. Osmanischer Bereich," in: *Lexikon des Mittelalters* IV: 1058.
Tilmans, K. (1991), "The Origin of the Empire and the Tasks of the Prince: Neglected Renaissance Mirrors-of-Princes in the Netherlands," *Humanistica Lovaniensia* 40: 43–72.
Tougher, S. (2012), "Reading between the Lines: Julian's *First Panegyric* on Constantius II," in: J. Baker-Brian and S. Tougher (eds.), *Emperor and Author: The Writings of Julian the Apostate*, Swansea, 19–34.
Virgilio, B. (2003), *Lancia, diadema e porpora. Il re e la regalità ellenistica*, 2nd edition, Pisa. (First edition Pisa 1999.)
Walbank, F. W. (1984), "Monarchies and Monarchic Ideas," in: *Cambridge Ancient History VII, 1*, 2nd edition, Cambridge, 62–100.
Watt, J. W. (2012), "Julian's *Letter to Themistius* – and Themistius' Response?," in: J. Baker-Brian and S. Tougher (eds.), *Emperor and Author: The Writings of Julian the Apostate*, Swansea, 91–103.
Weber, G. (2003), "J. Manuel Schulte, Speculum Regis. Studien zur Fürstenspiegel-Literatur in der griechisch-römischen Antike, Münster/Hamburg/London (LIT Verlag) 2001 (rev.)," *Klio* 85: 479–82.
Weber, M. (1904), " Die ‚Objektivität' sozialwissenschaftlicher und sozialpolitischer Erkenntnis," *Archiv für Sozialwissenschaft und Sozialpolitik* 19: 22–87.
Weithman, P. (2001), "Augustine's Political Philosophy," in: E. Stump and N. Kretzmann (eds.), *The Cambridge Companion to Augustine*, Cambridge, 234–52.
Wienand, J. (2012), *Der Kaiser als Sieger. Metamorphosen triumphaler Herrschaft unter Constantin I.*, Berlin.
Witschel, C. (2008), "The *Res Gestae Divi Augusti* and the Roman Empire," in: F. H. Mutschler and A. Mittag (eds.), *Conceiving the Empire: China and Rome Compared*, Oxford, 241–66.
Zimmermann, M. (1998), "*Speculum regnorum et aularum: Die Rezeption Herodians vom 15.-18. Jh.*," *Chiron* 28: 287–322.

Persian Mirrors for Princes

Pre-Islamic and Islamic Mirrors Compared

Seyed Sadegh Haghighat

MIRRORS FOR PRINCES are treatises on governance distinguished from political philosophy and political jurisprudence (*fiqh-i siyāsī*) in the Iranian and Islamic intellectual traditions. Chronologically speaking, they are categorized into two major groups: mirrors for princes from pre-Islamic Iran and the ones from the Islamic era. In spite of the discernible differences between the two, they have in common similar political ideas and a shared intellectual tradition. Fine specimen of the first group are *Nāma-yi Tansar* (The Letter of Tansar)[1] and *'Ahd-i Ardashīr*[2] (*Ardashīr's* Testament), both originally written in Pahlavi, though no Pahlavi version is extant. Abū Muḥammad 'Abd Allāh Rūzbih b. Dādūya (d. ca. 139/757), known as Ibn al-Muqaffa' has translated the first one from Pahlavi into Arabic. The second is a collection of advice from the Sasanian dynast Ardashīr I (d. 242 CE) to his governors and deputies throughout the Persian empire. These two mirrors from pre-Islamic Iran are important to this chapter, as it will focus on the works of the Islamic era, i.e. the works of Ibn al-Muqaffa', as well as *Siyāsatnāma* (also known as *Siyar al-mulūk*)[3] *by Niẓām* al-Mulk (d. 485/1092) and *Marzbānnāma*[4] by Marzbān b. Rustam b. Sharwīn (12th century). The latter was translated by Sa'duddīn al-Warāwīnī from the Ṭabari language to Farsi between 612/1215 and 617/1220. Emphasis is also placed on the ways in which the Islamic treatises are influenced by the pre-Islamic ones while adapting their contents to their own historical context.

A.K.S. Lambton and M.A. Emam Shushtari, the translator of *Nāma-yi Tansar*, as we shall see, believe in the influence of pre-Islamic Iranian mirrors on the Islamic ones, while Javād Ṭabāṭabā'ī sees Islamic mirrors as a "continuation" of Iranian ones,[5] arguing for an ideology of "Iranshahri" or what

1. Ed. Mīnuvī 1975.
2. Ed. 'Abbās 1969.
3. Ed. Darke 1962.
4. Ed. Rushan 1976.
5. Ṭabāṭabā'ī 2003, 46.

might be called "Iranopolis," and Davood Feirahi observes them as independent treatises influenced by their own historical context.[6] What confirms the first idea is that the essence of pre-Islamic and Islamic mirrors seems alike, and what confirms the second hypothesis is that the concept of aura of kings (Persian *farra*) does not predominate in mirrors from the Islamic era. According to Ṭabāṭabā'ī, Niẓām al-Mulk's *Siyāsatnāma* draws on pre-Islamic advice literature and develops a new theory of Persian kingship, which despite some references to Islam, the Qur'an, the *hadith* and the records of the caliphs, remains essentially alien to the caliphate.[7] In other words, historical context is not important, since mirrors from widely divergent contexts reveal similar contents. Analyzing these two opposing ideas, this study proposes that Islamic mirrors are influenced by both Iranian intellectual traditions and by their own historical context. This is also the position adopted by Omid Safi in his study on the relationship between the production of knowledge and social and political conditions in the Saljuq era. The focus in this study will be on the relationship between religion and state. In this regard, concepts such as *farra*, governance (*khshathra)*, expediency, justice and goodness (*asha*), will be discussed. Religion and political power are often described as twins in the pre-Islamic and Islamic periods, though the "Big Brother"[8] of political power always has been superior to religion.[9]

Students of Iranian mirrors are invariably constrained by the fact that these mirrors are only available in manuscripts dating from the Islamic period; which has made content analysis unavoidable. However, Foucauldian discourse analysis may provide a new and productive method for comparing the two groups of mirrors for princes, thus shedding new light on the relationship between knowledge and political power. Although discourse analysis, in general, is a common term for a number of approaches to analyzing written and unwritten texts, the objective of this method, especially in the present discussion, is to find coherent sequences of sentences and speech acts. The basic difference between discourse analysis and textual linguistics is that discourse analysis seeks to reveal socio-psychological characteristics of the author rather than studying the structure of the text in question. As Chouliaraki explains:

> [t]he Foucauldian concept of discourse sets up a constitutive relationship between meaning and power in social practice. Every move to meaning-making comes about from a position of power—power both structuring and structured by the social positions

6. Feirahi 2003, 74–5.
7. Ṭabāṭabā'ī 2012.
8. Borrowed from Orwell 1950 passim.
9. Safi 2006 passim.

> available within the practice. ... Foucault does not, however, postulate that meaning and power pre-exist in an inseparable state as causal conditions of existence for social practice—as ontological aprioris of the social world.[10]

Adopting discourse analysis as its primary methodological tool, this study hopes to demonstrate similarities between Iranian and Islamic mirrors, a "hypothetical" influence on the latter by the former, as well as specificities of Islamic mirrors that are determined primarily by their own historical contexts.

E. I. J. Rosenthal in his *Political Thought in Medieval Islam* has presented political philosophy, political *fiqh*, and mirrors for princes as a trinity.[11] While philosophers debated the scope of human reason, the ideal society and how to attain it and the nature of revelation, jurists argued about interpretations of the *sharīʿa*, i.e. Islamic law, to govern private and public life. Mirrors for princes instructed kings, especially young ones, on certain aspects of rule and behavior to reinforce their power. Rosenthal's tripartite classification, however, seems inadequate in that mirrors are not properly typified therein.[12] Mirrors may rely on reason, *fiqh*, narrations, fables, history and so on, but their style and method is not as significant as their overarching objective, which is the preservation of power. That overarching theme is present in almost all mirrors—cases in point are *Nasīḥat al-mulūk* by al-Ghazzālī (d. 504/1111), *Nasīḥat al-mulūk* of al-Māwardī (d. 450/1058), *Siyāsatnāma* of Niẓām al-Mulk and *Irshādnāma* of Mīrzā-yi Qummī (d. 1195/1816). For this reason, we can differentiate between al-Ghazzālī's *Iḥyā' 'ulūm al-dīn* and his *Nasīḥat al-mulūk*, since the first is a religious book, while the second is a mirror for princes. In the latter al-Ghazzālī has argued: "God has chosen two kinds of people: prophets and kings. According to tradition, kings are the shadows of God on earth, so we should like and obey them. The Holy Qur'an says: 'Obey Allah, the messenger and those in authority' (Q 4:59)."[13] While Patricia Crone in her study on medieval Islamic political thought has accorded mirrors to the Sunni tradition,[14] several Shiʿi mirrors exist as well.

Between Text and Context

According to contextualism, a text should be interpreted in its context, rather than as an independent entity. In this chapter, a contextualist meth-

10. Chouliaraki 2008, 674–5.
11. Rosenthal 1962, 115–21.
12. Feirahi 2003, 27–31.
13. Al-Ghazzālī, *Nasīḥat al-mulūk*, 322.
14. Crone 2004, 254–81.

od is necessary, as mirrors for princes, pre-Islamic and Islamic ones alike, are often written in the form of stories to reinforce the authority of kings, or what Jennifer London has dubbed as "speaking through the voice of another." [15] In her dissertation London used this term to refer to the rhetorical technique of translating or interpreting a story or saying to convey a political point and effect political action. For her, "political action" connotes how the translator or author uses an ancient source to challenge political ideas in his own environment. Her suggestion, however, is that the particular genre (e.g. literary, philosophical, etc.) used by individual scholars allowed them to achieve a particular sort of political action.[16] Hence, it is impossible to understand the meaning of these texts without knowing the historical situation of the polity in question. The authors of mirrors expressed their perspectives on political subjects, how rulers ought to think, act and organize society, by translating and interpreting stories and sayings, in widely different political and social contexts.

What follows in this chapter is a brief contextual introduction of several specific mirrors, from pre-Islamic Iran as well as the Islamic period. *Nāma-yi Tansar* claims to have been written in seventeen parts in about 570 CE by a Zoroastrian priest who served as advisor to the first Sassanid monarch, Ardashīr I, and was translated into Arabic by Ibn al-Muqaffaʿ. Though Ibn al-Muqaffaʿ's Arabic version is lost, Ibn-i Isfandiyār's Persian rendering of it, made in the early 13th century and embedded in his *Tārīkh-i Ṭabaristān*, reveals its content. *ʿAhd-i Ardashīr*, or "Ardashīr's Testament," is a collection of the dynast's teachings on good governance, addressed to his son and heir. The Pahlavi original is lost, but an Arabic rendition dating probably to the late Umayyad period is extant.[17] *Siyāsatnāma* was presented to Malikshāh, the Saljuq dynast by his vizier, Niẓām al-Mulk, right before the vizier's assassination in 485/1092. Niẓām al-Mulk was a pivotal figure who bridged the political gap between both the Abbasids (132–656/750–1258) and the Saljuqs (11th–13th centuries) against their various rivals such as the Fāṭimids (296–566/909–1171) and the Būyids (320–447/932–1055). According to Yavari, "Niẓām al-Mulk was asked by Malikshāh to prepare a manual for good governance, shedding light on the ways and manners of past kings, just rule and stable polities. Repetitious and faculty in its factual contents, Niẓām al-Mulk's string of anecdotes tie together pre-Islamic kings, Aristotelian tidbits, stories related to Prophet Muhammad and episodes from the lives of earlier caliphs."[18]

15. London 2009, 1.
16. London 2009 passim.
17. ʿAbbās 1969 (introduction), 33–4.
18. Yavari 2008a, 47–8.

Omid Safi has written on the intricate relations between the Saljuqs and a number of well-known Sufi Muslims and jurists of the time, explaining how orthodoxy in the structure of *madrasas* and Sufi *khānqāhs* legitimized Saljuq power.[19] That intricate relationship between power and knowledge is evidence for the necessity of a contextual approach to *Siyāsatnāma*. To confirm Feirahi's idea, *Siyāsatnāma* is a text influenced by Iranian mirrors on the one hand, and by the relationship between religion, knowledge and Saljuq power on the other. It and other Islamic mirrors are not simply "continuations" of Iranian mirrors as Ṭabāṭabā'ī has argued.

In addition to the translation of *Nāma-yi Tansar*, which has been referred to, Ibn al-Muqaffaʿ was responsible for a couple of other important translations. His Arabic rendition of *Kalīla wa Dimna* from Middle Persian is considered the first masterpiece of Arabic literary prose. A Middle Persian collection of animal fables mostly of Indian origin, and involving two jackals, Kalīla and Dimna, the text is prefaced by a putative autobiography of Burzūya and an account of his voyage to India. Ibn al-Muqaffaʿ was able to articulate his genuine views on how princes ought to behave and order society through his translation of fables from Middle Persian (Pahlavi) into Arabic.[20] Two other important works in Arabic are ascribed to Ibn al-Muqaffaʿ, *al-Adab al-kabīr* and *al-Adab al-ṣaghīr*[21], but only the first one can be accepted as his. The first of its four parts is a very brief rhetorical retrospect on the excellence of the ancients' legacy, clearly Sasanian, of spiritual and temporal knowledge. The second is a miniature mirror for princes. The addressee, seemingly the caliph's son, is apostrophized as one in pursuit of the rule of seemly conduct (*adab*).[22]

Marzbānnāma, ascribed to Marzbān b. Sharwīn, ruler of Ṭabaristān, written between 607/1210 and 622/1225,[23] and to which we shall refer in further detail below, is another treatise on good governance disguised as an animal fable. In *Marzbānnāma*, there is a dialogue between Malikzāda, as the symbol of good governance, and Dastūr, as the symbol of bad governance. While Malikzāda stresses governance based on honesty, rationality, justice, equity, truth, kindness and good deeds, Dastūr's government is based on power, wealth, lie and trick. Without any doubt, the structure of this book is influenced by *Kalīla wa Dimna*, and both of them are influenced by Iranian mirrors for princes, though they should be interpreted in their own socio-political contexts.

19. Safi 2006 passim.
20. London 2009.
21. Ibn al-Muqaffaʿ, *Al-Adab al-kabīr wa al-adab al-ṣaghīr*.
22. Latham 1997.
23. al-Warāwīnī, *Marzbānnāma*, 59–68.

Religion

Although it seems that Zoroastrianism and Islam have little in common, mirrors for princes have tried to use both religions to reinforce the authority of kings, commonly known as *farra*. Patricia Crone has argued that Muslims perceived Zoroastrianism as a dualist religion as it was blended with Manichaeism,[24] and one of the arguments for positing a close relationship between the two religions is the background and murder of Ibn al-Muqaffa' himself, who was a Persian thinker and a Zoroastrian convert to Islam. He was murdered at the order of the second Abbasid caliph al-Manṣūr (95–158/714–75), reportedly for heresy or bad faith (*zandaqa*), but in fact, for a complex of political and religious reasons.

The most important difference between pre-Islamic and Islamic mirrors in this regard is that there was a clash between Islamic *madhāhib* (denominations) such as Shias and Sunnis, or between Ḥanafīs and Shāfi'is in Abbasid era. According to Niẓām al-Mulk, a good vizier is either a Shāfi'ī or a Ḥanafī.[25] Therefore we should analyze *Siyāsatnāma* in the context of the rule of the Turks, and the tenets of their Ḥanafī creed.[26] Although there are similarities between mirrors before and after Islam, each should be analyzed in its own context.

The Aura of Kings

In most ancient Iranian texts, kingship is equated with the possession of the right aura and considered as a gift from God. For example, Ardashīr Babakān's Naqsh-i Rustam inscription, which dates to 1000 BCE, illustrates a bas-relief of Ardashīr riding a horse in front of the supreme deity Ahūrā Mazdā, who is also riding a horse and delivering the symbol of kingship to Ardashīr. A stone inscription above Ardashīr's horse reads in three languages, "Ardashīr is king of kings of Iran who is blessed by God. (He is) the son of Bābak Shāh."[27]

The Farsi *farra* (aura) is derived from Middle Persian *xwarrah* wherein *xwar/hwar* denotes the sun, and the verb *hwar* to lighten or to glorify. Accordingly, *farra* is the source of legitimacy and a sacred power bestowed on kings by God. As Fatḥullāh Mujtabā'ī explains: "*xwarrah/hwarrah* is an abstract example of light which can be observed in all classes including the rulers, guardians and the workers, in the story of Ardashīr (when he was

24. Crone 2004, 254.
25. Yavari 2008a, 53–4.
26. Makdisi 1973, passim.
27. Moradi Ghiasabadi 2012.

going to the war and saw a sheep), and in the aura of kings, etc."[28] Ardashīr introduced himself to people as the representative of God on earth,[29] having the authority to use force against his opponents.[30] As an abstract concept denoting distinction and supernatural guidance, *farra* is akin to the light of prophecy, possessed by Zoroaster and Muhammad and the Imams—this latter as per the Shīʿī creed alone. Henri Corbin has equated *ḥikmat al-ishrāq* of Suhrawardī (509–87/1155–91) with *xwarrah* and the light of prophets.[31] The power in the arms of Rustam, the warrior-hero of Firdawsī's (329–411/940–1020) *Shāhnāma*, and the holiness of the hoopoe and the Sīmurgh in ʿAṭṭār's *Manṭiq al-ṭayr* are some examples of *farra* in texts from the Islamic era. In ʿAṭṭār's text (513–626/1119–1229), the birds of the world gather to decide upon a king. The hoopoe, the wisest of them, suggests that they should find the legendary Sīmurgh, a mysterious bird in Iranian mythology which is a symbol often found in Sufi literature. When the group of thirty birds finally reaches the residence of the Sīmurgh, all they find is a lake in which they see their own reflection.

According to Niẓām a-Mulk the condition for the happiness of kings in this world and the other one is the aura given by God.[32] He states: "In every age and time God chooses one member of the human race and, having endowed him with godly and kingly virtues, entrusts him with the interests of the world and the well-being of the servants, He charges that person to close the doors of corruption, confusion and discord, and he imparts to him."[33]

In analyzing these quotes, four points become evident: First is the confluence of textualism and contextualism insofar as methodology is concerned. According to contextualists, such as the theorists of Marxism and sociology of knowledge, our understandings are reactions to the reality around us. Hence, there would be no essence to ideas such as the imamate. A theory of confluence, however, suggests that although a text should be interpreted in its context, religious concepts maintain their original essences. Secondly, in Suhrawardī's iteration, the *Shāhnāma* and its hero, Rustam, are put in mystical terms, another example of content adapting to new historical circumstances. In fact, Suhrawardī has changed the position of Rustam from a warrior-hero to an exemplar of mystical stories. Thirdly, most Iranian kings, including the most recent one, Mohammad Reza Pahlavi (r. 1941–1979), have displayed a belief of sorts in the *farra* of kings. The main difference be-

28. Mujtabāʾī 1973, 91–2.
29. ʿAbbās 1969, 25.
30. Ibid., 80.
31. Corbin 1990, 118.
32. Niẓām al-Mulk, *Siyāsatnāma*, 81.
33. Ibid., 9.

tween pre-Islamic and Islamic notions of kingly *farra* is that the Zoroastrian tenet justified the former, whereas the latter was legitimated via Islamic teachings. As concept, *farra* has itself changed over time. *Farra* was at least partially Islamized after the first/seventh century, and further on, lost some of its centrality following the fragmentation of the Islamic polity beginning in the fourth/tenth century. As mentioned before, Ṭabāṭabā'ī sees "continuation" in this regard, but the contention of this study has been that *farra* in the Islamic era should be interpreted in a more religious context. Over time, the *farra* of caliphs has been normalized and secularized, a development that is particularly noticeable in the Umayyad period (41–133/661–750).

Governance (*khshathra*)

Khshathra (Avestan) is the nodal point of power in Iranian treatises on governance. In fact, Iranian kingship cannot be understood without this concept. As a concept, it has three components: firstly, as God's sovereignty or *khshathra vairya*, secondly as beneficent power, or *hu khshathra*, and finally as evil power, or *dej khshathra*.

Another good example for the influence of Iranian mirrors on the Islamic ones is the juxtaposition of Iranian viziers with Muslim kings (Arabs or Turks for the most part). Based on the relationship between power and knowledge, Iranian viziers have advised Muslim kings in the framework of mirrors. Furthermore, Niẓām al-Mulk advocated for the division of power in the kingdom between the administrative and judicial branches, as well as a strictly hierarchical division of peoples into social classes, both reminiscent of pre-Islamic social organization. So, the form of hierarchical division of powers in the Islamic era is influenced by the pre-Islamic one.

For context, Ibn al-Muqaffa''s *Risāla fī l-ṣaḥāba*, which discusses specific problems confronting the nascent Abbasid regime, may be instructive. While it may be true that this book should not be considered as a proper mirror for princes as Patricia Crone has argued,[34] its story of fallen princes and murdered viziers accords with a salient theme in mirrors for princes, which have been characterized as "kisses of death."[35]

Religion and Government

Religion and state are routinely considered as twins in the Islamic as well as pre-Islamic eras. But, what is meant by this metaphor? Does it imply that

34. Crone 2004, 260.
35. Yavari 2008a, 68.

governance should be in the hands of clerics? A close relationship between religion and government is not limited to Iran and Islam. As Yavari states in the case of *Siyāsatnāma*:

> The veiled nature of advice that permeates this literature is reinforced by the many ways in which politics and religion are mixed in medieval texts. The absence of political and religious spheres does not of course imply that the two are not separated. It only means that religion and politics are locked in a bitter struggle of power and authority, and that the political never succeeded on the religious unless it appropriated the form and content of religious arguments.[36]

This understanding is confirmed in *al-Adab al-ṣaghīr*. There the prince is urged to promote men of religion to take advice, when necessary.[37]

The relationship between Niẓām al-Mulk and Malikshāh was like the one between a father and his son. Meanwhile Niẓām al-Mulk himself was the victim of plots in the court.[38] Obedience is due to kings, he argued, since God himself has so decreed: "Obey God, the Prophet and the rulers" (Q 4:59). The one who disobeys the rulers, opposes the Prophet, and the one who disobeys the Prophet, opposes God.[39] According to him, one of the king's duties is to be knowledgeable about the *sharīʿa* and to honor men of religion.[40] The point is that he argued it by two quotations: the first is from Islamic narrations and the second is attributed to Ardashīr. According to a hadith narrated from the Prophet: "*ʿulamā'* [i.e. religious scholars] are trustees of me except when they obey the kings."[41] Ardashīr says: "The king who can't deal with the elite, can't improve other people's affairs."[42]

The relationship between religion and kingship in mirrors after the rise of Islam was colored by the *sharīʿa*. Mirrors continued to be written after the rise of Islam for two reasons: the contradiction between *sharīʿa* and political rationality on the one hand, and pursuing "power politics" on the other. Lambton has seen a continuation of the structure of Iranian governance in the Islamic period.[43] For this reason medieval historians such as al-Masʿūdī and al-Ṭabarī have used Iranian mirrors such as *Nāma-yi Tansar* in their chronicles.[44] As mentioned before, kingship was considered superior

36. Yavari 2008a, 50.
37. Ibn al-Muqaffaʿ, *Al-Adab al-kabīr wa al-adab al-ṣaghīr*, 293.
38. Yavari 2008b, 353.
39. Niẓām al-Mulk, *Siyāsatnāma*, 22.
40. Niẓām al-Mulk, *Siyāsatnāma*, 78.
41. Majlisī (d. 1111/1699–1700), *Biḥār al-anwār*, 2: 110.
42. Niẓām al-Mulk, *Siyāsatnāma*, 80.
43. Lambton 1988, 7.
44. Al-Masʿūdī (d. 346/957), *Murūj al-dhahab*, 60.

to religion in both pre-Islamic and Islamic treatises. Ardashīr himself had specified the form of religious shrines and their social and political roles. The same pattern, i.e. the superiority of kingship to religion, persisted in the Umayyad and Abbasid eras. Because of the centrality of government in the Abbasid period, al-Māwardī divided leadership into *istikfā'* and *istilā'*. He has distinguished two types of rule: one freely conferred by the caliph, *istikfā'*, and rule by conquest, *istilā'*. These types of governments should be understood in the context of Abbasid era. Emam Shushtari, the contemporary Persian translator of *Nāma-yi Tansar*, holds that all Islamic mirrors are influenced by Sassanid texts.[45] As we have seen, however, Islamic mirrors are not simple imitations of the Iranian ones. Although Islamic mirrors were influenced by the latter, they reflect their own political contexts, and reveal what Foucault has called the inter-relationship between power, knowledge, and religion in that historical milieu.

45. ʿAbbās 1969, 13.

Bibliography

ʿAbbās, I. (ed.) (1348/1969), *ʿAhd-i Ardashīr*, tr. M. ʿAlī Emām Shushtarī, Tehran.

Amir Arjomand, S. (1994), "ʿAbd Allāh Ibn al-Muqaffaʿ and the ʿAbbasid Revolution," *Iranian Studies* 27: 9–36.

Chouliaraki, L. (2008), "Discourse Analysis," in: T. Bennett and J. Frow (eds.), *The SAGE Handbook of Cultural Analysis*, London, 674–98. (Online version http://eprints.lse.ac.uk/21564/1/Discourse_analysis_(LSERO_version).pdf [9/19/2013]).

Corbin, H. (1990), *Falsafa-yi Īrānī wa falsafa-yi taṭbīqī*, tr. J. Ṭabāṭabā'ī, Tehran, Tus.

Crone, P. (2004), *Tārīkh-i andīsha-yi siyāsī dar Islām*, tr. M. Jaʿfarī, Tehran.

Feirahi, D. (2003), *Qudrat, dānish wa mashrūʿīyat dar Islām*, Tehran.

Al-Ghazzālī, Muḥammad (1982), *Nasīḥat al-mulūk*, tr. J. Humā'ī, Tehran.

Ibn al-Muqaffaʿ, ʿAbd Allāh (2001), *Al-Adab al-kabīr wa al-adab al-ṣaghīr*, Beirut.

Lambton, A. K. S (1988), *Continuity and Change in Medieval Persia: Aspects of Administrative, Economic, and Social History, 11th-14th Century*, [New York].

Latham, J. D. (1997), "Ebn al-Moqaffaʿ," *EIr* VIII: 39–41. (Updated online version at http://www.iranicaonline.org/articles/ebn-al-moqaffa [8/22/2013].)

London, J. A. (2009), *Speaking Through the Voice of Another: Forms of Political Thought and Action in Medieval Islamic Contexts*, PhD dissertation, University of Chicago.
Majlisī, Muḥammad Bāqir (1983), *Biḥār al-anwār*, Qom.
Makdisi, G. (1973), "The Sunni Revival," in: D. S. Richards (ed.), *Islamic Civilization, 950–1150*, Oxford, 155–67.
Al-Mas'ūdī, Abū l-Ḥasan (1991), *Murūj al-dhahab*, tr. A. Payāndah, Tehran.
Mīnuvī, M. (ed.) (1354sh/1975), *Nāma-yi Tansar*, 2nd ed. Tehran.
Muradi Ghiyasābādī, R. (2012), "Evolution of the Names Iran, Arya, and Fars (Persia) in Ancient Texts," *http://ghiasabadi.com/what-is-iran-en.html* [9/19/2013].
Mujtabā'ī, F. (1973), *Shahr-i zībā-yi Aflāṭūn wa shāhī ārmānī dar Īrān-i bāstān*, Tehran.
Niẓām al-Mulk (1962), *Siyar al-mulūk [Siyāsatnāma]*, ed. Hubert Darke, Tehran.
Orwell, G. (1950), *1984*, New York.
Rosenthal, E. I. J. (1962), *Political Thought in Medieval Islam*, Cambridge.
Safi, O. (2006), *The Politics of Knowledge in Premodern Islam: Negotiating Ideology and Religious Inquiry (Islamic Civilization and Muslim Networks)*, Chapel Hill.
Ṭabāṭabā'ī, J. (2003), *Zawāl-i andīsha-yi siyāsī dar Īrān*, Tehran.
—— (2012), "An Anomaly in the History of Persian Political Thought," unpublished manuscript.
al-Warāwīnī, S. (tr.) (1355sh/1976), *Marzbānnāma*, ed. Muḥammad Rushan, Tehran.
Yavari, N. (2008a) "Mirrors for Princes or a Hall of Mirrors: Niẓām al-Mulk's *Siyar al-mulūk*, Reconsidered," *Al-Masāq: Islam and the Medieval Mediterranean* 20: 47–69.
—— (2008b), "Niẓām al-Mulk," in: A. Rippin (ed.), *The Islamic World*, London, 351–9.

Sultanic Rule in the Mirror of Medieval Political Literature

Stefan Leder

WRITINGS ON THE APPROPRIATE CONDUCT of rulers, the organization of rule, its aims and justification, pervade Arabic and Persian literature, and both literatures are interconnected via translations and borrowings in this realm. Together they constitute a robust textual corpus produced over centuries by Muslim authors from Spain to India and from Central Asia to the Sahara. One may distinguish various genres within this field of writing, even if boundaries are often blurred: political testaments in epistolary form, mirrors for princes offering counsel—in itself a varied genre—including treatises on ethics and political philosophy designed to give advice to rulers; handbooks on political administration; works on law or more particularly state law; works on political philosophy proper; *adab* compendia collecting sayings and exempla about the recommendable conduct of rulers; and historiography presenting exempla of good or remarkable rule.

Political Discourse

In the following, our interest in political literature is related to the first, most prolific and persistent group in an attempt to retrieve aspects of the political thought it conveys. This perspective is necessarily analytical and selective. The literary character of the mirror for princes genre is often daunting and prevalently manifest in elaborate style, artful composition and selective compilation from a large repertoire of established traditions. It thus tends to take precedence over political discourse. The politico-moralist idiom which pervades this literature is also not directly supportive of the discussion and negotiation of political issues. The conjunction of ethics and power, or the idea that rule is sustained when it obliges to the norms of the good and recommendable conduct, is a basic presumption in most of the writings in this realm, except for those advocating an a-moralist application of autonomous techniques of power. Somewhat in contrast to these trends we are giving attention to those aspects of discourse that refer to regula-tive habitual institutions and thus transcend political ethics centered on the ruler's person. What we are aiming at, in other words, is to demonstrate that political conceptualization in our texts includes a notion of good rule as it results from the functioning of the ruler's agencies and their aiming at the common good.

Established conceptions, current discursive conventions and elements of common knowledge about statecraft abound of course, and references to issues related to the authors' time tend to remain opaque and random and therefore need to be inferred from the context. But this does not diminish their explanatory potential for the history of political thought. Medieval authors, or many of them, indeed responded to concerns and problems they perceived, however conventional their literary approach might have been. This takes us beyond the exploration of conventional thematic perspectives, but does not deny other readings which may emphasize the authors' directly pragmatic strategies, for instance.[1]

The pre-modern literature of mirrors for princes, or a considerable part of it, may thus be read as political literature and a contribution to the evolution of political thought. Irrespective of its normative attitude, it engages in discussing the premises, objectives and perils of structure and organization of the polity. In this respect, it discusses how to justify power through the good that it brings, and reflects how political structures favoring unrestricted autocratic rule were perceived and countered. Authors eventually recommend strategies in reaction to what they perceived of a problematic reality.

The general mood is to advise rulers to seek a remedy and exhort them to comply with their duties. In general, there is no articulation of claims that could be made against them. From this point of departure, Patricia Crone emphasizes the generic difference between this kind of political articulation and modern concepts: "The single most important difference between contemporary Western political thinking and the Islamic tradition is that contemporary thought focuses on freedom and rights whereas the Islamic tradition focuses on authority and duties. This separates contemporary political thought from all pre-modern societies."[2] Such dichotomy may however be too rigorous, and it also tends to encourage an apodictic dismissal of the political significance of pre-modern literature.[3] It may therefore be more rewarding to inquire whether we can deduce that governmental ethics centered on the person of the ruler are combined with, or even were trans-

1. Marlow 2004, 169-94.
2. Crone 2013, 554.
3. "their effectiveness was limited," Crone 2013, 557.

formed into, concern for human and material resources based on the reality of political administration.

The most general approach to such a notion may be found in critical assessments which evidence an author's awareness of problematic issues. An obvious example is presented by Ibn Ẓafar the Sicilian (d. 1169 or 1172 CE), for instance, where he comments on dynastic rule in his *Consolation for the Ruler During the Hostility of Subjects*:

> Uprisings (of the people) are aimed against sovereigns whose crown is a hereditary right. Brought up in the midst of plenty, most are inclined to indolence while being persuaded that their capacity to govern is inherent in them. Moreover, most of them believe that the virtues of their illustrious forefathers live on in them, but they do not see any necessity for exertion on their parts.[4]

This passage is extant in one particular manuscript of the work, whereas many others do not include it.[5] This circumstance may be indicative of the statement's delicate nature, as it suggests that a lack of efficacy exposes governments to the challenges of (legitimate) upheaval, even if it is somehow relativized, as the ensuing discussion gives occasion to denounce the unrest of people as not being motivated by corruption and repression of the king, but by ignorance and greed. However, by addressing a particular issue related to the historical situation, it also reveals a common trait of mirrors for princes addressing local sovereigns. There are other passages of this kind, such as a description of pretended piety revealing the intent to defraud.[6]

Political Frameworks

Ibn Ẓafar himself edited his work twice, dedicated to an unknown ruler in Syria facing a situation of upheaval, and then in 1159 CE to Muḥammad b. Abī l-Qāsim al-Qurashī (Ibn al-Ḥajar) the Sicilian Amīr of the Muslims under Norman rule.[7] Just as in his case, the reflection of political issues rather appears within a political framework that grants authority and responsibility to the local rulers addressed. It is thus related to the concept of sovereign local rule which gradually took shape from the eleventh century onwards. The notion of local responsibilities can be presumed to have subsisted ir-

4. Translation of *Sulwān al-muṭā'*, see Ibn Ẓafar, *The Just Prince*, 242.
5. Ibn Ẓafar, *Sulwân al-muṭâ'*, 128. Available Arabic editions do not include this passage such as the ones of Damaj (Beirut 1995), 222-3, or al-Buḥayrī (Cairo 2001), 86.
6. Ibn Ẓafar, *The Just Prince*, 278; Ibn Ẓafar, *Sulwân al-muṭâ'*, 167.
7. Ibn Jubayr (d. 1217 CE), *Riḥlat Ibn Jubayr*, 341.

respective of the caliphate's habitual claim to paramount authority and the adherent politico-theological ideology. But when the *shar'ī* ideal of a political authority invested by the caliph lost significance in favor of local rule as an independent institution of governance including the administration of the religious-judicial apparatus, a new political paradigm gained ground.[8] Whereas concepts of a divinely ordained duality of spiritual and worldly powers (prophet and king, caliph and sultan) preceded and accompanied this political process,[9] the political role of the Saljuqs was crucial. Patrons of the re-establishment of Sunni Islamic rule, they introduced a new division of power which did not leave significant temporal power to the caliph.[10] The Saljuqs also established the ruler's title Sultan which became with the end of the twelfth century a widely spread term used for independent local rulers. Sovereignty in this context implies the necessity of a monopoly on the legitimate use of violence *(qahr)*, and is often postulated by use of pastoral, natural, or religious metaphors. Autonomous sovereignty is repeatedly circumscribed by a formula according to which the ruler is the shadow of God on earth (*al-sulṭān ẓillu Llāh fī l-arḍ*). This formula appears regularly in advice literature and Islamic tradition since the eleventh century and is related to the Iranian tradition of divine right.[11] Islamic tradition, using *sulṭān* in its impersonal signification of political authority, refers to God's support (*al-sulṭān 'izzatun min Allāh*) granted for the most visible (strongman) (*aẓhar 'ibādihī*) apt of fulfilling the task.[12]

The *Siyāsatnāma* (The Book of Government or Rules for Kings) attributed[13] to Niẓām al-Mulk (d. 1092 CE), conceives the sultan's rule as an autonomous institution based on the Persian tradition of kingly rule. As the book was transplanted to India by Fakhr Mudabbir's *Ādāb al-mulūk* (ca. 1260 CE)[14] and found several emulators there, such as Abū l-Fażl 'Allāmī's (d. 1602 CE) well known *Ā'īn-i Akbarī*, it is an influential testimony for the concept of sovereign rule. On the Arabic side, the *Counsel on Princely Manners* (*Kitāb al-Ishāra*), written by Muḥammad b. al-Ḥasan al-Murādī (d. 1096 CE) in the context of rising Almoravid rule in North Africa, is entirely based on traditions of political wisdom, ethics and philosophy. The author may have reckoned that the importance of Islamic law was sufficiently brought forward by Almoravid propaganda, and thus paid no heed to *shar'ī* legitimacy.

8. Woods 1999, 4-6.
9. Arjomand 2013, 84.
10. Tor 2013, 532-4.
11. Arjomand 1984, 94; and Arjomand 2013, 90.
12. al-Ḥākim al-Nīsābūrī (d. 1014 CE), *al-Mustadrak 'alā l-ṣaḥīḥayn*, vol. 3, 6, no. 4260.
13. Khismatulin 2008.
14. Ahmad 1962, 121-3.

Another approach is exemplified by the Mālikī expert of law and tradition, al-Ṭurṭūshī (d. 1126 CE), who wrote a detailed treatise on the principles of rule, completed in Fustat in 1122 CE. His book gives evidence of the author's preoccupation with matters of Islamic *fiqh,* as it is meant to demonstrate the comprehensiveness of Islamic norms rather dealing with the practicalities of the organization of rule.[15] The synthesis of both trends, political wisdom and the integration of *sharīʿa* norms appears established later in the twelfth century when the conventions and political reality of local sovereign law had taken shape.

Kingship and Sultanic Rule

Whereas a "sultanic political culture"[16] can be distinguished conceptually from the Islamic polity under the premises of the caliphate, the two paradigms, sultanate and caliphate, were not neatly separated. The caliph's confirmation of the rulers' authority continued as a practice and according to local circumstance even after the fall of the Baghdad caliphate. In some Muslim milieus, the ideological significance of the caliphate survived its abolishment in 1922 CE and the subsequent constitutional transformation under Mustafa Kemal Atatürk in 1924 CE.

Neither can we speak of a homogenous terminology of sultanic rule. Local rulers used various titles including king (*malik, pādshāh*), and also, in the Maghrib, Commander of the Muslims (*amīr al-muslimīn*). Some of these titles were used in combination with the title sultan.[17] The distinction between sultanate and imamate could be obliterated by individual authors according to their prospects. Ibn ʿAṭiyya al-Ḥamawī, a Syrian author writing in the second decade of the 16th century, assigns the obligations and tasks of the just *imām* to the Ottoman sultan Selīm I.[18] Outside of mainstream Sunnism, the Ibāḍī doctrine advocated a synthesis of political leadership and religious guidance reflected by use of the term Imamate.[19]

15. al-Ṭurṭūshī, *Sirāj al-mulūk.*

16. Dakhlia 2002, 1196.

17. See for instance the inscription from Nasrid Granada of 1348: *mawlānā amīr al-muslimīn al-sulṭān al-mujāhid al-ʿādil Abū l-Ḥajjāj Yūsuf .... b. al-Walīd b. Naṣr* (Lévi-Provençal 1931, 156–7, no. 171); or the inscription on the Damascus citadel from 1209–10 CE of the Ayyubid Sultan al-Malik al-ʿĀdil (d. 1218 CE): "Our Patron, the Sultan Malik al-ʿĀdil, defender (sword) of the mundane and religious realms, master (sultan) of the army of the Muslims ordered to erect the blessed tower (*amara bi-ʿimārat hādhā l-burj al-mubārak mawlānā al-sulṭān al-Malik al-ʿĀdil sayf al-dunyā wa l-dīn sulṭān juyūsh al-muslimīn* (Sobernheim 1922, 6.)

18. al-Ḥamawī, *al-Naṣāʾiḥ al-muhimma.*

19. Gaiser 2010, 8-9.

In spite of these variances and distinctions, the term sultan was in use from the Muslim West to India, and we may employ the term sultanate by way of simplification as a distinct political paradigm of independent local rule in general. Sultanic rule absorbed the Iranian tradition of kingship, but was reconcilable with the norms of the *sharīʿa,* whereas the term kingship tends to be seen in contrast to the Islamic ideal of apostolic succession to the Prophet thus representing worldly rule. In this vein, the notion of a division between "the legitimate vicarage of God and the profane kingship,"[20] even if historically imprecise and systematically inconsistent, was irreversible. It was expressed by Muslim authors, as al-Azmeh observes, sometimes in a melancholic tone. A tenacious expression of this notion is given by Ibn Khaldūn who wrote the first version of his groundbreaking *Muqaddima* between 1376-8 CE: When praising the companions of the prophet as representatives of an uncorrupted sober caliphate uninterested in worldly gains, he says in his chapter on the transition of power from the caliphate to kingship, they "refused kingship and its appearances, and disregarded its manners and customs in order to avoid the vanity (*al-bāṭil*) which these enwrap."[21]

Good Rule and Political Discourse

Ibn Khaldūn's analytical approach was critical of the exhortatory style which he recognized especially in al-Ṭurṭūshī's aforementioned mirror.[22] This reservation must derive from his postulation of an appropriate methodology for studying the history of civilization. His stance seems also to be induced by skepticism with regard to the political regimes of the epoch. In this light, Ibn Khaldūn would have cultivated doubt concerning the effects of political counsel, in accordance with his assessment that retention of power was the most important force driving politics in his time. This consideration is not far from what Ibn Ẓafar, above, was referring to, but it is more fundamental as he relates a deplorable political practice to a political discourse which is purely affirmative.

> Reasonable political order (*siyāsa ʿaqliyya*) is of two types: One type consists of balancing the general or public interest (*al-maṣāliḥ ʿalā l-ʿumūm*) with the interests of the sultan in retaining his rule. Such was the political order of the Iranians, abiding by wisdom. – [But] God has made this superfluous for us in the religiously defined polis (*milla*), and on the ground of the caliphate, as the rules of *sharīʿa* (i.e.

20. al-Azmeh 2001, 164.
21. Ibn Khaldūn, *al-Muqaddima, Kitāb al-ʿIbar,* 357.
22. Ibn Khaldūn, *al-Muqaddima, Kitāb al-ʿIbar,* 65.

> law of divine origin) make good for public and particular interests as well as for rules of good conduct. The imperatives of political rule are also incorporated in them. The second type consists in preserving the interest of the ruler, and how the rule is secured through coercion (*qahr*) and protraction (*istiṭāla*). Public interest here is subordinated (*wa takūnu l-maṣāliḥ al-'āmma fī hādhihī taba'an*). This is the political order of the rulers of the world, Muslims and unbelievers, even if Muslim rulers follow the requirements of the Islamic *sharī'a* in their politics as far as their efforts reach. As a consequence their principles (*qawānīn*) [i.e. of politics] combine *sharī'a* rules, ethics, the natural laws of society, and necessary measures of preserving supremacy and *'aṣabiyya*, esprit de corps. Orientation (*iqtidā'*) for this type of political order is found in divine law, in the comportment of the wise and in history.[23]

Ibn Khaldūn's pessimistic vision seems to deny the existence of any coherent normative or theoretical framework capable of determining objectives in politics. As a consequence, politics is about maintaining power. His assessment is linked to what he sees as the decisive and compelling momentum of Islamic history, the emergence of the religiously defined polity (*milla*), where "the rules of *sharī'a* make good for public and private interest."[24] However, this felicitous time is lost in history.

His thought is not compelling. One may argue that the major obstacle for making the demand of good rule politically implementable is not the loss of good guidance through an unselfish caliphate, but rather disinterest in (or despair of) the political matrix of the sultanate.[25]

Successful rule is generally believed to depend on observing a number of principles each of which embraces the two aspects of rule: legitimate sovereignty and good governance. Political thought therefore regularly reiterates a number of components of good rule, which approximate the tenets of righteous and therefore legitimate rule.

Justice is the heart of political teaching. The obvious practical advantages are illustrated by the persuasive circle of justice, variously attributed to Persian and Greek authors and extent in many redactions. It connects the maintenance of kingship with the proper state of the army, which necessitates sufficient revenue from economic activity, which in turn does not

23. Ibn Khaldūn, *al-Muqaddima, Kitāb al-'Ibar,* 520-1.

24. Ibn Khaldūn, *al-Muqaddima, Kitāb al-'Ibar,* 521.

25. Ibn al-Azraq, the most important pre-modern Arab recipient of Ibn Khaldūn's *Muqaddima*, pursued this approach: Ibn al-Azraq (d. 1491 CE), *Badā'i' al-silk.*

occur without justice.[26] The paramount importance of justice is also conveyed by its conceptualization as an autonomous institution. According to a well-known saying, extant in several texts, including Ibn Taymiyya's (d. 1376 CE) legal opinions, "God supports that rule which practices justice, even if it is exercised by unbelievers, but does not give support to unjust rule, even if exercised by Muslims."[27] It may appear at first glance contradictory when the same author is found to state that sixty years of unjust rule are preferable to one day without rule.[28] But in fact both statements are coherent, since justice (*'adl*) is granted by governance which depends, according to the logic of sultanic rule, on the authority of the ruler.

Justice and the Common Good

In political literature justice is not only referred to as an abstract principle, but also appears as practices of good rule serving the common good. When the exigencies arising from the principle of justice are explained, contemporary expectations and political visions are exposed.

'Abd al-Raḥmān [b. Naṣr] al-Shayzarī dedicated his work *The Pursuit of the Right Path in Princely Policy Making* to Sultan Saladin (d. 1193 CE).[29] He also authored a work on market inspection (*ḥisba*),[30] a medical treatise on marriage and sexuality,[31] as well as a book on love.[32] In his treatise, *sunna*, or Islamic tradition, i.e. the Qur'an and the teachings of the Prophet, play a prominent role, a feature which suits Ayyubid politics: Sunni Islam was cultivated as a resource of mobilization and as conceptual framework for creating political unity. As usual, justice appears as a practical, moral, religious duty—an inevitable obligation. It is the field of politics per se, where demands are negotiated, support is secured or lost, where kingdoms are maintained or squandered, at least in the light of counsels for rulers. Justice represents the most important element of political practice in the service of the common good. For Shayzarī, justice is a comprehensive principle, an obligation to the law of God, which is accessible by reason and therefore not bound to the *sunna*.[33]

26. Lambton 1962, 100; for the octagon of justice see also Forster 2006, 61-2.
27. Ibn Taymiyya, *Majmū' al-fatāwa*, 6: 168 and 410: *inna Llāh yanṣuru l-dawla al-'ādila wa in kānat kāfiratan, wa lā yanṣuru l-dawla al-ẓālima wa in kānat mu'minatan.*
28. Ibn Taymiyya, *Majmū' al-fatāwa*, 6: 322 and 340.
29. al-Shayzarī (d. 1193 CE), *al-Nahj al-maslūk.*
30. al-Shayzarī, *Nihāyat al-rutba.*
31. al-Shayzarī, *al-Īḍāḥ.*
32. Semah 1977.
33. al-Shayzarī, *al-Nahj al-maslūk*, 98-9.

> Be aware that justice (*ʿadl*) is accomplished only when kings keep to ten features [of good rule]: (1) Erecting the lighthouse of religion and preserving its cultic practice; thereby inciting people to integrate their religion into their daily practice in an adequate measure without neglect nor exaggeration.[34]

The author obviously advocates moderation in the fulfillment of religious obligations:

> (2) The sultan must also protect Islamic territories (*bayḍa*) and his subjects from heretics, aggressors, and evildoers; (3) undertake public construction to improve roads and highways; (4) protect his subjects against transgressions by government officials and members of the nobility, for otherwise he is accountable for their mishaps. (5) The sultan's fifth duty is to ensure that his subjects are protected from the army and state employees, so that officials would not reduce their income or delay the transfer of their pay which would let them be exposed to latencies stripping them of everything they possess.[35]

One can easily recognize the struggle against corruption in this last paragraph.

> (6) His sixth duty is attending *maẓālim* court hearings regularly and settling quarrels between people on the grounds established by Islamic law.[36]

This refers to real practice. Saladin's predecessor, Nūr al-Dīn Maḥmūd b. Zangī, erected a court building in Damascus in about 1163 CE. Saladin himself presided court hearings there while in Damascus.[37]

The organization of regular audits is mandated in the seventh duty, when the sultan is invited to (7) "carefully measuring remuneration from the state treasury according to the rank of people and thereby avoiding parsimonious or extravagant treatment."[38] The Sultan's eighth task is (8) "the application of penalties for crimes mentioned in the divine law,"[39] when the author asks for a system of penalties commensurate with the stipulations of the *sharīʿa*, rather than one based on the whims of the ruler or his agents who are thus placing themselves above the law. In the ninth duty, the sultan is asked to

34. al-Shayzarī, *al-Nahj al-maslūk*, 98.
35. al-Shayzarī, *al-Nahj al-maslūk*, 98.
36. al-Shayzarī, *al-Nahj al-maslūk*, 99.
37. Rabbat 1997, 3-28.
38. al-Shayzarī, *al-Nahj al-maslūk*, 99.
39. al-Shayzarī, *al-Nahj al-maslūk*, 99.

safeguard against nepotism, by (9) "appointing capable, trustworthy and trained people to official positions."[40] Finally, the Sultan is charged with:

> (10) implementing the stipulations issued by qadis and market inspectors, executing what they could not achieve out of the lack of executive power. The king has to perform what law demands. When the king acts according to these ten features of justice, he applies the right of God (*kāna mu'addiban li-ḥaqq Allāh*) with respect to his subjects. In return, he is entitled to receive their obedience, and merits their support. When he refrains from it, he deviates from justice preferring injustice (*jawr*) [which is a crime]."[41]

The concept of the right of God here incorporates two aspects. As God is the master of mankind, he does not invest the sultan with rule over man, but with rule over His creature (*wallānā amr 'ibādihī*).[42] In this sense the sultan's rule is subordinated, obliged to correspond with God's will to do good (*amaranā an nuḥassina*) and practice justice.[43] This general principle implies that people – given that they respect God's rules – are entitled to be treated corresponding to God's stipulations, which is the condition on which they pay obedience to the ruler. What this means in earthly rule is explained by Shayzarī in the passage above.

Even if a close study of this text reveals parallels in other works of the genre, it remains obvious from the work's context, that the author's assessment is not the product of a literary tradition, but a deliberate pronouncement of faith, confirming established practice and postulating this practice as a precondition for successful rule. Frankish presence in the Islamic lands in this period catalyzed the ideologization of society, wherein religious authority gained favor, especially among the urban populations of the Bilād al-Shām.[44]

Duality of Political Power and Religious Authority

Sultanic rule, although principally unrestricted and legitimated by divine right, was not itself the source of religious authority. The indispensable alliance between worldly and religious authority was structured by the intersecting realms of judiciary, education, institutional religious services etc.,

40. al-Shayzarī, *al-Nahj al-maslūk*, 99.
41. al-Shayzarī, *al-Nahj al-maslūk*, 99.
42. Ibn al-Azraq, *Badā'i' al-silk*, 2: 543.
43. Ibn al-Azraq, *Badā'i' al-silk*, 2: 543.
44. Leder 2011, 81-101.

which were partly funded and at least co-directed by the agencies controlled by the ruler. On the other hand, the autonomous spiritual and juridical resources of religious authority, its cohabitation with popular strata of society and political and social impact is referred to in political literature, either as a challenge and potential danger, or as a source of guidance and righteousness. The necessity of balancing political power and religious authority constitutes a historical matrix of political thought that is applied by authors to circumstantial contexts. The discussion may go beyond rather theoretical reference to concepts and turn to particular policies.

Al-Ḥasan b. ʿAbd Allāh al-ʿAbbāsī was a civil servant, probably in the tax department, and completed his work, *Āthār al-uwal fī tartīb al-duwal* (Teachings of the Ancients on the Organization of Dynastic Rule), in August 1309 CE, a few months after Baybars II al-Malik al-Muẓaffar Rukn al-Dīn Manṣūrī Jāshnakīr, who is his addressee, came to power.[45] The author wrote his treatise in troubled years, when the concept of dynastic succession, which the Mamluk Sultan Qalawūn tried to install, was challenged—and finally abrogated—by competing military rulers. Being also a historian, he pursues a clearly political approach to his task of giving political counsel.[46]

From the outset one may think that the author keeps to the traditional outline of advice literature by explaining the design of the virtuous state (*al-dawla al-fāḍila*). The fictitious tale of the virtuous king is the raison d'être of advice literature, as it postulates an interrelation between power and morality. But under the circumstance of his time, when competing military leaders aspired to climb the throne solely on the basis of military power and political alliances, sovereignty, its legitimacy and conditions had to be defined more carefully.

An advocate of the supremacy of political power, he disregards Islamic legitimacy as a basis for political rule. The caliphate is a mandatory rule (*wilāya ʿalā l-nās*).[47] Sovereignty is generally a divine right, a grace bestowed by God (*faḍlun ilāhiyyun yunʿimu Llāhu bihī ʿalā man yaṣṭafīhi min khalqihī*).[48] The above-mentioned formula according to which the ruler is the shadow of God on earth (*al-sulṭān ẓillu Llāh fī l-arḍ*)[49]—a formula which is a staple of advice literature and the Islamic tradition since the eleventh century—is employed by ʿAbbāsī in a critical position. Unlimited power upends criticism and resistance, and is hazardous to both the ruler and those obliged to deal with him. It also breeds abuse of power. Obedience, moreover, is not just

45. al-ʿAbbāsī (d. after 1307 CE), *Āthār al-uwal*. See also: Marlow 1995, 101-20.
46. al-Ṣafadī, (d. 1317 CE), *Nuzhat al-mālik*. See also Little 1970, 38-9.
47. al-ʿAbbāsī, *Āthār al-uwal*, 68.
48. al-ʿAbbāsī, *Āthār al-uwal*, 75.
49. al-ʿAbbāsī, *Āthār al-uwal*, 139.

a univocal obligation of the ruler's subjects, but a contractual relationship (*kullu man ḥaqqaqa l-ṭāʿata li-ghayrihī, tahaqqaqat al-ṭāʿatu li-nafsihī*).[50]

Religious law, *sharīʿa*, and its agents, the religious scholars, are closely connected to political rule which is meant to defend the *sharīʿa*.[51] *Sharīʿa* is the basis of their authority, and those who claim licenses exempting them from the law, are wrongdoers.[52] Religious claims more generally are suspect, as they are considered to be primarily a source of authority for political contenders. The coalition between the sultanic sovereign and religion, as recommended here, appears to be precarious. Religious authority must be controlled and tamed, as it may spread error, and incite doubts and skepticism. Men of religion may intend to acquire political power by making use of their religious authority, they may declare to possess exclusive insight into the matters of law, thus make claim of licenses, exempting themselves from the law which they impose on others; men of religion may incite rebellion in the name of ascetic ideals, and in history, the author says, men of religion often organized movements which led to the creation of powerful dynasties.[53]

According to the author's assessment, religious authority constitutes an important rival to state power. He recommends dealing with it like the "kings of the west" (*mulūk al-gharb*) who are vigilant and try to make use of religious authority only when it confirms their position.[54]

The ruler's justice is a moral obligation and instrumental to successful rule. According to its two-dimensional nature, it is based on the human disposition (*hay'a*)[55] towards equilibrium (*musāwāt*), and constitutes a general principle of avenging injustice (*inṣāf al-maẓlūm min al-ẓālim*). However, the ruler's faculty to apply justice in both its regards, is restricted by his absolute power: surrounded by a necessarily subservient entourage complaints are filtered or dismissed at an early stage. ʿAbbāsī recommends here the conventional remedy: the good ruler (*al-malik al-rashīd*) must seek consultation (*mushāwara*).[56]

Religious Law (*sharīʿa*) versus Political Rule (*siyāsa*)

A different approach to the division of power between political and religious authority appears in a pamphlet which advocates for the authority of Islamic law and its experts. Sibṭ b. al-Jawzī's work, *al-Jalīs al-ṣāliḥ* (The

50. al-ʿAbbāsī, *Āthār al-uwal*, 100.
51. al-ʿAbbāsī, *Āthār al-uwal*, 116.
52. al-ʿAbbāsī, *Āthār al-uwal*, 116.
53. al-ʿAbbāsī, *Āthār al-uwal*, 115-6, 124-7.
54. al-ʿAbbāsī, *Āthār al-uwal*, 127.
55. al-ʿAbbāsī, *Āthār al-uwal*, 68.
56. al-ʿAbbāsī, *Āthār al-uwal*, 121.

Trustworthy Companion), was written in the span of forty days during the months of Muḥarram to Ṣafar of 613 AH, roughly May to June 1216 CE, probably for the Ayyubid prince al-Malik al-Ashraf Mūsā (d. 1237 CE).[57] It gives advice to the aspirations of a religious scholar at the time of the strategic alliance between political rule and Sunnī scholars. The author is critical of political rule, blaming the application of law, disregarding the *sharīʿa,* and rejecting the claim of contemporary authorities that this is justified by the principle of *siyāsa—siyāsa* as the authority to act outside of the framework of law—as this would imply that the *sharīʿa* is deficient and must be complemented by the juridical opinion of rulers. This is in his eyes unacceptable, as the *sharīʿa* contains all aspects of *siyāsa.*[58] Sibṭ b. al-Jawzī balances his critique of contemporary politics by stressing the religious character of his admonition. Deliberating on the Islamic tradition is the mechanism through which he promotes his views and shields himself from criticism. At the end of a chapter on injustice or tyranny (*ẓulm*), he adds a passage in rhymed prose, to deliver a sermon using religious imagery of punishment. It exposes the disturbing consequences of a disequilibrium caused by political injustice, because, as he says, ignoring the complaints of the governed does not protect against the retaliation (*tha'r*) that the oppressed will seek.[59] This is more than an abstract thread, of course, because Sibṭ b. al-Jawzī is a public speaker, a religious orator famous for delivering moving sermons that captivate his audience. His treatise, therefore, gives support and at the same time challenges political rule. Neither distance from practical politics, nor a lack of theoretical substance, diminishes the political character of this work, which employs the theme of injustice to bolster the claim of religion to political relevance.

Ethics and Piety

The rules of ethical conduct constitute a codex that obliges, by virtue of its benefits, concern for the prosperity and well-being of the governed dominions. The concept of the virtuous ruler is in essence, therefore, not a function of piety or religious commitment, but may instead serve to emphasize a worldly order of good rule. As we learn form an author writing in a rather provincial setting in the Jazira, non-religious ethics are not only instrumental in establishing the imperatives of appropriate conduct of rulers, but may also provide a sphere of values that are unrelated to religion. Muḥammad b. Manṣūr b. al-Ḥaddād's *Precious Jewel for Princely Rule* was

57. Sibṭ b. al-Jawzī, *al-Jalīs al-ṣāliḥ*, 17. See also Kronholm 1989-90, 81-91.
58. Sibṭ b. al-Jawzī, *al-Jalīs al-ṣāliḥ*, 55.
59. Kronholm 1989-90, 88.

written for Lu'lu' Badr al-Dīn al-Malik al-Raḥīm who was the sovereign of Mosul in the first half of the 13th century (1232-59 CE).[60] A freedman of the Zangid al-Malik al-ʿĀdil Nūr al-Dīn Arslān, al-Malik al-Raḥīm did not dispose of dynastic legitimacy, but received a diploma from the caliph in Baghdad when his rule was established. The author combines Islamic wisdom with maxims and models of early Islamic Arab history highlighting "Arab" values from the eighth and ninth centuries—which in turn draw from the glorified pre-Islamic Arab past—such as forbearance (*ḥilm*), charity (*ʿafw*), nobility (*makārim al-akhlāq*), and vigor (*murū'a*). The Islamic legacy is thus placed into a larger mould of pluralistic composition, inspired probably by the spirit of Arab tribes and their impact on local affairs.

Ibn Ḥaddād's consideration of values and regards of political order is significant in that he justifies his approach by distinguishing a religious political order (*siyāsat al-dīn*) which is functional in performing the obligations (*farḍ*), from a sphere of worldly politics (*siyāsat al-dunyā*), which is functional in fostering civilization (*ʿimārat al-arḍ*). Both are united by the common goal of applying justice, "which grants a stable rule and cultivates the ruler's domain; because he who neglects religious obligations violates himself (*ẓalama nafsahū*), and he who does damage (*kharraba*) to the world violates the right of others."[61] Justice here does not emanate from divine law, it is not a legal principle derived from the *sharīʿa*, but rather a state of equilibrium, a middle ground which corresponds to the will of God[62] and yet includes the virtues that support politics (*siyāsa*) and accommodate the exigencies of various situations.[63] In this vein, justice is a carefully calibrated middle. The author professes a secular model of the appropriate, one that pursues the common good (*siyāsat al-maṣlaḥa*),[64] and he does so by providing a value fundament of Arab ethics as a model and goal.

In contrast, ʿAlī b. ʿAṭiyya al-Ḥamawī's (d. 1530 CE) *Counsels*, written for the Ottoman sultan Selīm I (reg. 1512-20 CE), conveys the worldview of an author preoccupied with moral theology, one with a Sufi imprint.[65] Individual piety is to be practiced in an environment characterized by disturbances of public order and moral decay.[66] Since the author displays awareness of the manners and social affairs of his time, his doctrine of personal conduct and moral practice rooted in Islamic ethics relates to a vision of how the polity should be organized. This perspective does not only stimulate his

60. Ibn al-Ḥaddād (flourished 1251 CE, date of the autograph), *al-Jawhar al-nafīs.*
61. Ibn al-Ḥaddād, *al-Jawhar al-nafīs*, 75-6.
62. *Al-ʿadl mīzān Allāh fī l-arḍ*, Ibn al-Ḥaddād, *al-Jawhar al-nafīs*, 79.
63. Ibn al-Ḥaddād, *al-Jawhar al-nafīs*, 87.
64. Ibn al-Ḥaddād, *al-Jawhar al-nafīs*, introduction (as-Sayyid) 57.
65. al-Ḥamawī, *al-Naṣā'iḥ al-muhimma.*
66. See also his *ʿArā'is al-ghurar.*

reprimand of widespread decadence, marked by the use of alcohol and indecent behavior, but also makes him chastise corruption and misconduct and urge remedial action.[67] The author's critical stance brought him rebuke and defamation, when people rejected his rigorist position.[68] Seeing himself as an outsider, the author deplores the depravity of the Sultan's entourage, comprised of false men of religion.[69] As the passage cited below may demonstrate, he demands the sultan's attention to grievances and to exacting standards of probity among his agents as constitutive of his own moral authority. He therefore addresses the head of the government as Imam.[70] That the Ottoman sultan was the Defender of the Holy Cities of Mecca and Medina since 1516 may have been an additional inspiration to his approach.

> If rulers control themselves and their agents, avoid injustice and covetousness that leads to wrongdoing and seizing the property of others, prevent favoritism among their agents, stop wrongdoing and tyranny emanating from their staff (*su'āt*), assure that their armed forces observe God's law and commands, ensure that people of their entourage, whether rich or poor, do not act unjustly by accepting gifts or bribes (*barṭīl*), or fodder for their animals, or unauthorized hospitality (hospitality which is not reimbursed), and that they do not exercise pressure on the people, and do not oppress them through excessive taxation,[71]

only then may they be faithful to God and lay rightful claim to the title of just ruler, or simply, *imām*.

The author's tone also gives insight into public disorder, which is apparent in more detail from contemporary historiography.[72] His explication of piety is embedded in a narrative that calls for remedying social ills, righting wrongs and elevating the wellbeing of the populace. Islamic political thought—although prolific, especially in the twelfth and the thirteenth centuries, and engaged with the practical aspects of governance and political life—has been mostly set aside in the contemporary period, overshadowed by a more global lineage of political thought favored by Muslims and Arabs today.

67. al-Ḥamawī, *al-Naṣā'iḥ al-muhimma*,130.
68. al-Ḥamawī, *al-Naṣā'iḥ al-muhimma*, preface (al-ʿIlwānī), 14.
69. al-Ḥamawī, *al-Naṣā'iḥ al-muhimma*, 124-5.
70. al-Ḥamawī, *al-Naṣā'iḥ al-muhimma*, 130.
71. al-Ḥamawī, *al-Naṣā'iḥ al-muhimma*, 129-30.
72. See for instance the impunity of malefactors from the military: Martel-Thoumian 2008, 463.

Bibliography

al-ʿAbbāsī, al-Ḥasan b. ʿAbd Allāh (1989), *Āthār al-uwal fī tartīb al-duwal*, ed. ʿA. ʿUmayra, Beirut, 1989.

Ahmad, A. (1962), "Trends in the Political Thought of Medieval Muslim India," *Studia Islamica* 17: 121-30.

ʿAllāmī, Abū l-Fażl (1993), *The Āʾīn-i Akbarī*, ed. H. Blochman, 2 vols. in 3 parts, Frankfurt. (Reprint of the edition Calcutta 1872.)

Arjomand, S. A. (1984), *The Shadow of God and the Hidden Imam: Religion, Political Order, and Social Change in Shi'ite Iran from the Beginning to 1890*, Chicago.

—— (2013) "Perso-Islamicate Political Ethic in Relation to the Sources of Islamic Law," in: M. Boroujerdi (ed.), *Mirror for the Muslim Prince, Islam and the Theory of Statecraft*, New York, 83-106.

al-Azmeh, A. (2001), *Muslim Kingship. Power and the Sacred in Muslim, Christian and Pagan Polities*, London.

Crone, P. (2013), "Traditional Political Thought," in: G. Böwering et al. (eds.), *The Princeton Encyclopedia of Islamic Political Thought*, Princeton, 554-60.

Dakhlia, J. (2002), "Les Miroirs des princes islamiques: une modernité sourde?," *Annales 57:* 1191-206.

Forster, R. (2006), *Das Geheimnis der Geheimnisse.Die arabischen und deutschen Fassungen des pseudo-aristotelischen Sirr al-asrār/Secretum secretorum*, Wiesbaden.

Gaiser, A. R. (2010), *Muslims, Scholars, Soldiers. The Origin and Elaboration of the Ibāḍi Imāmate Traditions*, Oxford.

al-Ḥākim al-Nīsābūrī (2007), *al-Mustadrak ʿalā l-ṣaḥīḥayn*, ed. Ṣ. al-Laḥḥām, 4 vols., Amman.

al-Ḥamawī, ʿAlī b. ʿAṭiyya (1990), *Arāʾis al-ghurar wa gharāʾis al-fikar fī aḥkām al-naẓar*, ed. M. F. ʿA. al-Murād, Damascus.

—— (2000), *al-Naṣāʾiḥ al-muhimma li-l-mulūk wa l-aʾimma*, ed. N. al-ʿIlwānī, Damascus.

Ibn al-Azraq al-Andalusī, Abū ʿAbd Allāh (1977), *Badāʾiʿ al-silk fī ṭabāʾiʿ al-mulk*, ed. M. b. ʿAbd al-Karīm, 2 vols., Tunis.

Ibn al-Ḥaddād, Muḥammad b. Manṣūr b. Ḥubaysh (2012), *al-Jawhar al-nafīs fī siyāsat al-raʾīs*, ed. R. al-Sayyid, 2nd edition, Beirut.

Ibn Jubayr (1907), *Riḥlat Ibn Jubayr*, ed. W. Wright, 2nd. edition, rev. M. J. de Goeje, Leiden.

Ibn Khaldūn (2006), *al-Muqaddima, Kitāb al-ʿIbar wa dīwān al-mubtadaʾ wa l-khabar fī ayyām al-ʿarab wa l-ʿajam wa l-barbar wa man ʿāṣarahum min dhawī l-sulṭān al-akbar*, ed. I. Shabūḥ and I. ʿAbbās, Tunis.

Ibn Taymiyya, Taqī l-Dīn Aḥmad (2003), *Majmū' al-fatāwa Ibn Taymiyya*, CD-ROM, first edition, Riyad.
Ibn Ẓafar, Muḥammad b. 'Abd Allāh (1973), *Sulwân al-muṭâ' ossiano conforti politici*, Palermo.
—— (1995), *Sulwān al-muṭā' fī 'udwān al-atbā'*, ed. M. A. Damaj, Beirut.
—— (2001), *Sulwān al-muṭā' fī 'udwān al-atbā'*, ed. A. 'A. al-Buḥayrī, Cairo.
—— (2003), *The Just Prince. A Manual of Leadership, Including an Authoritative English Translation of the Sulwan al-muta' fi 'udwan al-atba' (Consolation for the Ruler during the Hostility of Subjects) by Muhammad ibn Zafar as-Siqilli*, tr. J. A. Kechichian and R. H. Dekmejian, London.
Khismatulin, A. (2008) "The art of medieval counterfeiting: the *Siyar al-mulūk* (the *Siyāsatnāma*) by Niẓām al-Mulk and the 'full' version of the *Naṣīḥat al-mulūk* by al-Ghazālī," *Manuscripta Orientalia* 14.1: 3-31.
Kronholm, T. (1989-90), "Dedication and Devotion. The Introduction to the *Kitāb al-Ǧalīs aṣ-ṣāliḥ* ascribed to Sibṭ Ibn al-Ǧauzī," *Orientalia Suecania* 38-9: 81-91.
Lambton, A. K. S. (1962), "Justice in the medieval Persian theory of Kingship," *Studia Islamica* 17: 91-120.
Leder, S. (2004), "Sunni Resurgence, Jihād Discourse and the Impact of the Frankish Presence in the Near East," in: S. Leder (ed.): *Crossroads between Latin Europe and the Near East*, Würzburg, 81-101.
Lévi-Provençal, E. (1931), *Inscriptions arabes d'Espagne*, 2 vols., Leiden.
Little, D. (1970), *An Introduction to Mamlūk Historiography*, Wiesbaden.
Marlow, L. (1995), "Kings, Prophets and the 'Ulamā' in Mediaeval Islamic Advice Literature," *Studia Islamica* 81: 101-20.
—— (2004), "The Way of Viziers and the Lamp of Commanders (*Minhāj al-wuzarā' wa sirāj al-umarā'*) of Aḥmad al-Iṣfahbadhī and the Literary and Political Culture of Early Fourteenth-Century Iran," in: B. Gruendler and L. Marlow (eds.), *Writers and Rulers: Perspectives on their Relationship from Abbasid to Safavid times*, Wiesbaden, 169-94.
Martel-Thoumian, B. (2008), "Pouvoir et justice sous les derniers sultans circassiens (872-922/1468-1516)," in: K. D'Hulster and J. van Steenbergen (eds.), *Continuity and Change in the Realms of Islam. Studies in Honour of Professor Urbain Vermeulen*, Leuven, 451-67.
al-Murādī, Muḥammad b. al-Ḥasan (1981), *Kitāb al-Ishāra ilā adab al-imāra*, ed. R. al-Sayyid, Beirut.
Rabbat, N. O. (1997), "The Ideological Significance of the *Dār al-'Adl* in the Medieval Islamic Orient," *IJMES* 27.1: 3-28.
al-Ṣafadī, al-Ḥasan b. 'Abd Allāh (2003), *Nuzhat al-mālik wa l-mamlūk fī mukhtaṣar sīrat man waliya Miṣr min al-mulūk*, ed. 'U. 'A. Tadmurī, Sayda.

Semah, D. (1977), "*Rauḍat al-qulūb* by al-Šayzari: A Twelfth Century Book on Love," *Arabica* 24: 187-206.

al-Shayzarī, ʿAbd al-Raḥmān b. Naṣr (1986), *al-Īḍāḥ fī asrār al-nikāḥ*, ed. M. S. al-Ṭurayḥī, Beirut.

—— (1994), *al-Nahj al-maslūk fī siyāsat al-mulūk*, ed. M. A. Damaj, Beirut.

—— (2003), "Nihāyat al-rutba fī ṭalab al-ḥisba," in: Muḥammad b. al-Ḥasan al-Murādī, *Kitāb al-Siyāsa aw al-Ishāra fī tadbīr al-imāra*, ed. M. Ḥ. M. Ḥ Ismāʿīl and A. F. al-Mazīdī, Beirut, 201-391.

Sibṭ b. al-Jawzī, Shams al-Dīn (1989), *al-Jalīs al-ṣāliḥ wa l-anīs al-nāṣiḥ*, ed. Ṣ. Fawwāz, London.

Sobernheim, M. (1922), "Die Inschriften der Zitadelle von Damaskus," *Der Islam* 12: 1-28.

Tor, D. G. (2013), "Sultan," in: G. Böwering et al. (eds.), *The Princeton Encyclopedia of Islamic Political Thought*, Princeton, 532-4.

al-Ṭurṭūshī (1994), *Sirāj al-mulūk*, 2 vols., ed. A. B. M. Fatḥī, Cairo.

Woods, J. E. (1999), *The Aqquyunlu. Clan, Confederation, Empire. A Study in 15th/9th Century Turko-Iranian Politics. Revised and expanded edition*, Salt Lake City.

Avoiding History's Teleology:

Byzantine and Islamic Political Philosophy

Johannes Niehoff-Panagiotidis[*]

THE PAST TWENTY OR SO YEARS have witnessed an exponential increase in new approaches in Islamic studies that go beyond collecting factoids, or half-cooked explanations – sociological as well as theological – for how, where, and when, Islam will trigger the next world war.[1] Among them, one offered by comparative political theory promises to avoid two mistakes: measuring the manifold political achievements of non-Western people, including their juridical, religious, philosophical heritage, insofar it had political repercussions – as it had mostly – according to Western models; and considering the manner of living of European and North American people as *per essentiam* linked to the success story of this part of the world, or, to use the argument *au rebours*, interpreting non-European *Lebensformen* (in the Schützian sense) in the light of their non-success, whatever this failure is supposed to be.

The assumption of Eurocentric models is that European science and scholarship is intrinsically linked from its very beginnings to the values of the Enlightenment and thus to the conviction that rationality as a scientific method or a political means of government is a privilege of this culture in the sense that it evolved by an historical teleology linked to the space occupied by it, the intellectual tools developed on this territory since the beginnings of ancient philosophy among the Greeks, and the fusion of liberalism and capitalism since the eighteenth century. This set of assumptions faces serious problems: Greek philosophy and science were virtually unknown in the Latin Middle Ages, no work of Plato (except a part of the *Timaeus*) having been translated into Latin before the twelfth century.[2] Byzantines and Arabs,

* I am grateful to my research assistant Gunna Bendfeldt, MA for her invaluable help in editing this article.

1. See March 2009, 532, n. 2 and Euben 1999. Some of these problems are being explored at the Berlin Graduate School Muslim Cultures and Societies (see www.bgsmcs.fu-berlin.de).

2. Boethius (d. about 524 CE) had only translated Aristotle's *Organon* and Porphyry's *Eisagoge*, thus leaving the *Metaphysics* out. On the other side, the complete *Corpus Aristotelicum* (except the *Politics*) was available in Arabic. The Byzantines had the whole corpus at their disposal. For a reassessment of the translation movement from Greek to Latin during the Middle Ages one should consult Berschin 1980 and the earlier but very fine work by Haskins 1927.

however, knew these texts, be it via translation, be it in the original. And they made use of them by translating, commenting, giving abstracts, teaching, and finding their own way through this immense bulk of tradition.[3] Though it is debated how much of it reached the Latin Middle Ages by translations and commentaries directly from the Greek (i.e. the Byzantines) or via an Arabic translation,[4] there can be no doubt that the Latin West had moved afar from the old centers of Mediterranean civilization in Late Antiquity.

As the Arab-Islamic Empire since its commencement occupied a great part of the former Roman Near East[5] (e.g. the old province of *Syria*, established by Pompey, in part co-extensive with Diocletian's *dioecesis Syria* during Late Antiquity with the capital Antioch/Anṭakya), the relation of the rising Islamic culture to the Graeco-Roman heritage poses a problem for European understanding, up to S. Huntington's book of 1998.[6] And this problem is posed by the Islamic concepts of rule, too. And it is here that Byzantium comes into play: All the difficulties in understanding links between Islamic civilization and European intellectual tradition, including reflections on righteous rule, appear or reappear when studying the heritage of the empire ruled from Constantine's capital. What is more, they appear tightened, since there is no question that the realm of the *Romaioi* (whence, Arabic *Rūm*) is the direct continuator of the Roman Empire, the heir of Greek philosophy and literature. Furthermore, this political unit is Christian, the Church of that Empire reciting the Gospels in their very language until today.

In a way, it is easier to keep Byzantium out of the questions touched upon so far, since this empire does not exist anymore. Some Byzantinists prefer to do so, by understanding their field as an ancillary to Medieval Studies, or to Classical Philology. The problem with this approach is that it closes the door on the investigation of long term sociopolitical currents of the region, such as the history of politics, religion and society in modern day Greece, Russia, the Balkans and perhaps to a lesser degree, Turkey. But most importantly, it hinders our understanding of the Orthodox Church today. It should be remembered that contemporary sources for the "Serbian Golgotha,"[7] for example, are transmitted in many languages – including Old Italian – but not in Serbian or Church Slavonic.

This paper seeks to explore Byzantine and Islamic concepts of governance in a comparative framework, to argue that the manifold affinities

3. See Gutas 1998, e. g. the introduction.

4. One of the most recent books in this field, Gouguenheim 2008, reveals the political overtones of the debate. For a more sober view on things one might consult Strohmaier 2012.

5. The expression is Millar's (see Millar 1994).

6. Huntington 1998.

7. Emmert 1990. On the special conditions for Balkan nationalism see below.

between the two traditions stem from their common roots in the political theology of Late Antiquity.

By way of introduction, a brief historical sketch of the relationship between the two fields, Byzantine and Arabic/Islamic studies is in order. Christian Oriental Studies is kept out of this discussion, since it is considered a discrete field.[8] Within the already small field of Byzantine studies,[9] only a few scholars specialize in the relations between Byzantium and Islam. Language proficiency is a contributing factor, but the dearth of scholarly interest should not be underestimated. Notable exceptions are G. Fowden,[10] W. Kaegi,[11] and I. Shahid.[12]

Comparative political theory is a task to be undertaken best if the researcher and his or her public tries to investigate along a small borderline to cut carefully the seam between written texts and political realities. In the field of Byzantine studies, this is an extremely thorny issue since there are very few specialists, and after the Enlightenment, Christian literature in Greek was largely neglected, at least until Peter Brown's work attracted the attention of scholars in the field. Thus, and as is the case also with Arabic texts, many important texts are still in manuscript form and not widely accessible.[13] Even rarer are translations, not surprising considering that the language of scholarship in Byzantium was Ancient Greek. A confluence of the above factors has undermined academic interest in this millenarian literature and modern theoretically-enriched studies on this subject are few and far between.[14] The existence of 'genre' in Byzantine literature is also very much debated and stretches from denial (A. Kazhdan) to genre-specific taxonomy (H. Hunger).[15]

Especially underserved is the field of Byzantine social and political thought.[16] This is partially due to the fact that Byzantine written consid-

8. The founding charter of this highly important field, the three-volume book by the Dominican LeQuien (LeQuien 1740/1958) is still compulsory reading on this subject.

9. At the present, fewer than ten universities where German is the language of instruction offer courses in Byzantine studies.

10. Fowden 2004.

11. Kaegi 1992.

12. Shahid 1984, 1989, 1995–2009, and many contributions by the same author, including his edition of Themistius 1974.

13. A good example is the treatise *On Political Science (peri politikēs epistēmēs)* from the age of Justinian that had been discovered on a Vatican palimpsest, edited (and falsely attributed to Petros Patrikios, *magister officiorum* under Justinian), and published by the cardinal A. Mai in a fragmentary state in 1827, v. Mai (1827); the next edition appeared in 2002 (Mazzucchi 2002), more than 150 years later.

14. Mullet 1992 gives an excellent introduction on the presuppositions for inserting these approaches into a literature that does not seem a promising field for this – at first sight.

15. Mullet 1992, 133–5.

16. Barker 1958.

erations about government can be understood only against the backdrop of the Classical, Hellenistic and Late Antique speeches and treatises - one might call them "Mirrors for Princes" - often to be found under the title *On kingship (peri basileias)*, such as the ones written by Isocrates (d. 336 BCE), Themistius (d. ca. 388 CE) and Synesius (d. after 412 CE).[17] In the heyday of structuralist and post-structuralist criticism, the very existence of *Fürstenspiegel* in Byzantium was brought under question.[18] One can hardly expect therefore that the situation concerning the comparative study of Byzantine-Arabic literature in the field of political theory is sufficient in any aspect.[19] It should be noted, however, that as far back as 1977, Sir Steven Runciman acknowledged similarities between Muslim and Byzantine political thought.[20]

Since the basic traits of Byzantine political philosophy and theology are sufficiently known,[21] only a skeletal presentation will suffice for our purposes: The *Romaioi* abstained of developing a political lore of their own. The scaffolding of political thought borrowed heavily from Antiquity: the king was the divine word incarnate (*logos empsykhos*),[22] the *imitation of God* (*mimēsis theou*).[23] The history of Byzantine political thought - speeches and treatises *on kingship* (*peri basileias*) - comprises 1800 years, stretching from Isocrates to the establishment of the Empire. Watersheds in this gradual Christianization of Hellenistic themes and topoi - whence their integration into Byzantine political thought - are speeches by the philosopher and later bishop of Cyrene Synesius,[24] a pupil and admirer of Hypatia, and by the court philosopher and short-time prefect of Constantinople, Themistius, one of whose speeches, to Emperor Julian, the "Apostate," allegedly (more probably, from the time of Theodosius I., d. 395 CE), was translated into Arabic.[25] Much material has been lost; but important fragments have been preserved by Joannes Stobaeus in the fifth century, together with Athenaios (2nd/3rd century CE),

17. Barker 1958 and Dvornik 1966 are first attempts. Runciman 1977 is a useful overview.

18. The most important contributions are Odorico 2009; Reinsch (forthcoming); but also Prinzing 1988. Agapetus Constantinopolitanus, Theophylact of Ochrid, Thomas Magister 1981 is a collection of important texts in German translation by Blum.

19. Niehoff-Panagiotidis 2003 is a first attempt.

20. Runciman 1977, 2. His view that the caliph was not seen as the Viceroy of God should be reconsidered, v. i.

21. Apart from Dvornik 1966 and Runciman 1977 one should mention Beck 1952, despite its title: In fact, the book is valid for the whole of Byzantium; see especially 76–95 ("The Byzantine Monopoly").

22. 'Archytas' in Joannes Stobaeus 1911, 82.

23. *On Political Science* (v. supra n. 13), Mazzucchi 2002, 19.6; 21.11 and 14 (and passim), v. the index in Mazzucchi 2002, 137.

24. Synesius of Cyrene 1973 and 1999.

25. Themistius, *Risālat Thāmisṭiyūs*; Themistius, *Epistula*; Crone 2004, 151, 186; on the dating see Shahid in Themistius, *Epistula*, 78-9.

the most important compiler of ancient literature. Excerpts on politics and economics are preserved in the fourth book of his *florilegium* (*Anthologion*). Chapter seven, *Issues on kingship* (*hypothēkai peri basileias*[26]), preserves (under names such as Archytas, Diotogenes, Ekphantos, and Sthenidas) fragments by neo-Pythagorean authors of dubious authenticity, on kingship, often lost otherwise.[27] In one of these, as usual kept in Hellenistic pseudo-Doric, typical for Pythagorean and pseudo-Pythagorean writings, "Ekphantos"[28] calls the king the Divine Word insofar as it *dwells on the earthly land* (*tan epigēion oikeusa khoran*).[29] In other words, the author sketches a theory of the *widespread divine word* (*logos spermatikos*) even before Christianity became the leading religion of the Roman Empire. The consequences are clear: At the same moment when the new faith became the official religion of state, the emperor – formerly pagan – was refashioned as the *vicarius Christi*.[30]

This shift, best understood through the work of Eusebius of Caesarea (d. ca. 337–40 CE) and his *Life of Constantine*,[31] did not change too much: The emperor remained if not God on earth, then his *emanation*.[32] The world had a new center, the Christ-loved Roman emperor residing in Constantinople, the *City preserved by God* (*polis theophylaktos*), but the cult, including the one representing the monarch as sun-god, the hegemony of political Hellenism in the empire, did not. And what is more: This Roman empire, as the last one before the Second Coming, assumed thus an eschatological function.[33] The end of this empire was understood as the end of the world, evident in the glosses (9th century?) to the geographical tract of Kosmas Indikopleustis (6th century).[34]

That this set of convictions was also shared by leading members of the clergy is evidenced in the writings of Athanasios, patriarch of Alexandria (d. 373 CE), who was by no means uncritical towards his – mostly Arian – monarchs, and therefore spent most of the time of his reign in exile. His *Apology*

26. Ch. six, *That monarchy is the best*, deals with cognate topics.

27. Joannes Stobaeus 1911, 249–95. The next chapter, as often with Stobaeus, deals with the opposite, tyranny (*psogos tyrannidos*). On the genuineness, see below.

28. According to Frede 1997, 942, s. v. [2] the fragments preserved in Joannes Stobaeos under this name are a falsification of the second or third century CE, perhaps inspired by Jewish thought. This would make them even more interesting for our question. For this literature see Burkert 1962.

29. Joannes Stobaeus 1911, 278.12–20. Cf. also Runciman 1977, 21.

30. This is a much investigated topic, see Peterson 1926 and 1935; Baynes 1934; Beck 1952, 76–95; Dvornik 1966, 2: 611–58; Runciman 1977, 5–25. In fact, every kind of thinking about the Eastern European manner of ruling has to take this into consideration.

31. Eusebius of Caesarea 1999, an excellently commented English translation.

32. In Greek *problēsis theou*, Beck 1952, 78.

33. Mango 1980, 201–17 (chapter 11), gives a still not superseded introduction into the topic of Byzantine state apocalypticism.

34. Schneider 2010, 64–5, actually an anonymous commentary to the book of Daniel. See also the bibliography given by Schneider.

against the Gentiles, admittedly an early work, dating to a time before he entered into conflict with Constantius II, comprises a range of topics common to Hellenistic treatises on kingship, while the Christian difference is – at least to a modern reader – gradual, not essential.[35]

By the sixth and seventh centuries, the gap that existed between Christianity and the Roman state had but disappeared. This is shown by the relevant treatises: Apart from *On Political Science* mentioned above (see n. 13), there is, on a more popular level, the oldest Byzantine mirror for princes by Agapetos the deacon which was also translated into Latin.[36] Justinian I (d. 565 CE), for example, did not hesitate in arresting a recalcitrant pope (Vigilius) as he was celebrating mass in Rome and shipping him to Constantinople. And Leo III (717–40 CE) described himself proudly as "priest and king" to another pope, thus claiming for the Byzantine emperor the tradition of sacred kingship stemming from Melchizedek, David and Solomon.[37]

The question is if it was this Byzantine concept of sacred kingdom that influenced the emerging caliphate of the Muslims. This question did not remain without debate: Tyan as early as 1954 spoke in favor of this hypothesis,[38] while Crone and Cook,[39] restated by Crone 1986,[40] have spoken against it, pleading instead for a Samaritan origin. We cannot resolve the problem once and for good here but the following point deserves mention: The most striking similarity between the Arab-Islamic concept of legitimate power and Byzantine theory of kingship (*basileia*) is absence of the Augustinian split between *civitas terrestris* and *civitas caelestis*. Though this difference was to be obliterated at some point during European history, the fundamental distinction, drawn by St Augustine regarding the conquest of Rome in 410 CE, assigns all empires, including the Roman one, in which St Augustine had been born and bred, to the *civitas terrestris*.[41] This Augustinian construction (exemplar is *De civ. Dei* XVII, 4) is absent in both Byzantine and Islamic conceptions of politics.[42]

35. Athanasios 1946, 85–8; the work was probably written during his exile in Trier (335–7 CE). The passage is discussed *in extenso* by Dvornik 1966, 2: 731–42.

36. Agapetos Diakonos 1995.

37. Runciman 1977, 72 and 177, citing Mansi 1901/1960, 12: col. 976. Byzantine "Caesaropapism" is discussed by Dagron 2003.

38. Tyan 1954, 439.

39. Crone and Cook 1977, 26–7.

40. Crone 1986, 114, with modifications towards an internal genesis.

41. It is impossible here to give even a sketchy bibliography of works on the topic; for that, see Brown 1969, 299–312.

42. Runciman 1977, passim. It is thus hardly comprehensible if Crone 1986, 115 tries to draw this distinction inside Byzantine civilization. True, it had existed once, but had been effaced beginning with Constantine. And in the time of Justinian and Heraclius (610–41) it had since a long time ceased to have much significance.

From this basic constellation, i.e. the persistence of the Constantinian model of rule in the East, many similarities in imperial representation can be explained: not only the title *khalīfa*[43] which sounds like a translation of *vicarius*[44] (and in the transmission of which the Samaritan term *ḥlyft Yhwh*[45] might have played a role)[46], but also imperial representation in architecture, as in the Dome of the Rock (*qubbat aṣ-ṣakhra*),[47] or in rhetoric and poetic imagery. To cite but one example: the metaphor of the religious/political leader who acts like light (e.g. he restores sight to blind men) is common to both the Byzantine mirror for princes *On Political Science* (*peri politikēs epistēmēs*),[48] and to Umayyad poetry.[49]

In the triumphal entry of Heraclius into Jerusalem in 630 as the messiah/king, the Muslims had a vivid example, within reach of their own historical memory, given that the Byzantine-Sassanid wars were fought during the Prophet's lifetime (see Sura 30, beginning).[50] And since Mu'āwiya I (r. 661–80) received the *bay'a*, according to the *Maronite Chronicle*, in Jerusalem,[51] and it was during his caliphate that the title *khalīfat Allāh* gained currency, it seems hardly a coincidence that he was criticized for his *hiraqliyya*.[52] Thus the later identification of 'Uthmān b. 'Affān (r. 644–56), the third of the rightly guided caliphs and ancestor to the Umayyads, as the first bearer of this title, may be considered as propaganda in support for the dynastic claims of the Umayyads.

It is quite plausible that Byzantine writings on state and rule, including the aforementioned speech by Themistius,[53] circulated in the former eastern parts of the Byzantine empire as part of its Late Antique heritage, and thus were not foreign to medieval Islamic thinkers, including al-Fārābī (d.

43. For the evolution of the title Crone 1986, 4–23 and passim; Sourdel 1977 and Lambton 1977.

44. Paret 1974.

45. Crone 1986, 115, n. 39 with reference to Crone and Cook 1977, 178, n. 71.

46. Since Samaritanian is a dialect of Aramaic, the second language of the Empire, and since the root is attested in Syriac, too (Brockelmann 1928, col. 235–7), as in many Semitic languages, including Sabaic, it looks as if the Arabic word is, at least partially, a calque; a phenomenon not rare in Arabic, though Fränkel 1886 does not mention this possibility for the Islamic title.

47. Grabar 2006.

48. Mazzucchi 2002, 59: 10; 63: 17 and 32: 10.

49. Crone 1986, 34–40; Niehoff-Panagiotidis 2012, 127–30.

50. Niehoff-Panagiotidis 2013, 259.

51. Cited according to Howard-Johnston 2010, 170, 190, 481–7 who redates the text to 660.

52. The discussion, also including a possible older title, *khalīfat rasūl Allāh*, originally launched by I. Goldziher, is carried out by Crone 1986, 4–23 (esp. 4 and 11–2) and 111–5, including the elimination of Abū Bakr; less polemical is the article in the *EI*² (see Sourdel 1977 and Lambton 1977).

53. Crone 2004, 165–96 and supra.

950). This could explain the fact that one of the few translations made from Arabic into Greek was, though achieved much later, the standard Oriental "mirror for princes" (*Kalīla wa Dimna*), undertaken under Alexios I Komninos (d. 1118 CE) by the physician and astronomer Symeon Seth (d. 1086 or 1087 CE), a *Rūmī* from Antioch in Syria, the former capital of the *dioecesis Orientis*. By then, however, the Byzantine Empire stood much transformed.[54]

54. Mullett and Smythe 1996; Niehoff-Panagiotidis (forthcoming).

Bibliography

Agapetos Diakonos (1995), *Der Fürstenspiegel für Kaiser Justinian*, ed. R. Riedinger, Athens.

Agapetus Constantinopolitanus, Theophylact of Ochrid, Thomas Magister (1981), *Byzantinische Fürstenspiegel*, tr. W. Blum, Stuttgart.

Athanasius of Alexandria (1946), "Oratio contra gentes," in: *Patrologia Graeca* 25: 3–96.

Barker, E. (1958), *Social and Political Thought in Byzantium. From Justinian I to the Last Palaeologus*, Oxford.

Baynes, N. H. (1934), "Eusebius and the Christian empire," *Annuaire de l'Institut de philologie et d'histoires orientales* 2: 13–8.

Beck, H.-G. (1952), *Theodoros Metochites. Die Krise des byzantinischen Weltbildes im 14. Jahrhundert*, München.

Berschin, W. (1980), *Griechisch-lateinisches Mittelalter: von Hieronymus zu Nikolaus von Kues*, Bern.

Brockelmann, C. (1928), *Lexicon Syriacum*, Halle.

Brown, P. (1969), *Augustine of Hippo*, London.

Burkert, W. (1962), *Weisheit und Wissenschaft. Studien zu Pythagoras, Philolaos und Platon*, Nürnberg.

Crone, P. (1986), *God's Calif. Religious authority in the first centuries of Islam*, Cambridge.

—— (2004), *Medieval Islamic Political Thought*, Edinburgh.

—— and M. Cook (1977), *Hagarism: the making of the Islamic World*, Cambridge.

Dagron, G. (2003), *Emperor and priest: the imperial office in Byzantium*, Cambridge.

Dvornik, F. (1966), *Early Christian and Byzantine Political Philosophy. Origins and Background*, 2 vols., Washington D. C.

Emmert, Th. A. (1990), *Serbian Golgotha: Kosovo 1389*, Boulder.

Euben, R. (1999), *Enemy in the Mirror*, Princeton.

Eusebius of Caesarea (1999), *Life of Constantine*, tr. A. Cameron and S. G. Hall, Oxford.

Fowden, G. (2004), *Quṣayr 'Amra: art and the Umayyad elite in late antique Syria*, Berkeley.
Fränkel, S. (1886), *Die aramäischen Fremdwörter im Arabischen*, Leiden.
Frede, M. (1997), "Ekphantos," in: H. Cancik and H. Schneider (eds.), *Der Neue Pauly*, 16 vols., Stuttgart and Weimar, 3: 941–2.
Gouguenheim, S. (2008), *Aristote au Mont Saint Michel: les racines grecques de l'Europe chrétienne*, Paris.
Grabar, O. (2006), *The Dome of the Rock*, Cambridge, Mass.
Gutas, D. (1998), *Greek language - Arabic culture. The Graeco-Arabic translation movement and early 'Abbāsid society (2nd to 4th/8th to 10th centuries)*, London.
Haskins, Ch. H. (1927), *The Renaissance of the Twelfth Century*, Cambridge.
Howard-Johnston, J. D. (2010), *Witnesses to a world crisis: historians and histories of the Middle East in the seventh century*, Oxford.
Huntington S. P. (1998), *The clash of civilizations and the remaking of world order*, London.
Joannes Stobaeus (1911), *Ioannis Stobaei anthologium*, ed. C. Wachsmuth and O. Hense, vol. 4, 1, Berlin.
Kaegi, W. E. (1992), *Byzantium and the early Islamic conquests*, Cambridge.
Lambton, A. K. S. (1977), "Khalīfa. (ii) In political theory," in: *EI*[2] IV: 947–50.
LeQuien, M. (1740), *Oriens Christianus*, 3 vols. Paris [Reprint Graz 1958].
Mai, A. (1827), *Scriptorum Veterum Nova Collectio*, vol. 2, Rome.
Mango, C. (1980), *Byzantium: Empire of New Rome*, London.
Mansi, J. D. (1901/1960), *Sacrorum conciliorum nova et amplissima collectio*, 12 vols., Paris, Graz.
March, A. F. (2009), "What Is Comparative Political Theory?," *The Review of Politics* 71: 531–656.
Mazzucchi, C. M. (2002), *Menae patricii cum Thoma referendario De scientia politica dialogus*, Milan.
Millar, F. (1994), *The Roman Near East: 31 BC - 337 AD*, Cambridge, Mass.
Mullett, M. (1992), "The Madness of Genre," *Dumbarton Oaks Papers* 46: 133–43.
Mullett, M. and D. Smythe (eds., 1996), *Alexios I Komnenos, vol. 1: Papers*, Belfast.
Niehoff-Panagiotidis, J. (2003), *Übersetzung und Rezeption. Die byzantinisch-neugriechischen und altspanischen Adaptionen von Kalīlah wa-Dimna*, Wiesbaden.
—— (2012), "Byzanz und der Islam. Von der Kontingenzbewältigung zur aneignenden Übersetzung," in: A. Speer (ed.), *Knotenpunkt Byzanz: Wissensformen und kulturelle Wechselbeziehungen*, Berlin, 123–44.

—— (2013), "Wie wurde die Mittelmeerwelt islamisch?", in: P. Eich and E. Faber (eds.), *Religiöser Alltag in der Spätantike*, Stuttgart, 257–75.
—— (forthcoming), "The Pañcatantra (Kalīlah wa-Dimna) and Greek Literature."
Odorico, P. (2009), "Les miroirs des princes à Byzance: Une lecture horizontale," in: P. Odorico (ed.), *"L'éducation au gouvernement et à la vie." La tradition des 'règles de la vie' de l'antiquité au moyen-âge. Actes du colloque international Pise, 18 et 19 mars 2005*, Paris, 213–46.
Paret, R. (1974), "Ḫalīfat Allāh – Vicarius Dei: ein differenzierender Vergleich," in: P. Salmon (ed.), *Mélanges d'Islamologie (Festschrift A. Abel)*, Leiden, 224–32.
Peterson, E. (1926), *Εἷς Θεός. Epigraphische, formgeschichtliche und religionsgeschichtliche Untersuchungen*, Göttingen.
—— (1935), *Der Monotheismus als politisches Problem. Beitrag zur Geschichte der politischen Theologie im Imperium Romanum*, Leipzig.
Prinzing, G. (1988), "Beobachtungen zu ‚integrierten' Fürstenspiegeln der Byzantiner," *Jahrbuch der Österreichischen Byzantinistik* 38: 1–32.
Reinsch, D. R. (forthcoming), "Bemerkungen zu einigen byzantinischen ‚Fürstenspiegeln' des 11. und 12. Jahrhunderts," in: H. Seng and L. M. Hoffmann (eds.), *Studies in Byzantine History and Civilisation* 6, Turnhout, 404–19.
Runciman, S. (1977), *The Byzantine Theocracy*, Cambridge.
Schneider, H. (2010), *Kosmas Indikopleustes, Christliche Topographie. Textkritische Analysen, Übersetzung, Kommentar*, Turnhout.
Shahid, I. (1984), *Byzantium and the Arabs in the fourth century*, Washington, DC.
—— (1989), *Byzantium and the Arabs in the fifth century*, Washington, DC.
—— (1995–2009), *Byzantium and the Arabs in the sixth century*, 3 vols., Washington, DC.
Sourdel, D. (1977), "Khalīfa. (i) The history of the institution of the caliphate," *EI*[2] IV: 937–47.
Strohmaier, G. (2012), *Zwischen Islamismus und Eurozentrismus: Mosaiksteine zu einem Bild arabisch-islamischen Erbes*, Wiesbaden.
Synesius of Cyrene (1973), *Sul regno*, ed. and tr. A. Garzya, Naples.
—— (1999), *Sulla regalità*, ed. C. Amande and P. Graffigna, con una nota di L. Canfora, Palermo.
Themistius (1970), *Risālat Thāmisṭiyūs ilā Yūlīyān al-malik fī l-siyāsa wa tadbīr al-mamlaka*, ed. M. S. Sālim, Cairo.
—— (1974), *Epistula de re publica gerenda*, ed. and tr. I. Shahid, Cambridge, Mass.
Tyan, E. (1954), *Institutions du droit public musulman, vol. 1: Le califat*, Paris.

The King's Beautiful Body

On the Political Dilemmas of Ideal Government

Hans-Joachim Schmidt

THE PURSUIT OF HAPPINESS must be the purpose of all political regimes. This was the point Thomas Aquinas (1225–1274) depicts in the first chapter of his treaty *De regno*, written in the seventies of the 13th century and arguing on the basis of an Aristotelian point of view then available due to the translation in Latin of the political oeuvre of Aristotle.[1] Which form of government was the best one to promote the *bonum commune?* Thomas responds in the second chapter rather unambiguously: It is the monarchy, the rule of one person. The welfare of any organized group is based on the preservation of its unity. The rule of many or a group will result in disagreement, thus undermining unity, peace, and the common good. Thomas' arguments derive from a large range of allegories that are not merely rhetorical, but serve strategically to provide evidence. In the same manner that a doctor does not debate curing a sick person, a ruler should not ponder the maintenance of unity in the community under his rule. A number of persons could not move a ship in one direction unless they work together under the command of one chief. Examples from nature confirm the need for unity assured by one man rule. There, actions have a singular source. In the human body, the heart moves all other parts.[2] Among the bees there is one queen bee. The whole universe has one God who is its maker and master. Nature is in accord with reason, because every plurality derives from unity. Human behavior and human community emulate nature, consequently reason, and therefore the prescription given by God.

Thomas provides further evidence from Ecclesiastes: "Be solicitous to preserve the unity of the spirit in the bond of peace." The legitimacy of monarchy is also apparent from experience. Communities that are not ruled by one person are torn by dissension and disputes without peace, whilst communities under a single king enjoy peace and justice and they delight in the abundance of wealth. The conclusion seems to be clear: only a monarchy can

1. Hertling 1911; Grabmann 1934; Steenberghen 1955; Dunbabin 1965, 65–85; Flüeler 1992.

2. Struve 1978.

conduct human society to its inherent aim: peace and welfare and individual happiness.

But in the following chapter Thomas Aquinas sketches an unexpected and scathing critique of one person rule. There is only a change of terminology. Whilst the best form of government is the one exercised by a king, the worst one is exercised by a tyrant. The opposition of the two terms does not change the fact that one man rule can be the best or the worst achievement of political organization. Even more disturbing is that the difference between these two forms of government is not predicated upon divergent forms of acquiring power. The tyrant is not defined by usurpation, personal defects, or the lack of virtue. The difference is solely the function of the uses to which power is put. Where the king preserves unity and peace, the tyrant produces quarrel and war. The efficacy of one man rule entails both beneficial and adverse ramifications. The consequence of tyranny is that private interests are pursued in preference of the common good. According to Thomas, evil results from tyranny, but not from its origins. The worst effect of tyranny is that it prevents the subjects from becoming virtuous and from creating bonds of friendship. The mutual distrust makes it even more difficult to overthrow the tyranny. Dissension undermines comity and abrogates the pursuit of both the common good and individual happiness.[3]

Thomas follows Aristotle when enumerating the positive and negative aspects of one person rule. In shaping the problem as if the very best and worst could be subsumed under the same form of government, however, he carves a separate path for himself. In effect, Thomas poses a dilemma. One possible exit strategy would be to elaborate on the virtuous ruler. Thomas refuses to adopt this solution. Every human being is, as Thomas states, dependent on the help and cooperation of his community. All men are sinful creatures, and incapable of safeguarding unity in the political community. Thus, trust in the individual virtues of a monarch will not safeguard against tyranny. Therefore the ideal government discussed in the second chapter seems to be a mere utopian program without any chance for realization. But on the other hand, the principle that the multitude must be made subservient to unity is a necessary one. The ethical dichotomy of the two forms of government does not detract from crafting a structural analogy; the best is not very different from the worst; the monarchy has the same basic characteristics as the tyranny. The only difference, i.e. the moral qualification,

3. Thomas Aquinas, *De regno ad regem Cypri*, 419–71; about the authorship, the manuscripts and the reception of work: ibid., 421–44; Demongeot 1928; Gilson 1957, 329–30; Gilby 1958, 294; Wilks 1963, 1–11; Tierney 1982; Flüeler 1987, 193–239; Blythe 1994, 39–45; Schmidt 1996, 339–57; Kempshall 1999, 83–9.

doesn't prevent from similarities in other fields of definition. Thus the question of the best form of government results in a paradox.

This paradox is not resolved in Thomas' treatise on kingship. In fact, he even sharpens the dilemma. If driven by fear of tyranny people impede monarchy they render impossible the best form of government. And every monarchy is always vulnerable to tyranny. The theoretical antagonism is transformed into a dynamic historical process, wherein monarchy and tyranny are linked by systematic as well as historical concerns.

What Aquinas presents toward a resolution of the dilemma are procedures to mitigate the autocratic exercise of power whilst still preserving its theoretic legitimacy. Autocracy must be tempered with institutions for the provision of advice and consultation. In this manner, the practical solution offered to the dilemma of good governance is not the realization of the best form of government, but a compromise in the interest of minimizing damage to the community. *Cum autem inter duo ex quorum utroque periculum imminet eligere oportet, illud videtur potissime eos que sequitur minus malum.*[4] ("Because of two things provoking dangers, one must be chosen; it is better to choose this one which is less harmful.") Not an *optimum* but a *minus malum* ("lesser worse") is the realistic aim that can be realized in human affairs. A hierarchy of values established to promote the common good is needed to put aside mere individual aims and interests, even those of the king. The monarch's function as a creator of the common good cannot be derived from any personal characteristics. The perfection of goodness demands even more: to bring others to promote goodness. The political body in its totality is linked with an individual ruler, but without any individual pre-eminence. Therefore the kings have to choose counsellors whose function is to weaken royal power, to prevent hasty decision making and to schedule alternative projects. Only an institutional framework that is not based, however, on a legal organization of defined competences provides the chance to direct the king on the path of good governance. Thomas writes: *Deinde sic disponenda est regni gubernatio ut regi iam instituto tyrannidis subtrahatur occasio.*[5] ("Then you have to dispose the administration of the realm in order that there wouldn't be the occasion to establish tyranny.")

Therefore, Thomas Aquinas doesn't present a catalogue of moral qualities the kings must have; nor does he entertain a regiment of moral edification to assure the existence of a good king. Thomas seems skeptical of moral education, and the possibility of individual perfection. The cooperation of many, gathered at the royal court, was the only measure to put the monarch on the path of a moderate and less harmful ruling.

4. Thomas Aquinas, *De regno ad regem Cypri*, 454.
5. Thomas Aquinas, *De regno ad regem Cypri*, 454.

Far from privileging the monarchy as the best form of political organization, as some modern scholars aver,[6] Thomas in other texts even favors as the best form of government a mixed one. The argument in the *Summa theologica* is directed more to institutional structures than to the person of the ruler. Thomas insists that individual virtue is enforced, and even enabled, only through a good assembly of proper laws and customs. He writes in a more explicit manner in his commentary on the *Politics* of Aristotle that every king needs the cooperation and even the normative framing of his power with the notables of his realm. *Iudici et magistri constituti* ("established judges and administrators") were put in a position which Thomas describes as *pars in principatu* ("part in administration").[7] They collaborated with the king, but were not in competition with him, and their authority was nevertheless demarcated by law. The argumentation goes further than in the treaty on the kingship where the collaborators are not equipped with juridical competences. Thus it is not surprising to find Thomas' unfinished work, *De regno*, completed by his fellow Dominican friar Ptolemy of Lucca (1236–1327) with quite a different orientation: The latter favored a genuine republican government in which power is exercised by many.[8]

The paradox was carefully avoided in the Aristotelian commentary of Albertus Magnus (d. 1280), a fellow Dominican and contemporary of St Thomas. The tyrant's unique interest in increasing his own material profit was in contrast to the king's investment in ameliorating the benefit of his subjects,[9] thus the discerning of king from tyrant was rendered more substantive.

Good governance, presented as paradox, however, would hardly gain favor with a royal court. To gain royal sanction, it was necessary to provide monarchy with the biological continuity assured in a dynasty. Familial succession had to be combined with individual eminence. The king must be an ideal man and the eminence in virtue would have to result in a lineage best endowed to exercise power. The king's body was tied to that of his progeny. Excellence thereby acquired corporal form; but the promise of excellent offspring that the formula entailed was flimsy at best. How could a monarch guarantee the physical fitness and moral probity of his progeny?

The fissures in dynastic succession acquired added urgency beginning in the thirteenth century, when ecclesiastical and lay criticism of royal legitimacy gathered pace, and the king was compelled to project an aura of natural superiority in response. In the writings of ecclesiastical authorities,

6. Schramm 1963, 250.
7. Thomas Aquinas, *Sententiae in libros Politicorum*, 262, 263, 271.
8. Thomas Aquinas, *Opuscula philosophica et theologica*, 3–170.
9. Albertus Magnus, *Super Ethica*, 230, 240, 632–3; Lambertini 1987, 464–78.

dynastic succession determined by birthright compared unfavorably with merit based appointments, as was the rule governing the appointment of priests and bishops. The king's body generated by family ascendancy had no value. This was the argument Pope Gregory VII (r. 1073–1085) expressed in his letter to Hermann, bishop of Metz from 1073 to 1090, which was integrated in the *Decretum Gratiani* and cited in later canonical collections.[10] The warm reception of Aristotle's political philosophy destabilized royal legitimacy too, by obliging kings to promote the common good, the state and the subjects of the realm. But the unreliability of dynastic succession meant that it could not be relied upon to produce consistently rulers that conformed to the ecclesiastical demand for support of their institutions or to the Aristotelian requisite of promoting public utility. The danger posed by the coming into power of a deceitful and undeserving heir could not be ignored , and confidence in the merits of the *stirps regni* ("the descendant to kingship"), still a strong basis of royal prestige in the high Middle Ages, was contested by ecclesiastical authors undermining the legitimacy of secular power. Peter Damian (d. 1072 or 1073) and Manegold von Lauterbach (d. after 1103) were among its strongest critics; the latter arguing that any ruler revealed as useless could be legitimately overthrown.[11]

Preparing a king for office turned into a primordial challenge in the late Middle Ages. The prince was in need of education in morals and manner, skills and temperament to preserve royal supremacy and cater to the demand for utility. Regardless of acquired skills, however, the king himself was to be placed over and above his vassals and subjects, for without it his legitimacy was at risk. It wasn't sufficient to frame kingship institutionally, as Thomas Aquinas had suggested, but the king himself, his person, spirit, force and body had to be prepared. Efforts to promote kingly perfection included not just the cultivation of skills and virtues, but regarded as well aspects of his physical appearance. The corporal perfection of the monarch was understood as a prelude to the proper exercise of his office. The king's body was the obvious constituent link to dynastic succession. Thomas' dilemma of averting tyranny while preserving monarchical rule was resolved by placing the king in a dynamic process that would edify his corporal and spiritual selves, to ensure that the right man sat at the top of the secular hierarchy.

A text extant in the Western world alone in at least 200 manuscripts written since the end of the twelfth century provided an answer to the dilemma of cultivating perfect rule. The Latin translation of the pseudo-

10. Caspar 1920–3, 544–63; *Corpus iuris canonici*, ed. Friedberg, col. 756.

11. Petrus Damiani, *Liber gratissimus*, 31; Manegold von Lautenbach, *Ad Gebehardum Liber*, 365; Hartmann 1970, 47–145; Fuhrmann 1975, 21–42.

Aristotelian *Secretum secretorum*, available originally in Arabic, amplified the necessity of physical excellence in the fulfilment of royal duties.[12] Aristotle is said to have given the following advice to his pupil Alexander the Great: *Convaluit Alexander in sanitatis observacione per observanciam sui sani consilii.*[13] ("Alexander prospered as he was in observation of his health by observation of the safe advice given to him.") Advice on health concerns was linked to political issues by the fact that the ruler must perfect bodily ability and beauty to perform his duties well. The Catalan version of the text stressed this idea of the *regimento de la sanidat* ("health regime"). A regiment of corporal care is needed to ensure the regimentation of secular affairs: *neçessario pora al regimiento de aquesti mundo* ("the necessary thing for the regime of this world"). There is no political power without corporal health.[14] Physical prowess is a top priority in this text. The king's body serves as departure point for any political action. The tradition of the Indian kings, who appeared once a year before their subjects, fully ornamented, robed in precious cloths and parading the beauty of their body, is an example to follow by every ruler. It is a service to the state: *curam et operam quam circa rempublicam fideliter gessit ostendere.*[15] ("One has to perform the task to sustain loyally the state.") The exterior of the king must conform to his inner qualities, to expose them to the public and to enhance his prestige in the eyes of his subjects as well as those of foreigners.[16] Olfactory sensation in addition to the visual aspect should contribute to the exquisiteness of the body.[17] Beautiful voice and subsequent beautiful speech enhance the king's appearance.[18] In this discussion, the body creates beauty. What beautifies the king's physical appearance is his healthy constitution, which has to be cultivated by a strict dietary regime from his very youth until his last breath. Opposition between health and illness underlines the discourse. Physical excellence not only empowers the king to exercise his duties, especially the military one, but also to awe his subjects and to evidence the excellence of his soul, and testify to the superiority of his lineage. The presentation of the king's body should be considered as great privilege to his people. His body and his robe have to be worshiped; they should create reverence and love among the royal

12. Williams 2003, 7–141; Forster 2006, 1–19.

13. Steele 1929, 37.

14. Heredia, *The Aragonese Version of the Secreto Secretorum*, 31, 32; on the Hispanic reception of the *Secretum secretorum*: Bizzarri 1999, 9–14; Bizzarri and Rucquoi 2005, 7–30; Forster 2010, 106–8.

15. Steele 1929, 49.

16. Forster 2006, 94–5.

17. Steele 1929, 69; Roche 2009.

18. Steele 1929, 48, 69.

subjects. This must be taught to the children in any town of the realm, as an English version explained.[19]

The very detailed medical advice presented in the second part of the text under the title *De regimine sanitatis* ("the regime of health") is justified for the *regimen huius mundi* ("the regime of secular affairs").[20] Without a healthy body, nothing can be achieved in the state. The *potential* ("power"), that is the capacity of acting, depends on the *sanitas* ("health").[21] Without detailing here the many recommendations for eating, drinking, sleeping, hygiene, corporal exercises and medical care, all based on ancient rules of medicine,[22] it must be stressed that the main concern was the preservation of the inherently corruptible body, and thereby prolonging the life of the ruler in order to extend his government and therefore to maximize the utility of his political actions. Having a good and healthy body is, according to the *Secretum secretorum*, the king's most important obligation.[23] The physiognomy of the king has to demonstrate his inner virtues, whence the physiognomy indeed originates, but also is their reflection, since the corporal is more than just an outside form, it is inextricably connected to the soul. The cultivation of one's physiognomy is also a cultivation of the soul.[24] The principle admitted in the *Secretum* that the external aspect of a person is not necessarily an unambiguous reflection of the characteristics of his soul notwithstanding, the text presumes the interface of both.[25] A beautiful body is therefore not only a sign of a perfect person, but its material proof. The ideal man must be beautiful, and the king the first. Physiognomy as inherited is not therefore unelectable; it can and must be improved upon. These recommendations are surely intended exclusively for kings and their courtiers; the *Secretum* is very often included with manuscripts on natural philosophy and natural history. But the views offered in the *Secretum* cannot be dissociated from political thought in the West.

That the body is beautified by design is replicated in the most copied mirror for princes in Western late medieval culture, Giles of Rome's (d. 1316) *De regimine principum*.[26] Although the author warns against founding royal majesty on corporal characteristics and on physical beauty, because these

19. Steele 1898, 12–3.
20. Steele 1929, 64.
21. Steele 1929, 42.
22. Ullmann 1970, 97.
23. Steele 1929, 64–97.
24. Steele 1929, 67.
25. Steele 1929, 70–2; Schauwecker 2007, 7–17, 33–7, 71–138, 430.
26. Aegidius Romanus, *De regimine principum*; Berges 1938, 211–9; Miethke 1993, 83–94; Boureau 2002, 25–50; Perret 2011, 241–91.

are susceptible to change and cannot result from the intellectual acuity,[27] nevertheless, in another chapter, the same Giles required the prince to ensure the beauty of his body. He should marry a beautiful woman to ensure the beauty of his heir who would perpetuate the royal dynasty and political power. Every subject and every prince must provide for the beauty of his wife and his children. *Ex pulchris nascuntur pulchri* ("from beautiful people beautiful people are born"). The best age to procreate is 36 for men and 18 for women. In this manner *procreantur filii magis perfecti* ("more perfect sons will be created"). Sexual intercourse must be prevented for men under the age of 21; for their generative strength will increase after that and result in superior offspring.[28]

Procuring the future of the ruling dynasty is not the only benefit to be derived from the king's physical perfection. The beauty of the king's body will win him friends in high places; notables will be conducted to submitting to his rule, so coercive measures will not be necessary. Opulence in attire is intrinsic to the king's ability to wield power, so the king must be liberal in the provision of materiel for himself and his family. The *exteriora bona* ("the exterior goods"), as Giles wrote, are essential and not mere accidental attributes, as they contribute to harmony in the state. Analogous to the harmony that is guaranteed in the royal marriage by the attractiveness of the king and his queen, corporal beauty will also secure the loyalty of the body politic.[29] Thus, corporal beauty is not a matter of random inheritance, but rather fashioned by design and through meticulous planning.

The preparation of the body of the future king also includes, as Giles exposes in his treaty, the education of the prince. Cultivating bodily strength and as a result, physical beauty is an important part of Giles of Rome's educational curriculum. Offspring must be perfect *in anima et in corpore* ("in soul and body").[30] Physical training is the main focus of education during the first seven years while the intellectual capacities are too raw to be trained. Moderation in every corporal activity is provisioned: The prince and the future king have to desist from excessive eating and drinking. Any concupiscent affect must be rejected, for it is harmful to the body. Instruction in moderation is especially important in the early years, as young people do not make use of their reason and often fail to resist harmful sensual pleasures. Control over the body and physical pleasure is analogous to rule over subjects.[31] To strengthen the young body, princes have to engage in physi-

27. Aegidius Romanus, *De regimine principum*, fol. 21a–3a.
28. Aegidius Romanus, *De regimine principum*, fol. 191a.
29. Aegidius Romanus, *De regimine principum*, fol. 150b–2a.
30. Aegidius Romanus, *De regimine principum*, fol. 178b.
31. Aegidius Romanus, *De regimine principum*, fol. 188b–91a.

cal games. The body must also be trained to adopt pleasing gestures, which the king must put in commotion sparingly, to secure the intended end. The mastering of gesture is an evident requisite for the monarch, who has to refrain when interacting with subjects and foreign dignitaries, from wild gesticulation as well as body movements that diminish corporal splendor and therefore the integrity of the monarch. A placid demeanor will conduce to the performance of beauty.

The *exercitatio* of the body is also useful to spiritual edification. For this, Giles of Rome relies on Aristotle's argument in *Politics*. Vincent of Beauvais (d. *c.* 1264), a contemporary of Giles and also author of a mirror for princes made a similar argument, underling the more distinctive role of physical training for princes, who are protected from physical labor but obliged to exercise royal duties—civilian as well as military.[32] In the description of Alexander the Great, Vincent of Beauvais stressed the beauty of his body, accomplished by noble birth and corporal training.[33] For Guibert of Tournai (d. 1284), who authored yet another mirror for princes, attention to the king's body will procure longevity of both life and rule. His healthy constitution will make possible a solid political constitution.[34]

The human disposition to goodness, as Thomas Aquinas stated, has to be awakened and trained. Perfectibility is an exhortation to materialize potential. The king's body served as the link to his predecessors, thus bestowing legitimacy on his rule. Because the body is vulnerable to corruption and decay, however, it must be subject to rigorous training. An unfit physique will harm the soul and sabotage the proper exercise of power. To resolve the dilemmas evoked earlier, between monarchy and tyranny and between hereditary successions a strict educational regime was advocated, and even a mild exercise in eugenics, to ensure the physical prowess of the prince's offspring. The king's beautiful body was a public body and therefore a political instrument. Much was made of the corporal splendors of kings and princes in the medieval chronicles, for example in *Gesta Frederici* of Otto of Freising describing the corporal perfection and beauty of emperor Frederic I.[35] Even physical imperfection was not considered sufficient to obviate the king's dedication to beauty, as demonstrated in the examples of Otto IV (emperor 1209–1218) or Louis IX of France (r. 1226–1270), whose devastation of the body in penitentiary rites supposed the pre-existence of its beauty, for otherwise the denigration would have no value.[36] Beauty was included in the

32. Vincent of Beauvais, *Speculum doctrinale*, 9; Gabriel 1967.
33. Vincent of Beauvais, *Speculum historiale*, 118.
34. Guibert de Tournai, *Education des rois et des princes*.
35. Otto Frisigensis et Rahewinus, *Gesta Frederici* , 708.
36. Hucker 1996, 337–41 ; Le Goff 1996, 291–300.

king's virtues, but not merely as an instrument to augment his prestige and power, for it could also be sacrificed and by that it could be purified. It was a pawn that could be transformed in order to obtain other profits, spiritual and eternal ones. But this does not diminish the importance of being beautiful. It was a moral requirement imposed on kings by the mirror for princes. Fitness for the royal office rested upon the fitness of the royal body. Beauty as a requisite may have enjoyed a long life, but it gained additional import in the thirteenth century, when corporal perfection was no longer attributed to biological inheritance, but cultivated through a strict regimen of physical training and elaborate criteria for the selection of spouses, to ensure the physical beauty of the king's progeny. In Western mirrors for princes, beauty was no longer considered an organic good, but was rather an artefact, sculpted by active intervention and elaborated design.

Bibliography

Aegidius Romanus (1656), *De regimine principum*, Rome.

Albertus Magnus (1987), *Super Ethica*, ed. W. Kübel, Münster.

Berges, W. (1938), *Die Fürstenspiegel des hohen und späten Mittelalters*, Leipzig.

Bizzarri, H. (1999), "El secretoum secretorum Pseudo-Aristotélico en Castilla. Una consecuencia de la censura parisina," in: R. E. Penna and M. A. Rosarossa (eds.), *Studia Hispanica Medievalia*, vol. 3, Buenos Aires, 9–14.

Bizzarri, H. and A. Rucquoi (2005), "Los espejos de principes en Castilla entre Oriente e Occidente," *Cuadernos de historia de España* 79: 7–30.

Blythe, J. (1994), *Ideal Government and the Mixed Constitution in the Middle Ages*, Princeton.

Boureau, A. (2002), "Le prince médiéval et la science politique," in: R. Halévi (ed.), *Le savoir du prince du moyen âge aux Lumières*, Paris, 25–50.

Caspar, E. (ed.) (1920–3), Das Register Gregors VII., Berlin.

Demongeot, M. (1928), *Le meilleur régime politique selon Saint Thomas*, Paris.

Dunbabin, J. (1965), "Aristotle in the Schools," in: B. Smalley (ed.), *Trends in Medieval Political Thought*, Oxford, 65–85.

Flüeler, C. (1987), "Mittelalterliche Kommentare zur Politik des Aristoteles und zur pseudo-aristotelischen Oekonomik," *Bulletin de philosophie médiévale* 29: 193–239.

—— (1992), *Rezeption und Interpretation der aristotelischen Politica im späten Mittelalter*, Amsterdam.

Forster, R. (2006), *Das Geheimnis der Geheimnisse. Die arabischen und deutschen Fassungen des pseudo-aristotelischen Sirr al-asrār / Secretum secretorum*, Wiesbaden.

——(2010), "Transmission of Knowledge through Literature: The Literary Frames of the pseudo-Aristotelian 'Sirr al-Asrār' and 'Kitāb al-Tuffāḥa'," *Eos* 97: 101–17.

Friedberg, E. (ed.), (1879), *Corpus iuris canonici*, vol. 1, Leipzig.

Fuhrmann, H. (1975), "'Volkssouveränität' und 'Herrschaftsvertrag' bei Manegold von Lautenbach," in: S. Gagnér (ed.), *Festschrift für Hermann Krause*, Cologne, 21–42.

Gabriel, A. L. (1967), *Vinzenz von Beauvais. Ein mittelalterlicher Erzieher*, Frankfurt.

Gilby, T. (1958), *Principality and Polity: Aquinas and the Rise of State Theory in the West*, London.

Gilson, E. (1957), *The Christian Philosophy of St. Thomas Aquinas*, London.

Grabmann, M. (1934), *Studien über den Einfluß der aristotelischen Philosophie auf die mittelalterlichen Theorien über das Verhältnis von Kirche und Staat*, Munich.

Guibert de Tournai (1914), *Education des rois et des princes*, ed. A. de Porter, Louvain.

Hartmann, W. (1970), "Manegold von Lautenbach und die Anfänge der Frühscholastik," *Deutsches Archiv zur Erforschung des Mittelalters* 26: 47–145.

Heredia, J. F. de (1999), *The Aragonese Version of the Secreto Secretorum*, ed. L. Kasten, Madison.

Hucker, U. B.(1996), *Kaiser Otto IV.*, Hannover.

Hertling, G. von (1911), *Zur Geschichte der aristotelischen Politik im Mittelalter*, Kempten and Munich.

Kempshall, M. S. (1999), *The Common Good in the Late Medieval Political Thought*, Oxford.

Lambertini, R. (1987), "Individuelle und politische Klugheit in den mittelalterlichen Ethikkommentaren (von Albert bis Buridan)," in: J. A. Aartsen and A. Speer (eds.), *Individuum und Individualität im Mittelalter*, Berlin and New York, 464–78.

Le Goff, J. (1996), *Saint Louis*, Paris.

Manegold von Lautenbach (1891), "Ad Gebehardum Liber," ed. K. Francke, in: *Monumenta Germaniae Historica. Libelli de lite imperatorum et pontificum*, vol. 1, Hannover, 300–430.

Miethke, J. (1993), "Politische Theorien im Mittelalter," in: H.-J. Lieber (ed.), *Politische Theorien von der Antike bis zur Gegenwart*, Bonn, 47–156.

Otto Frisigensis et Rahewinus (2000), *Gesta Frederici*, ed. A. Schmidt, Darmstadt.

Perret, N.-L. (2011), *Les traductions françaises du De regimine principum. Parcours matériel, culturel et intellectuel d'un discours sur l'éducation*, Leiden.

Petrus Damiani (1891), "Liber gratissimus," ed. L. de Heinemann, in: *Monumenta Germaniae Historica. Libelli de lite imperatorum et pontificum*, vol. 1, Hannover,15–75.
Roche, M. (2009), *L'intelligence d'un sens. Odeurs miraculeuses et odorat dans l'Occident du haut moyen âge*, Turnhout.
Schauwecker, Y. (2007), *Die Diätetik nach dem Secretum secretorum in der Version von Jofroi de Waterford*, Würzburg.
Schmidt, H.J. (1996), "König und Tyrann. Das Paradox der besten Regierung bei Thomas von Aquin," in: F. Burgard, C. Cluse and A. Haverkamp (eds.), *Liber amicorum necnon et amicarum für Alfred Heit. Beiträge zur mittelalterlichen Geschichte und geschichtlichen Landeskunde*, Trier, 339–57.
Schramm, P.E. (1963), "Das Alte und das Neue Testament," in: *La Biblia nell'Alto Medioevo. Settimane di studio del Centro Italiano di Studi sull'Alto Medieveo, 26 apr.-2 mag. 1962*, Spoleto, 229–56.
Steele, R. (ed.) (1898), *Three Prose Versions of the Secretum Secretorum*, London.
Steele, R. (ed.) (1929), *Secretum secretorum cum glossis et notulis fratris Roger*, Oxford.
Struve, T. (1978), *Die Entwicklung der organologischen Staatsauffassung im Mittelalter*, Stuttgart.
Thomas Aquinas (1886), *Opuscula philosophica et theologica*, ed. A.M. de Maria, Città di Castello.
—— (1979),"De regno ad regem Cypri," in: idem, *Opera omnia*, vol. 42, ed. H.F. Dondaine, Rome, 419–71.
—— (1980), "Sententiae in libros Politicorum," in: idem, *Opera omnia*, vol. 4, ed. R. Busa, Stuttgart, 248–73.
Tierney, B. (1979), "Aristotle, Aquinas, and the Ideal Constitution," *Proceedings of the Patristic, Medieval and Renaissance conference* 4: 1–11.
—— (1982), *Religion, Law, and the Growth of Constitutional Thought*, Cambridge.
Ullmann, M. (1970), *Die Medizin im Islam*, Leiden.
Van Steenberghen, F. (1955), *Aristotle in the West*, Louvain.
Vincent of Beauvais (1664–1665, reprint 1995), *Speculum historiale*, Graz.
—— (1664–1665, reprint 2010), *Speculum doctrinale*, Graz.
Wilks, M. (1963), *The Problem of Sovereignty in the Later Middle Ages*, Cambridge.
Williams, S.J. (2003), *The Secret of Secrets. The scholarly career of a pseudo-Aristotelian text in the late Middle Ages*, Ann Arbor.

The "Book of the Pearl on the Ruler" in *The Unique Necklace* by Ibn 'Abd Rabbih

Preliminary Remarks

Isabel Toral-Niehoff

"KNOWLEDGE IS POWER" – in pre-modern Islamicate culture, this was a well-known idea.[1] Scholars surrounded rulers, and rulers sought the proximity of scholars. Many hadith and aphorisms favor and recommend the acquisition of knowledge and some even subordinate kings to scholars and sages: "Princes rule over people, but scholars rule over princes."[2] Islamicate culture was, in fact, a "sapientalist" society, where knowledge was a main criterion for the demarcation of social prestige and the legitimization of hierarchy.[3]

Knowledge may refer to expertise in a particular field (*'ilm*, corresponding to "science," or "scholarship"), or it may designate a broader wisdom that includes a certain attitude, morality, and behavior. In classical Arabic, the term *adab* refers to this latter kind of knowledge.[4] It designates that knowledge which results from "taking a little bit of everything" (*al-akhdh min kull shay' bi-ṭaraf*), and defined a cultivated person (*adīb*). An *adīb* was able to speak about any topic and delighted his environment by his good manners and the agreeable social attitude of a civilized individual. "If you want to be a scholar, you should aim at one field of learning; if you want to be an *adīb*, then take the best of everything."[5]

Thus, an *adab* encyclopedia ideally combines the universalism of an encyclopedia with the aesthetic attitude of *adab*: it is a well-selected anthology of all the things precious a person should know to carry on an exquisite conversation, in order to be considered cultivated. *Al-'Iqd al-farīd* (Unique Necklace), whose first section is the topic of this article, is one of the earliest and most representative examples of this genre.

1. See the survey of quotations in van Gelder 1997. The generous support of a research project (FF 12010-16314) directed by Dr. Cristina de la Puente and funded by the Spanish Ministry of Science and Innovation, which allowed me to consult relevant bibliographies in Spain, is hereby gratefully acknowledged.
2. Van Gelder 1997, 243–4.
3. Fierro 2009, 104.
4. Rosenthal 1970, 240–77; see Biesterfeldt 2002, 47; Gutas 1981, Marlow 2007.
5. Van Gelder 1997, 244–5.

In the context of the present volume, *al-'Iqd al-farīd* is a very significant text, since its first parts are considered as one of the earliest examples of Arabic mirrors for princes.[6] In the following, I shall discuss some of those sections, although the results have to be very preliminary, mainly because *al-'Iqd al-farīd* has been remarkably neglected by scholarship until now, and its central aspects remain unstudied.[7] Therefore, I will firstly address some general points important for a study of *al-'Iqd al-farīd*.

Al-'Iqd al-farīd – Authorship and Context

Al-'Iqd al-farīd was composed in the heyday of the second Umayyad caliphate (929–1031) in Andalusia. Its author, Ibn 'Abd Rabbih (860–940), was a cultivated member of the ruling elite at the court in Cordova: He came from a local family whose members had been clients (*mawālī*)[8] of the Umayyads since the emir Hishām I (788–796).[9] His teachers were Mālikī *fuqahā'* and *muḥaddithūn* who had travelled to the East in search of knowledge: Baqī b. Makhlad (816–889),[10] Muḥammad b. Waḍḍāḥ (815–899),[11] and a scholar named Muḥammad b. 'Abd al-Salām al-Khushanī (833–899), who is said to have introduced much poetry, *akhbār* and *adab* from the Islamic East to Andalusia.[12] Ibn 'Abd Rabbih himself is said to have never left the Peninsula. In spite of his education as *faqīh*, he became more a man of letters than a jurist, and functioned as a court poet since the start of the emir 'Abd Allāh's (888–912) reign. He reached the apogee of his career at the court of caliph 'Abd al-Raḥmān III (912–961).[13]

Content

Authored by a belle-lettrist who never left Andalusia, *al-'Iqd al-farīd* is based almost exclusively on Oriental material imported previously to the peninsula through various channels. The complicated issue of the sources of *al-'Iqd al-farīd* has been discussed in detail by Walter Werkmeister in his

6. Richter 1932, 72–9.

7. See the bibliographical survey in Werkmeister 1983, 42–3; to this add Veglison 2011 and her bibliography 120–3; and the bibliography in Ibn 'Abd Rabbih, *'Iqd*, tr. Allen, xxiii–iv.

8. *Mawālī* is not used for converted locals like in the Islamic East; these were called *muwallad in* Andalusia. The Umayyad *mawālī* in Andalusia were a small, privileged group, closely attached to the dynasty, and mostly composed by former war captives, cf. Fierro 1999.

9. Fierro 1999, 89.

10. Fierro 1989, 78–9; Monés 67–9.

11. Fierro 1989, 79–81; Monés 66–7.

12. Werkmeister 1983, 254–6.

13. For his biography, cf. Werkmeister 1983, 16–26.

meticulous and highly recommendable study of 1983. His investigation is especially meritorious since the majority of the traditions or *akhbār* quoted in *al-'Iqd al-farīd* (some 10,000–12,000) are anonymous, i.e., without any attribution (only 2101 mention the name of their transmitter, including 582 with some kind of *isnād*).[14] Werkmeister's conclusions have stimulated a broader scholarly debate about form and content of the early *akhbār* and the issue of written vs. oral transmission in early Islam. By comparing the variants and parallels Werkmeister demonstrated that *al-'Iqd al-farīd* relies mostly on the rather informal material circulating in the scholarly circles or *ḥalqāt*,[15] and that Ibn 'Abd Rabbih rarely used written, fixed books.

Authorial Voice

Like most other authors of *adab* collections, Ibn 'Abd Rabbih scarcely ever speaks directly to the reader, but remains rather hidden in the background. Therefore, it is quite complicated to establish the intention and meaning of this work that appears at first sight to be a random selection of aphorisms and quotations. Excepting the introduction and some passages at the beginning of each book, the author adopts the role of a compiler of valuable material of the past: "I have compiled this work and selected its jewels (*jawāhir*) from the choice gems of literature and the best picks of eloquence."[16] However, this statement should not be interpreted as a sign of (maybe topical) modesty, nor should its emphasis on the author's lack of creativity and his humble respect for preceding savants be taken at face value. On the contrary, Ibn 'Abd Rabbih argues that a worthwhile selection of material is not only very commendable, but the utmost achievement for any wise man, since "Selecting speech is more difficult than composing it (*ikhtiyār al-kalām aṣ'abu min ta'līfihī*). They say: 'A man's selection demonstrates his mind'."[17] In his view, he is just following the model of his wise precursors, because "every one of them [i.e. wise men] has given his utmost and done his best to summarize the beautiful ideas of the ancients and to select the gems of the sayings of past generations (*fī ikhtiṣār badī' ma'ānī l-mutaqaddimīn wa ikhtiyār jawāhirih*) ... they have done this so profusely that their summaries have needed summarization, and their selection have needed further excerpting."[18] The underlying idea is that of a perennial, transcultural and cumulative wisdom,

14. Werkmeister 1983, 46.
15. Cf. the conclusive chapter in Werkmeister 1983, 463–9.
16. Ibn 'Abd Rabbih, *'Iqd*, 1: 16; Ibn 'Abd Rabbih, *'Iqd*, tr. Allen, 2.
17. Ibn 'Abd Rabbih, *'Iqd*, 1: 16; Ibn 'Abd Rabbih, *'Iqd*, tr. Allen, 2.
18. Ibn 'Abd Rabbih, *'Iqd*, 1: 15–6; Ibn 'Abd Rabbih, *'Iqd*, tr. Allen, 1.

which is to be found in successive utterances by wise men who themselves relied on the sayings of previous generations. In so doing, Ibn 'Abd Rabbih is following the precedence set by wise men of the past.

These statements render a decisive key for interpreting *al-'Iqd al-farīd*: they indicate that, excepting the short paratexts, which are therefore particularly significant, its message is embedded in the formal structure of the text, the organization of its material, and the normative criteria deployed in the selection process.

Organization of *Al-'Iqd al-farīd*

An exhaustive discussion of *al-'Iqd al-farīd*'s organization is an important *desideratum*, but would go beyond the scope of this article.[19] It is sufficient for our purposes to emphasize that structure is central to an adequate excavation of the text's meaning. *Al-'Iqd* is a very delicate, conscious composition, wherein all parts are interrelated in a sophisticated architecture, which merits exploration as a message in its own right. Questions of balance between frivolity and sobriety, semantic ranking, aesthetics and instruction were probably leading organizational principles; as well as the political agenda connected to the establishment of the Second Umayyad regime (929–1031).[20] The omission of *isnād*, for example is less a sign of provincial backwardness than a deliberate choice justified as adherence to certain aesthetic criteria.[21] Furthermore, the title *Unique Necklace* is not only ornamental, but points to the structure: knowledge is presented as a necklace of 25 precious pearls, and, following this metaphor, each book-title corresponds to the name of a gem or pearl, expressing both the quest for "the best" as jewels, and of the *jawhar* or essence of the things[22]. There is probably a yet unexplored correspondence in content between the books named after opposing jewels.[23] Each book is divided into chapters, which in turn consist of short independent narrative units or *akhbār* (singular *khabar*). The division in *akhbār* is a common compositional form in Arabic prose literature and especially in historiography. Like in other cases, most of these *akhbār* are also transmitted in other *adab* collections and in historical compilations (though often with

19. For the organization, see Werkmeister 1983, 27–43 and Veglison 2011, 19–26; however, both studies are rather descriptive and do not go into details.

20. Martínez-Gros 1992 does not discuss *al-'Iqd al-farīd* in his work.

21. Ibn 'Abd Rabbih, *'Iqd*, 1: 17; Ibn 'Abd Rabbih, *'Iqd*, tr. Allen, 3; cf. Werkmeister 1983, 44–6.

22. Van den Bergh 1957.

23. Cf. however Werkmeister 1983, 28 who denies any connection between the books named after corresponding jewels.

slight variations), so that we should read them not only in the context of *al-'Iqd al-farīd*, but also within the inter-textual web of cognate texts.[24] This multi-textuality and strong inter-textuality is a salient feature of *adab* and Arabic prose literature in general which cannot be ignored when interpreting an individual *khabar*.

Al-'Iqd al-farīd is subdivided into the following books:[25]

1. The Book of the Pearl on Rulership and Authority[26] (*Kitāb al-lu'lu'a fī l-sulṭān)*
2. The Book of the Nonpareil Jewel on Warfare (*Kitāb al-farīda fī l-ḥurūb*)
3. The Book of the Chrysolite on Generous Men and Gifts (*Kitāb al-zabarjada fī l-ajwād wa l-aṣfād*)
4. The Book of the Nacre on Delegations (*Kitāb al-jumāna fī l-wufūd*)
5. The Book of the Coral on the Etiquette of Addressing Kings (*Kitāb al-marjāna fī mukhāṭabat al-mulūk*)
6. The Book of the Ruby on Knowledge and *adab* (*Kitāb al-yāqūta fī l-'ilm wa l-adab*)
7. The Book of the Gem on Proverbs (*Kitāb al-jawhara fī l-amthāl*)
8. The Book of the Emerald on Sermonizing and Asceticism (*Kitāb al-zumurruda fī l-muwā'aẓa wa l-zuhd*)
9. The book of the Mother-of Pearl on Condolences and Elegies (*Kitāb al-durra fī l-ta'āzī wa l-marāthī*)
10. The Book of the Unique Jewel on Genealogy and Virtues of the Arabs (*Kitāb al-yatīma fī l-nasab wa faḍā'il al-'arab)*
11. The Book of the Adorable Jewel on the Speech of Bedouins (*Kitāb al-masjada fī kalām al-a'rāb)*
12. The Book of the Flanking Jewel on Responses (*Kitāb al-mujannaba fī l-ajwiba*)
13. The Book of the Middle Jewel on Orations (*Kitāb al-wāsiṭa fī l-khuṭab*)
14. The Book of the Second Flanking Level on Signatures, Sections, Opening Formulae and Stories of Secretaries (*Kitāb al-mujannaba al-thāniya fī l-tawqī'āt wa l-fuṣūl wa l-ṣudūr wa akhbār al-kataba*)
15. The book of the Second Adorable Jewel on Caliphs, their Histories, and Battles (*Kitāb al-masjada al-thāniya fī l-khulafā' wa l-tawārīkh wa ayyāmihim*)

24. I have studied some of the traditions of Book 21 in an earlier article (Toral-Niehoff 2010).

25. Cf. also the telling visualization of the "necklace" in Werkmeister 1983, 28.

26. See below on the translation of *sulṭān.*

16. The book of the Second Unique Jewel on Reports about Ziyād, al-Hajjāj, the Ṭālibids and the Barmakids (*Kitāb al-yatīma al-thāniya fī akhbār Ziyād wa l-Ḥajjāj wa l-Ṭālibiyyīn wa l-Barāmika*)
17. The Book of the Second Mother of Pearl on the Battle Days of the Arabs (*Kitāb al-durra al-thāniya fī ayyām al-ʿarab wa waqāʾiʿihim*)
18. The Book of the Second Emerald on the Merits of Poetry, its Meter and its Scansion (*Kitāb al-zumurruda al-thāniya fī faḍāʾil al-shiʿr wa maqāṭiʿih wa makhārijih*)
19. The book of the Second Gem on Prosody and Metrical Irregularities (*Kitāb al-jawhara al-thāniya fī aʿārīḍ al-shiʿr wa ʿilal al-qawāfī*)
20. The Book of the Second Ruby on the Art of Song and Dissenting Opinions Thereof (*Kitāb al-yāqūta al-thāniya fī ʿilm al-alḥān wa ikhtilāf al-nās fīh*)
21. The Book of the Second Coral on Women and their Attributes (*Kitāb al-marjāna al-thāniya fī l-nisāʾ wa ṣifātihinna*)
22. The Book of the Second Nacre on False Prophets, Lunatics, Misers and Parasites (*Kitāb al-jumāna al-thāniya fī l-mutannabiʾīn wa l-marūrīn wa l-bukhalāʾ wa l-ṭufayliyyīn*)
23. The Book of the Second Chrysolite on the Nature of Humans and Other Animals and the contention for precedence among cities (*Kitāb al-zabarjada al-thāniya fī bayān ṭabāʾiʿ al-insān wa sāʾir al-ḥayawān wa tafāḍul al-buldān*)
24. The Book of the Second Nonpareil Jewel on Food and Drink (*Kitāb al-farīda al-thāniya fī l-ṭaʿām wa l-sharāb*)
25. The Book of the Second Pearl on Tidbits, Gifts, Jokes and Witticism (*Kitāb al-luʾluʾa al-thāniya fī l-nutaf wa l-fukāhāt wa l-hidāyā wa l-milaḥ*)

Reception

The full impact of *al-ʿIqd al-farīd,* inside and outside Andalusia, remains to be investigated. There is a famous statement by a Būyid vizier that is commonly quoted to illustrate the alleged lackluster reception the book met in the Orient ("this is our merchandise brought back to us"),[27] that conveys the dignitary's disappointment at the absence of authentic Andalusian material from *al-ʿIqd al-farīd*. However, this saying does not do justice to the text's reception in the East. It was a big success, not just because it remains extant in numerous manuscripts and is frequently excerpted;[28] but also as it was

27. As example, see Werkmeister 1983, 38.
28. Werkmeister speaks of about 100 MSS. extant (Werkmeister 1983, 38–9).

one of the earliest *adab* works ever printed, and has since been reissued in an amazing number of (mostly non-critical) editions.[29] *Al-ʿIqd al-farīd's* elevated stature in the Arab world is also reflected in its selection, along with al-Jāḥiẓ's (d. 868 or 869) *Kitāb al-Bukhalāʾ* as the only works of *adab* included the prestigious "Masterpieces of Islamic Civilization" series, which "was established in order to acquaint non-Muslims with the contribution Islam has given to human civilization as a whole" by means of translations of emblematic books of Arabic and Islamic culture into English.[30]

Al-ʿIqd al-farīd as Advice Literature

Perennial wisdom, knowledge and moral advice are central themes of *al-ʿIqd al-farīd*: As any *adab* work, it contains much moralizing and instructive elements, so that we will find many aspects associated with advice and/or wisdom literature spread over the whole work.[31] It is a typical instance of what Louise Marlow has called a "hybrid mirror"[32] in which the genre intersects with many other forms of literature. Reflecting a rather aristocratic, elitist world-view, *al-ʿIqd al-farīd* addresses mostly cultivated, courtly men and therefore people close to the centers of power or potential "advisors." However, there are some books within *al-ʿIqd al-farīd* that conform more specifically to the genre of *Fürstenspiegel*, by giving "advice to rulers and their executives on politics and statecraft," where "the ruler's comportment towards God and towards the subjects or *raʿiyya* whom God has entrusted to his charge," and "the conduct of warfare, diplomacy and espionage" is debated.[33] These are books 1, 2, 4, 5, 12, and 14. On that basis, Gustav Richter

29. The first edition from Būlāq dates from 1876. It was followed by eight other editions (cf. Werkmeister 1983, 41–2). Since then, there have been two other editions, cf. Ibn ʿAbd Rabbih, *ʿIqd*, tr. Allen, XIX. All of them are more or less based on the edition by Aḥmad Amīn, Aḥmad al-Zayn, and Ibrāhīm al-Abyārī (Cairo 1940–53), which is based on two manuscripts and the earlier prints, which in turn are based on unknown MSS. The edition by Amīn has an *apparatus criticus*, but considering the number of manuscripts extant, a revised, critical edition is a *desideratum*.

30. Ibn ʿAbd Rabbih, *ʿIqd*, tr. Allen, foreword by H. H. Sheikh Muhammad b. Hamad of Qatar (no page numbers). Sheikh Hamad is also patron of the Center of Muslim Contribution to Civilization, and the Editorial Board is composed of prominent scholars from the Arab world (cf. list after Foreword, no page numbers).

31. Marlow 2007, 34b: "Moralising and instructive elements are found in virtually all forms of *adab*." Cf. Marlow 2009, were she discusses the problems of definition and delimitation of the genre of "mirror of princes," advice and wisdom literature and its intersection with other genres.

32. This term is used by Marlow 2009, 526.

33. Bosworth 1992.

considered these books of *al-'Iqd al-farīd* as one of the earliest examples of Arabic *Fürstenspiegel* or mirror for princes.[34]

In the present study, I will concentrate on the first book of *al-'Iqd al-farīd*, which is dedicated explicitly to the topic of *sulṭān*. The term is difficult to translate accurately into English, because in Classical Arabic it may designate both, the abstracts "power" or "authority" as well as the "holder of power, authority," and its meaning is determined by its context.[35] However, it is important to note that in Umayyad Andalusia *sulṭān* never designates a formal political title, as it does in the East, where the title *sulṭān* was incorporated as part of the dynast's name (as with the Saljuq ruler Malikshāh [r. 1072–92] for instance) since the tenth century in the Būyid and the slightly later Ghaznavid periods. For the sake of consistency, I will use in the following the term "rulership."

Organization of the Book of the Pearl on the Rulership (*Kitāb al-lu'lu'a fī l-sulṭān*)

Having established the importance of organization of knowledge in *al-'Iqd al-farīd*, an adequate evaluation would benefit from a comparison with a cognate text that will illuminate certain aspects of the structure imposed by Ibn 'Abd Rabbih. In this regard, '*Uyūn al-akhbār* by the great polygraph Ibn Qutayba (213–276/828–889) is conventionally upheld not only as the model, but also as one of the main sources of *al-'Iqd al-farīd*, which was composed several decades later.[36] This assumption is due firstly to several similarities in the structure (both works are conceived as *adab* encyclopedias and both begin with chapters discussing similar topics), and in the second instance, to the fact that the two works share a great number of traditions. However, in terms of material, Werkmeister has shown convincingly that a written text of *'Uyūn al-akhbār* could not have been the source of *al-'Iqd al-farīd*, but that the parallels go back to a common fundus of circulating *akhbār*, which formed the material basis for both authors.[37] It is not even certain if *'Uyūn al-akhbār* as such had already reached Andalusia in the lifetime of Ibn 'Abd Rabbih.[38]

34. Richter 1932, 72–9.

35. In the translation Ibn 'Abd Rabbih (2007), it is sometimes translated as "ruler," sometimes as "authority" or "governance." Cf. Kramer and Bosworth 1997.

36. Cf. the discussion in Werkmeister 1983, 62–77; cf. also similarly Richter 1932, 72–9. Veglison 2011, 34–5 continues considering *'Uyūn al-akhbār* as an important source of *'Iqd al-farīd*.

37. Cf. Werkmeister 1983, 463–9.

38. Cf. Ramírez del Río, 49–55, where he discusses which works of Ibn Qutayba were known in Andalusia.

However, in terms of structure, a comparison of the organization of *'Uyūn al-akhbār* and *al-'Iqd al-farīd* remains a promising approach. The dissimilarities will help to clarify the specific agenda of each encyclopedia. Preliminary studies focusing on certain chapters have shown that the similarities are less striking than apparent at first sight, pointing to a specific agenda of *al-'Iqd al-farīd*, that differs from the one pursued in *'Uyūn al-akhbār*.[39] A comparison of Book 21 on women in *al-'Iqd al-farīd*[40] and the corresponding Book 10 in *'Uyūn al-akhbār*[41] has shown that the texts follow different approaches, *al-'Iqd al-farīd* being more focused on the woman as spouse and genealogical link, whereas *'Uyūn al-akhbār* enhances more the physicality and sexual attractiveness of women.[42] In the case of the two books on *al-sulṭān*, a topic placed as the first book in both encyclopedias, similarities as well as important divergences are discernible:

	Al-'Iqd al-farīd, Kitāb al-lu'lu'a fī l-sulṭān		*'Uyūn al-akhbār, Kitāb al-sulṭān*
1.	General definition (*ḥāja al-'imrān ilā l-sulṭān*)	1.	The position of the ruler, his good conduct and administration (*Maḥall al-sulṭān wa sīratuhū wa siyāsatuh*)
2.	Advising the ruler and the necessity of obedience (*naṣīḥat al-sulṭān wa luzūm ṭā'atih*)	2.	Selection of officials (*ikhtiyār al-'ummāl*)
3.	Qualities of the ruler's associates (*mā yaṣḥab bihī l-sulṭān*)	3.	Chapter on the companions of the ruler, his cultivated courtiers; disposing and censuring the ruler (*Bāb ṣaḥbat al-sulṭān wa udabā'ihī wa taghayyur al-sulṭān wa talawunnih*)
4.	Good administration and the well-being of the realm (*ḥasan al-siyāsa wa iqāma al-mamlaka*)	4.	Consultation and opinion (*al-mushāwara wa l-ray'*)
5.	Selection of officials (*ikhtiyār al-sulṭān li-ahl 'amalih*)	5.	Subjective assumption and opinion (*al-iṣāba bi-l-ẓann wa l-ra'y*)
6.	Promoting justice and correcting iniquities (*basṭ al-ma'dala wa radd al-maẓālim*)	6.	Pursuit of passions (*ittibā' al-hawā*)

39. Richter 1932, 72–9.
40. Ibn 'Abd Rabbih, *'Iqd*, 1: 20–111; Ibn 'Abd Rabbih, *'Iqd*, tr. Allen, 5–67.
41. Ibn Qutayba, *'Uyūn*, 1: 1–106.
42. Toral-Niehoff 2010.

	Al-'Iqd al-farīd, Kitāb al-lu'lu'a fī l-sulṭān		*'Uyūn al-akhbār, Kitāb al-sulṭān*
7.	Prosperity of the subjects in accordance with the prosperity of the ruler (*Ṣilāḥ al-ra'iyya bi-ṣilāḥ al-imām*)	7.	The secret, keeping it and giving it away (*al-sirr wa kitmānuhū wa i'lānuh*)
8.	Sayings about the king, his companions and ministers (*qawluhum fī l-malik wa julasā'ihī wa wuzarā'ih*)	8.	Secretaries and the chancellery (*al-kuttāb wa l-kitāba*)
9.	Characteristics of a just ruler (*ṣifat al-imām al-'ādil*)	9.	Treachery of the secretaries (*khiyānat al-kuttāb*)
10.	Glory of the humble ruler (*haybat al-imām fī tawāḍu'*)	10.	Judgment (*al-qaḍā'*)
11.	Propriety and empathy in dealing with subjects (*ḥasan al-sīra wa l-rifq bi-l-ra'iyya*)	11.	Testimonies (*fī l-shahādāt*)
12.	The ruler's gain from decisiveness and determination (*mā ya'khudh al-sulṭān min al-ḥazm wa l-'azm*)	12.	Judges (*bāb al-aḥkām*)
13.	Objection to the ruler and its appropriate response (*al-ta'arruḍ li-l-sulṭān wa l-radd 'alayh*)	13.	Injustice (*al-ẓulm*)
14.	The ruler's forbearance with men of religion and virtue on their being audacious with him (*taḥallum al-sulṭān 'alā ahl al-dīn wa l-faḍl idhā ijtara'ū 'alayh*)	14.	On imprisonment (*qawluhum fī l-ḥabs*)
15.	Consultation (*al-mashwara*)	15.	Permission (al-*ḥijāb*)
16.	Safeguarding secrets (*ḥafẓ al-asrār*)	16.	Courteousness in addressing the ruler and giving him advice (*al-talaṭṭuf fī mukhāṭabat al-sulṭān wa ilqā' al-naṣīḥa ilayh*)
17.	Permission (*al-ḥijāb*)	17.	Concealing obedience to the ruler (*al-khafwāt fī ṭā'atih*)
18.	Loyalty and betrayal (*bāb min al-wafā' wa l-ghadr*)	18.	Generosity in his praise (*al-talaṭṭuf fī madḥih*)

Al-'Iqd al-farīd, Kitāb al-lu'lu'a fī l-sulṭān	*'Uyūn al-akhbār, Kitāb al-sulṭān*
19. Appointments and dismissals (*al-wilāya wa l-'azl*)	19. Courteousness when apologizing to the ruler (*al-talaṭṭuf fī mas'ala al-'afw*)
20. Qualifications for judges (*bāb min aḥkām al-quḍāt*)	

A simple comparison will suffice to demonstrate the different structures of the two books. Overlapping topics are few, and they are ordered differently in the two texts: *al-'Iqd al-farīd* 1 = *'Uyūn al-akhbār* 1; *al-'Iqd al-farīd* 3 and 5 = *'Uyūn al-akhbār* 2; *al-'Iqd al-farīd* 8 = *'Uyūn al-akhbār* 3; *al-'Iqd al-farīd* 15 = *'Uyūn al-akhbār* 7; *al-'Iqd al-farīd* 16 = *'Uyūn al-akhbār* 7. Moreover, as has been already emphasized by Richter, *'Uyūn al-akhbār* includes in this book (sections 16–19) topics that *al-'Iqd al-farīd* discusses elsewhere (in books 5, 12 and 14).[43]

In terms of content, *al-'Iqd al-farīd* focuses more than *'Uyūn al-akhbār* on the importance of just governance, which to Ibn 'Abd Rabbih is based on the good, balanced interaction between ruler and ruled, in a relationship marked by mutual responsibility and exemplary conduct on the part of the ruler, who functions as the protector of the ruled and the warrant of civil and divine order (cf. sections 2, 4, 7, 9, 10, 11, 12, and 13). This implies a certain obligation of advice, and even of critique by the courtly companions of the ruler, who must rely on their input to behave morally. Therefore, the ruler should accept advice with forbearance (especially section 14 "The ruler's forbearance with people of religion and virtue on their being audacious with him.")[44] *'Uyūn al-akhbār*, on the other hand, discusses in more detail subjects related to the administration of justice (sections 4, 11, 12, 13, 14), a topic not addressed in this book of *al-'Iqd al-farīd.*

Moreover, a close reading of chapters with similar titles reveals different contents. One example is the section dealing with the selection of officials in the two texts (*al-'Iqd al-farīd* 5: *ikhtiyār al-sulṭān li-ahl 'amalih* and *'Uyūn al-akhbār* 2: *ikhtiyār al-'ummāl*).[45] In the first instance, there is a difference in material: there is only one *khabar* common to both.[46] Secondly, the discus-

43. Richter 1932, 73.

44. Cf. Fierro 2004, 128 for the legitimizing role of the *'ulamā''s* critique.

45. Ibn 'Abd Rabbih, *'Iqd*, 1: 33–8; Ibn 'Abd Rabbih, *'Iqd*, tr. Allen, 13–6; Ibn Qutayba, *'Uyūn*, 1: 14–7.

46. Ibn 'Abd Rabbih, *'Iqd*, 1: 34; Ibn 'Abd Rabbih, *'Iqd*, tr. Allen, 14 = Ibn Qutayba, *'Uyūn*, 1: 17: 'Adī b. Ar'āt (Governor of Basra 99–101/718–720) and Iyās b. Mu'āwiya on Qur'an readers.

sion in *al-'Iqd al-farīd* is significantly longer and more focused on historical *akhbār*, many of them featuring prominent Umayyad figures such as the caliphs 'Abd al-Malik (r. 685–705), 'Umar b. 'Abd al-'Azīz (r. 717–720), and their governors and judges including Iyās b. Mu'āwiya (d. 121/739), 'Umar b. Hubayra (governor of Iraq between 102/720 and 105/724), al-Mughīra b. Shu'ba (d. between 48/668 and 51/671) and Ibn Abī Waqqās (d. during Mu'āwiya's caliphate, between 661 and 680); and some to the exemplary rule of the righteous caliph 'Umar b. al-Khaṭṭāb (r. 634–644). In general, *al-'Iqd al-farīd* seems much more concerned with the selection of governors and judges (it starts with a tradition about Ibn Hubayra, the Umayyad governor of Iraq sending an official to Khurasan), whereas *'Uyūn al-akhbār* focuses more on the aspect of *wilāya* or designation of a successor, and on the legacy a predecessor bequeaths to his successor. Ibn Qutayba begins with an account of Abū Bakr's (r. 632–634) designation of 'Umar b. al-Khaṭṭāb as his successor,[47] and then goes on quote *Kitāb al-Tāj*, with a similar tradition from Khusruw Parwīz[48] addressing his son Shīrawayh.[49]

Good Governance in *Al-'Iqd al-farīd* – the Paratexts

We have already seen that the specific selection and arrangement of the material in *al-'Iqd al-farīd* gives relevant information on the concept of the "good ruler." There are also two relevant sections in the *Kitāb al-lu'lu'a fī l-sulṭān* where Ibn 'Abd Rabbih speaks directly to the reader to introduce the theme of "power,"[50] all written in a delicate, elegant rhyming prose (*saj'*):

> Ruling power (*sulṭān*) is the rein (*zimām*) of all things. It organizes rights, maintains punishments (*ḥudūd*), and is the hub around which religious and secular matters turn. It is God's protection of His country, and His shadow stretching over His servants. Through it, their wives are secure, their oppressors are deterred, and their frightened are safe.
>
> Therefore, it is incumbent upon him whom God has invested with

47. Ibn Qutayba, *'Uyūn*, 1: 14.

48. Khusruw II Parwīz, (Arabic Abarwīz) Sasanian king (ruled 591–628), the last great ruler of this dynasty. In later Islamic literature he became renowned for the splendor and luxury of his court and the love for his Christian wife Shīrīn. See Howard-Johnston 2010.

49. Sasanid king, Shīrawayh, Shīra or Shērōē Qubad II (ruled 628), son of Khusruw Parwīz. There are several traditions about Khusruw giving counsel to his son in *Kitāb al-Tāj*, see (pseudo) al-Jāḥiẓ 1914, Index (s.v. Shīrawaih b. Abarwīz).

50. Ibn Qutayba does not have any paratexts in his book. He starts his *Kitāb al-sulṭān* with several hadith.

> the reins (*izimma*) of His rule (*ḥukm*), whom He has made sovereign over the affairs of His creatures, whom He has specially favored with His beneficence, and whom He has firmly appointed to wield power (*sulṭān*) – it is incumbent upon him to care seriously about his subjects' interests, and to pay attention to the welfare (*marāfiq*) of the people obedient to him, in accordance with the honor that God has conferred upon him and the conditions of happiness (*asbāb al-sa'āda*) He has bestowed upon him.[51]
>
> It is unusual for the flock (*al-ra'iyya*) to be satisfied with the leaders (*a'imma*), to find no facile excuse for them, and to blame them when many a blamed person may be innocent. There is no way one can be safe from the (biting) tongues of the common people (*alsunat al-'āmma*), for the satisfaction of everyone (*riḍā al-jumla*) and the agreement of all (*muwāfaqat jimā'atihā*) are among impossible and unattainable things. Everyone has his share of justice and his place in government. It is the duty of the leader (*imām*) to rule his people by deeds that satisfy the majority. And it is the right of the ruled that their leader should accept their apparent obedience (*ḥusn al-qubūl li-ẓāhir ṭā'atih*) and turn away from disclosing their misdeeds. It is just as Ziyād said when he came to Iraq as a ruler: "O people, there were grudges and hostilities between you and me. I have put all that behind me and underfoot. He who has done good needs, let him increase them; and he who has done bad deeds, let him desist from them. If I know that someone among you hates me to high heaven, I will not expose him unless he reveals his innermost to me."[52]

The central themes of these passages are the obligations of the ruler, including the provision of welfare and security to the ruled and the maintenance of public and divine order. Second, the ruled are obliged to accept the rule of the sovereign and to show at least nominal obedience, although the agreement of all is impossible to attain.[53] It is remarkable how strongly these passages emphasize the moral duties of the ruler, whose power is restricted by ethic commitments.

The *Risāla* of al-Ḥasan al-Baṣrī

Another very relevant passage is a long letter attributed to al-Ḥasan al-Baṣrī (21/642–110/728), where this famous Basran preacher of the Umayyad pe-

51. This passage is followed by a quotation of Qur'an 22:41, which emphasizes the religious duties of those who had been invested in power by God.

52. Ibn 'Abd Rabbih, *'Iqd*, 1: 20–1; Ibn 'Abd Rabbih, *'Iqd*, tr. Allen, 5–6.

53. An interesting point, because it gives way to make the ruler accept a certain degree of dissatisfaction among the ruled.

riod addresses 'Umar b. 'Abd al-Azīz, who had, upon assuming the caliphate, asked al-Ḥasan for a description of the just ruler.[54] The letter, which is the only *khabar* transmitted in the section "Description of a just ruler (*ṣifat al-imām al-'ādil*)," deserves a detailed study that cannot be undertaken here; for the present, it is remarkable that the letter coincides almost perfectly with Ibn 'Abd Rabbih's ideas on the subject matter, discussed earlier.

Thus, the main issue of al-Baṣrī's *Risāla* is to emphasize the responsibility of authority that is always bestowed by God, and the duties of the ruler, who has to care for his subjects as their shepherd.[55] In fact, the ruler is responsible for both the divine and the political order, and protects the weak, much as a caring (and sometimes punishing) father would: "Be it known to you, O Commander of the Faithful, that God instituted the just ruler to be the redress of every wrong-doer, the discipline of every unfair person, the correction of every corrupt man, the strength of every weak one, the justice of every wronged being, and the refuge of every frightened individual (*i'lam, yā amīr al-mu'minīn, anna Allāh ja'ala l-imām al-'ādil qiwāma kull mā'il, wa qaṣd kull jā'ir, wa ṣilāḥ kull fāsid, wa quwwa kull ḍa'īf, wa naṣafa kull maẓlūm, wa mafza'a kull malhūf*)."[56]

Responsibility and exemplary commitment of the ruler to his religious and moral duties are central: "God has prescribed punishments (*ḥudūd*) to act as deterrents to wicked deeds and vile acts (*al-habā'ith wa l-fawāḥish*). So, what happens then, if these deeds and acts are committed by those responsible for implementing the punishments?"[57]

Preliminary Conclusions and Further Perspectives

This study has pointed to several topics that merit further discussion. A central challenge is to find an adequate method to establish the central content of *al-'Iqd al-farīd*, since the work, like most other *adab* collections, at first sight may appear as a mere collection of well-known quotations, without any original input by the author Ibn 'Abd Rabbih. As has been shown, one key approach is the close reading of the organizational framework, which is one of the main contributions of the collector. Further, in order to contextualize the specific selection and arrangement of the material, it has to be evaluated by comparing them to those in parallel works. This has been done

54. Ibn 'Abd Rabbih, *'Iqd*, 1: 50–2; Ibn 'Abd Rabbih, *'Iqd*, tr. Allen, 24–6. Not transmitted in *'Uyūn al-akhbār*. The only parallel seems to be in *Nihāyat al-'arab*, which goes back to *'Iqd*. The issues of the textual history of this text shall not be discussed here. Unfortunately, neither Ritter 1933 nor Suleiman 2006 discuss this letter in their studies on al-Ḥasan al-Baṣrī.

55. For this metaphor, cf. Crone 2004, 270.

56. Ibn 'Abd Rabbih, *'Iqd*, 1: 50; Ibn 'Abd Rabbih, *'Iqd*, tr. Allen, 24.

57. Ibn 'Abd Rabbih, *'Iqd*, 1: 51; Ibn 'Abd Rabbih, *'Iqd*, tr. Allen, 25.

here with the respective sections in *'Uyūn al-akhbār* and *Kitāb al-sulṭān*. Direct utterances by Ibn 'Abd Rabbih are rare; however, their content has proved to be consistent with the one previously established by the structural and comparative analysis of the quotations.

Good rule in Ibn 'Abd Rabbih's text certainly considers political authority as part of the divine order. Political power is bestowed by God to the ruler and implicates a huge moral responsibility, though only accountable to God. That divine origin ensures moral obligations for ruler and ruled alike: The ruler has to protect, guide and care for the ruled like a shepherd for his flock or a good father for his children, and in return, he is entitled to obedience. The ruler's function is to be the guarantor of social, moral and divine order; however, in spite of all this grandiosity, he remains human and fallible. Therefore, his advisers need to dispense with good advice, at times a risky venture.

These themes are encountered frequently in advice literature,[58] and may perhaps be germane to a courtly milieu. In *al-'Iqd al-farīd* – again as in many other mirrors – government is God's, but Islamic legitimation is remarkably absent, although hadith, Qur'an and quotations from pious men such as al-Ḥasan al-Baṣrī are used authoritatively. There is no discussion of the nature of the caliphate or the *sharī'a*, rather surprising since it was written in the early years of the Umayyad caliphate in Cordova. Ibn 'Abd Rabbih was a court poet, and although he had studied with fully-fledged *fuqahā'*, he seems to have identified more with the courtly culture, using as medium *adab* and poetry. His deliberate omission of *isnād* is significant and can be interpreted as a statement in favor of elitist aesthetics and against the inclusion in *adab* of methods of authorization borrowed from the *muḥaddithūn*, methods that he certainly knew, since his teachers are credited as having introduced hadith in al-Andalus. We have to consider that other *adab* authors of the same chronological context like Abū l-Faraj al-Iṣfāhānī certainly used *isnād* in their *adab*-collections.

Finally, there may be a very subtle, specifically Andalusian Umayyad message in the selection of traditions that remains to be investigated by comparing it to other, similar Eastern collections. Although the Umayyads were regularly idealized in *adab*, for example by al-Jāḥiẓ, it seems that figures like Mu'āwiya, 'Abd al-Malik and 'Umar b. 'Abd al-'Azīz and their governors are especially frequent subjects in *al-'Iqd al-farīd*. There are also some interesting *akhbār* which portray Abū Sufyān, the otherwise ill-famed forefather of the Umayyads, in a positive light;[59] the same applies to Hind b. 'Utba, the figura-

58. Marlow 1995, 101 and passim; Marlow 2007.
59. See for example Ibn 'Abd Rabbih, *'Iqd*, 1: 25–6; Ibn 'Abd Rabbih, *'Iqd*, tr. Allen, 8–9.

tive "mother" of the Umayyads.[60] The cast of personalities and the manner in which they are presented may also prove a fecund lens for scrutinizing the political and cultural agenda of this precious "necklace" of *adab.*

Notwithstanding these slight differences, the concept of good rulership conveyed by the "Book of the Pearl" in *al-'Iqd al-farīd* is fairly consistent with other works of advice literature composed in the Eastern parts of the Islamicate world: central topics are the ruler's responsibility, the importance of adequate advice and the divine origin of political power. Another parallel is that the material base of this book goes back to the same sources that circulated widely in the East (besides Qur'an and hadīth, there was also Indian, Greek, Persian and other pre-Islamic wisdom literature).

Finally, it is clear that although the Umayyad caliphate in Cordova was opposed to the Abbasids, the political literature of al-Andalus in this period followed mainly models and themes already set in Baghdad.

60. About Hind, cf. Toral-Niehoff 2013.

Bibliography

Bergh, S. van den (1957), "Djawhar," in: *EI*² II: 493–4.

Biesterfeldt, H. H. (2002), "Arabisch-islamische Enzyklopädien. Formen und Funktionen," in: C. Meier (ed.), *Die Enzyklopädie im Wandel vom Hochmittelalter bis zur frühen Neuzeit*, Munich, 43–84.

Bosworth, C. E. (1992), "Nasīḥat al-mulūk," in: *EI*² VII: 984–8.

Crone, P. (2004), *Medieval Islamic Political Thought*, Edinburgh (Reprint 2012).

Fierro, M. (1989), "The Introduction of Hadith into al-Andalus," *Der Islam* 66: 69–93.

—— (1999), "Los mawālī de 'Abdarraḥmān I," *Al-Qantara* 20: 65–95.

—— (2004), "La política religiosa de 'Abd al-Raḥmān III," *Al-Qantara* 25: 119–56.

—— (2009), "El saber enciclopédico en el mundo islámico," in: A. Alvar Ezquerra (ed.), *Las Enciclopedias en España antes de l'Encyclopédie,* Madrid, 83–104.

Van Gelder, G. J. (1997), "Compleat Men, Women and Books: On Medieval Arabic Encyclopaedism," in: P. Binkley (ed.), *Pre-Modern Encyclopaedic Texts. Proceedings of the Second COMERS Congress, Groningen, 1–4 July 1996,* Leiden, 241–59.

Gutas, D. (1981), "Classical Arabic Wisdom Literature: Nature and Scope," *JAOS* 101: 49–86.

Howard-Johnston, J. (2010), "Ḵosrow II," in: *EIr* (available at http://www.iranicaonline.org/articles/khosrow-ii, accessed on 5/22/2013).
Ibn 'Abd Rabbih (2007), *The Unique Necklace*, vol. 1, tr. R. Allen, Reading.
Ibn 'Abd Rabbih, Aḥmad b. Muḥammad (1990), *al-'Iqd al-farīd*, ed. A. Amīn, with an introduction by 'U. Tadmurī, 7 vols., Beirut.
Ibn Qutayba, 'Abd Allāh b. Muslim (1925–30), *Kitāb 'Uyūn al-akhbār*, 4 vols., Cairo.
(Pseudo) al-Jāḥiẓ (1914), *Le Livre de la Couronne. Kitab el-Tadj (Kitāb al-Tāj)*, ed. A. Zeki Pasha, Cairo.
Kramer, J. H. [revised by C. E. Bosworth] (1997), "Sulṭān (1.) In early Islamic usage and in the central lands of Islam," in: *EI*[2] IX: 849–51.
Marlow, L. (1995), "Kings, Prophets and the 'Ulamā' in Mediaeval Islamic Advice Literature," *Studia Islamica* 81: 101–20.
—— (2007), "Advice and advice literature," in: *EI*[3] 2007–1: 34–58.
—— (2009), "Surveying Recent Literature on the Arabic and Persian Mirrors for Princes Genre," *History Compass* 7: 523–38.
Martínez-Gros, G. (1992), *L'idéologie omeyyade*, Madrid.
Monés, H. (1964), "Le rôle des hommes de religion dans l'histoire de l'Espagne musulmane jusqu'à la fin du Califat," *Studia Islamica* 20: 47–88.
Mourad, Suleiman (2006), *Early Islam between Myth and History. Al-Ḥasan al-Baṣrī (d. 110H/728CE) and the formation of his legacy in classical Islamic scholarship*, Leiden.
Ramírez del Río, J. (2002), *La Orientalización de al-Andalus: Los días de los árabes en la Península Ibérica*, Seville.
Richter, G. (1932), *Studien zur Geschichte der älteren arabischen Fürstenspiegel*, Leipzig.
Ritter, H. (1933), "Studien zur Geschichte der islamischen Frömmigkeit. Ḥasan al-Basrī," *Der Islam* 21: 1–83.
Rosenthal, F. (1970), *Knowledge Triumphant. The Concept of Knowledge in Medieval Islam*, Leiden (Reprint 2007).
Toral-Niehoff, I. (2010),"«Sei seine Dienerin, dann wird er dein Diener sein!» Auf der Suche nach der idealen Ehefrau: Ibn 'Abd Rabbihi und sein Buch über die Frauen," in: R. Forster and Romy Günthart (eds.), *Didaktisches Erzählen. Formen literarischer Belehrung in Orient und Okzident*, Bern, 255–75.
—— (2013), " 'Paradise is at the Feet of the Mothers.' Some Preliminary Remarks Concerning the Figuration of Motherhood in Medieval Arab Literature," *Imago Temporis. Medium Aevum* 7: 45-58.
Veglison, J. (2011), *El collar único de Ibn Abd Rabbihi*, Madrid.
Werkmeister, W. (1983), *Quellenuntersuchungen zum Kitāb al-'Iqd al-farīd des Andalusiers Ibn 'Abdrabbih (246/860-328/940)*, Berlin.

A Scholar's Claims on Practical Politics

Nūr al-Dīn al-Rānīrī's Seventeenth-Century Malay *Bustān al-salāṭīn*[1]

Edwin P. Wieringa

On Sunday, 6 Muḥarram 1047/31 May 1637, Sheikh Nūr al-Dīn (b. 'Alī b. Ḥasanjī b. Muḥammad Ḥamīd) al-Rānīrī, who, as his *nisba* indicates, was a native from Rānīrī or Rander in Gujerat on the northwestern part of the Indian subcontinent, arrived on the northern tip of the island of Sumatra where he would leave an indubitable mark on the theological life of the Acehnese sultanate.[2] Although his sojourn in Aceh would only last barely seven years, when he was expelled, in 1644, and forced to return to his place of origin, in this brief period he produced a remarkable oeuvre, exceptional both for its sheer volume and for its profound learning.[3] His longest work, arguably "the longest text ever written in the history of traditional Malay literature,"[4] is the *Bustān al-salāṭīn fī dhikr al-awwalīn wa l-ākhirīn* (Garden of Kings, concerning the Recollection of the First and the Last). The rather long Arabic title, duly rhyming as Arabic convention prescribes, bespeaks an exhaustive, encyclopedic work.[5] Apparently, this was exactly what his royal benefactor had ordered: as Nūr al-Dīn explains in the introduction, the text was commissioned by Sultan Iskandar Thānī (r. 1636–1641) on 17 Shawwāl 1047/4 March 1638, who wanted him "to write a book in the Malay language

1. Although I had already made notes from the Leiden manuscripts of Book VI of the *Bustān al-salāṭīn* for this paper, at its final stage, through the good offices of Dr Paul Wormser (Paris), I could thankfully profit from a draft transliteration of this part, which had been prepared by the late Prof. Teuku Iskandar (Leiden). I am also grateful to Prof. Karel Steenbrink (Utrecht) who, back in 1994, when I was working on a catalogue of the oldest collection of Malay manuscripts of Leiden University Library (published as Wieringa 1998), provided me with a photocopy of the pre-final draft of Abdus Salam Arief MA thesis (without title, dated 1989), containing an edition of Book VI, chapter 2.

2. The date of arrival is not unproblematic: the *Bustān al-salāṭīn* mentions the year 1040 (see Steenbrink 1993, 3), but this was Thursday and too early, see Harun 2004, 48 n. 18. It is not impossible that this was not his first visit to Aceh; see Voorhoeve 1951, 357. On his full name, see Voorhoeve 1951, 356. On Rander, see Drewes 1955.

3. A recent list of his bibliography can be found in Wormser 2012, 47–55.

4. Harun 2009, xi.

5. On its long Arabic rhyming title, see Jones 1985, 7.

(*bahasa jawi*), containing stories on the denizens of the seven layers of the heavens and the seven layers of the earth, and to relate the deeds of kings of former times and later."[6] In other words, the aim was twofold: (1) to narrate a universal history and (2) to describe the manners of kings.[7] The *Bustān al-salāṭīn* thus belongs to the universal *Fürstenspiegel* (mirror for princes) genre, being a variant of *naṣīḥat al-mulūk* (Counsel for Kings), dedicated to *adab al-mulūk* (manners of kings) or *siyar al-mulūk* (conduct of kings).[8]

The *Bustān al-salāṭīn* is Nūr al-Dīn's most comprehensive work, occupying seven substantial books, and covering a wide range of learned material, from the creation of the heavens and the earth to physiognomy and medicine. However, it is a moot point to what extent anonymous hands, either by error or intent, have contributed in shaping the text as it has come down to us. Its great length made it expensive to copy and reduced its general appeal. According to Vladimir Braginsky, the *Bustān al-salāṭīn* is "an encyclopaedic compilation, so grandiose that no manuscripts have been preserved which contain all its books."[9] The extant manuscript witnesses are all rather young copies, fragmentary, and made by different copyists.[10] Pieced together, the complete text would comprise more than one thousand dense pages in print, but hitherto only a few sections have been made available through text editions, while large parts of it still languish unedited in manuscripts scattered around the world.

It is unclear when the *Bustān al-salāṭīn* was finished, if at all.[11] There is no conclusion with an authorial colophon formally stating its end. Estimated dates of possible completion depend on one's assessment of the authenticity of chapter 13 of Book II. The latter chapter explicitly deals with the history of Aceh, both the early period of the sultanate as well as contemporaneous events.[12] The last entry mentions the ascent to the throne of Sultana 'Ināyat Shāh (r. 1678–1688) in 1080/1678, but in that very year Nūr al-Dīn's bones had already rested for two decades in the soil of his place of birth, where he had died on 22 Dhū l-Ḥijja 1069/21 September 1658.[13]

6. Malay text in Steenbrink 1993, 3–4. The term *bahasa jawi* denotes the language of Sumatra, hence Malay, see Roolvink 1975, 2.

7. Harun 2004, 29.

8. See Marlow 2009, 526.

9. Braginsky 2004, 450.

10. Harun 2009, 28; Wormser 2012, 36.

11. Cf. the remark by Voorhoeve 1955, 153, "Encyclopedic work, begun in 1047, perhaps never finished." See also Riddell 2003, 817 who writes, "commenced in 1638 and probably never completed."

12. This chapter has been made available by Iskandar 1966 and is also included in Steenbrink 1993.

13. Voorhoeve 1959, 90.

Jelani Harun opines that the rather extensive description of the great funeral procession for Sultan Iskandar Thānī (who died on 6 Dhū l-Qa'da 1050/17 February 1641),[14] Nūr al-Dīn's erstwhile patron and protector, emanated from the latter's pen, suggesting that the *Bustān al-salāṭīn* was completed sometime around 1641 or 1642.[15] However, it is rather hard to believe that the report on the funerary rites constitutes some sort of eye-witness report by Nūr al-Dīn, for why should he have written about himself in the third person, whereas in other chapters he refers to himself as *fakir* (*faqīr*), which is the normal referent of convention used by traditional Malay writers? Furthermore, isn't it rather odd that in his alleged function as the supposed chronicler of Acehnese history he should have been appreciative about his archenemies at court whom he had persecuted by fire and sword? For example, about Sheikh Shams al-Dīn al-Sumatra'ī (d. 1630), whom he had vigorously attacked and even accursed in numerous polemical theological treatises, we read: "At that time Sheikh Shams al-Dīn ibn 'Abd Allāh al-Sumatra'ī passed away, at Sunday evening, at the time of the *'aṣr* prayer, at the twelfth of the month Muḥarram, in the year one thousand four hundred of the *hijra*. This sheikh was a scholar versed in all sciences and he was famous for his knowledge of mysticism and several books which he compiled."[16]

As Anne Grinter has shown, the last sections of Book II, dealing with local Acehnese history and the neighboring Malay world, are in all respects much too different from the rest of the *Bustān al-salāṭīn* to be counted as Nūr al-Dīn's own work.[17] As Paul Wormser points out, it is quite ironic that it was precisely this inauthentic part which has earned its supposed author the title of the first writer who had initiated modern Malay historiography.[18] In fact, Wormser is even skeptical about Nūr al-Dīn's authorship of the *Bustān al-salāṭīn* as a whole. In an attempt to explain the rather rough-and-ready condition of the text, his hypothesis is that Nūr al-Dīn may not have been its single author, but rather had employed a group of scribes assisting him by writing different bits and pieces for which he then took the credit.[19] This

14. This date in Iskandar 1966, 58 and Steenbrink 1993, 234, to which the chronicler adds that the Sultan had ruled for "four years, three months, six days."

15. Harun 2009, 27.

16. The Malay text can be found, with some minor variations, in Niemann 1907, 127; Van Nieuwenhuijze 1945, 15; Iskandar 1966, 35; and Steenbrink 1993, 218. Wormser 2012, 152 has translated this entry into French.

17. Grinter 1979.

18. Wormser 2012, 31, 33.

19. Wormser 2012. On this interesting philological problem, see Peacock 2007, 58 where a similar theory is discussed (but discarded).

theory is quite attractive as it would also explain how Nūr al-Dīn was able to produce such a relatively large work in only a few years' time (1638–1641/2?). However, there is no definitive proof that Nūr al-Dīn entrusted the writing to a scriptorium, and it remains puzzling why he should have accepted items of quite divergent quality. As the earliest extant manuscripts are all relatively young, it is hardly surprising that they appear to be very corrupt.

Whether sole author or editor of others' works, Nūr al-Dīn was in any case a compiler of textual material familiar from Arabic and Persian sources. As Wormser has meticulously demonstrated, the *Bustān al-salāṭīn* is the fruit of extraordinary erudition.[20] However, Nūr al-Dīn's heavy reliance upon "a repertoire of shared ideas"[21] raises questions about him as a thinker in his own right. Was he perhaps just copying and pasting, parroting other people's thoughts? If so, if he was merely rehashing old motifs and well-known *exempla* known to us from other sources, why should his mirror for princes be worthy of further study? However, as Louise Marlow reminds us, although "certain themes of advice literature have endured since antiquity in diverse cultural milieux... each example is strikingly individual, tailored to specific circumstances and specific writer-ruler relationships. The significance of a motif, however often it has been invoked before, is shaped with each utterance by the particularities of time, place, author, and audience."[22] In the case of the *Bustān al-salāṭīn*, too, the specific *Sitz im Leben* is in my opinion crucial for understanding Nūr al-Dīn's ambitious endeavor. As a foreigner lacking his own power base in local society, he was fully dependent on the ruler's patronage, but by producing a monumental mirror for princes he not only wished to please his master, but also intended to strengthen his own position as the king's mentor, seeking to guide his royal recipient. A brief background sketch, although necessarily sketchy and incomplete, may give an idea of the historical setting.

From information in the *Bustān al-salāṭīn* we know that Nūr al-Dīn was born into a diaspora Hadhrami Arab family of *'ulamā'* with some ties to Aceh. His paternal uncle, Sheikh Muḥammad al-Ḥamīd, had taught a wide range of Islamic sciences (covering logic, poetics, rhetoric, theology, and jurisprudence) in Aceh between 1580 and 1583, but as his students were keener on mysticism, he went to Mecca in order to gain more in-depth knowledge in that particular field. Returning to Aceh, Muḥammad al-Ḥamīd taught Sufism

20. Wormser 2012.
21. Expression used by Bray 2010, 33.
22. Marlow 2007, 55. Elsewhere I proposed a similar argument in the case of the "eternal return" of well-known (foreign) narrative material in traditional Malay adventure romances, see Wieringa 2011, 379.

from 1589 to 1604, succeeding in attracting considerable attention among the courtiers.[23] It may well be that Nūr al-Dīn's stellar career was due to his uncle's network. It has been speculated that Nūr al-Dīn's mother was Malay, but this is no more than a wild guess which should explain his mastery of Malay. There is little revelatory autobiographical information on this to be found in the *Bustān al-salāṭīn*: in its introduction Nūr al-Dīn merely employs the standard modesty trope of prefatory rhetoric by humbly stating that he obeyed his highness' command, although "my knowledge is limited and I have not much understanding of Malay (*bahasa jawi*)."[24]

Anyhow, this newcomer, "an intruder of Indo-Arab origin,"[25] very quickly became intimately involved in daily Acehnese politics as one of its key players. He was the ruler's principal religious adviser, holding the office of *Shaykh al-Islām,* which made him the supreme arbiter of Islamic doctrine. Sultan Iskandar Thānī wished to mark a clear break with the past, because under his patronage Nūr al-Dīn initiated a virulent witch-hunt against the local-born mystics and religious teachers whom Iskandar Muda (r. 1607–1636), his immediate predecessor, had just previously still favored.

It may seriously be doubted that the Sultan could grasp the fine intricacies of the theological disputes about mystical arcana among the quarreling clerics which, in the twentieth century, would spur a cottage industry in (Western) academia of learned text editions with additional commentaries and analyses.[26] However, dogma and the notion of orthodoxy and heresy directly touched upon the question of who could claim to be the sole possessor of Truth (with a capital T), intimately involving the ruler's "divine right" to impose his will on his subjects. Politically, redrawing the strict boundaries between the "orthodox" and the "heterodox" had the benefit for the newly installed non-Acehnese Sultan Iskandar Thānī of (re)creating the nation's identity and demonizing those who belonged to the *ancien régime.*

Nūr al-Dīn tried to remove the words of his predecessors from discourse, having the writings of the indigenous luminaries Ḥamzah al-Fanṣūrī (i.e. from Fanṣūr, better known as the seaport town Barus) and Shams al-Dīn of Pasai (Aceh's predecessor as center of Islamic studies), both from northern Sumatra, publicly burned for their allegedly heretical views.[27] To gauge the radicalism of this enterprise, it should be remembered that ever since the beginning of the seventeenth century Shams al-Dīn had been a most pow-

23. Malay text in Iskandar 1966, 33–4; Steenbrink 1993, 217.
24. Malay text in Steenbrink 1993, 4.
25. Takeshi 1984, 254.
26. For a succinct survey of this Islamologist literature, see Van Bruinessen 1998, 196–8.
27. Takeshi 1984, 254.

erful and influential theologian at the court of Aceh, being *Shaykh al-Islām* until his death in 1630.[28] Ḥamzah al-Fanṣūrī, too, was a big name: although his biography remains elusive, he must have been Shams al-Dīn's teacher and mentor. Echoes of Ḥamzah's mystical poems have continued to reverberate throughout the archipelago for centuries after his death.[29] Both men were renowned for their Sufi speculations on the seven grades of emanation of the *wujūdiyya*, teaching the "Unity of Being" (*waḥdat al-wujūd*): "If Hamza was the master of utilizing poetry for that purpose, then Shams al-Dīn has to be considered the master of prose."[30]

Apart from trying to literally extinguish their words, Nūr al-Dīn's prolific output may also be seen as an attempt to make a new start by crafting a new canon.[31] His polemical treatises against the adherents of "untrue" interpretations of *wujūdiyya* teachings are a case in point, but *Bustān al-salāṭīn* also testifies to this ambition.[32] Its title is remarkably close to that of *Tāj al-salāṭīn* (Crown of Kings), written as a "didactic mirror for rulers, nobility and commoners"[33] at the Acehnese court, in 1603, for Sultan 'Alā' al-Dīn (r. 1589–1604) by a certain Bukhārī who, depending on one's interpretation, may have been "of Johor" (*al-Johori*) or "the jeweler" (*al-Jawharī*) or perhaps both.[34] Nūr al-Dīn not only vied with his predecessor concerning the title of this mirror for princes, but also in subject matter, using a number of the same anecdotes to bring a lesson to life.[35]

Although belonging to the same genre, the two texts are quite different from one another. According to Braginsky, Bukhārī in all likelihood used the Persian original of *Naṣīḥat al-mulūk* (Counsel to Kings) attributed to al-Ghazālī (d. 1111),[36] which formed about two-thirds of *Tāj al-salāṭīn*.[37] As Braginsky points out, although the greater part may have been based upon a foreign, twelfth-century model, at least one chapter seems to have been specifically written with a view to a topical theme, viz. Chapter 21 on the relationship between Muslim monarchs (*raja yang Islam*) and their non-Mus-

28. For biographical details, see Van Nieuwenhuijze 1945, 15–6; Nasir 2010, 213–6.

29. Wieringa 2005, 391.

30. Nasir 2010, 215.

31. Braginsky 2004, 449.

32. Nūr al-Dīn, who was deeply versed in mysticism, was not opposed to *wujūdiyya* per se, but differentiated between "true" and "heretical" understandings of the doctrine of the unity of being, see Drewes 1986.

33. This categorization is from Braginsky 2004, 431.

34. On the author's name, see Braginsky 2004, 433–4.

35. Braginsky 2004, 449. For a more detailed comparison of the two works, see Wormser 2012, 177–83.

36. On the authorship of the *Naṣīḥat al-mulūk* see Crone 1987.

37. Braginsky 2004, 432, 485 n. 56.

lim subjects (*segala rakyat yang kafir*).[38] In this relatively short chapter (of no more than two and a half pages in a modern text edition) it is stated that the information for this section is based upon a book by the second caliph 'Umar I (r. 634–644) under whom the Muslims achieved their great conquests. The latter's regulations with the subjected infidels are included "in order that the Muslim monarchs below the wind will know the rules pertaining to their non-Muslim subjects."[39] The nautical term "below the wind" refers to insular Southeast Asia and, according to Braginsky, the subject matter of this particular chapter was pertinent for Aceh at the time, because the sultanate in the sixteenth and seventeenth century was a military and imperial center which rulers were warrior kings, making many conquests in "heathen" territory in Sumatra.[40]

Tāj al-salāṭīn would enjoy widespread favor for centuries in the archipelago, which has been attributed to "its adaptation of Persian wisdom to local conditions."[41] As Christiaan Hooykaas notes, until the early twentieth century, Bukhārī's work was still widely read in Java (in Javanese adaptations) by "royal personages, aristocratic ladies, court dignitaries and civil servants, subjects and even Muslim Chinese; this learned and verbose book even reached illiterate persons."[42] According to the ruler of Surakarta, Pakubuwana XII (1925–2004), "it is obligatory for all Javanese kings to read this text."[43] Hooykaas ascribes this enduring appeal to the rather simple, edifying character of *Tāj al-salāṭīn*, whereas Nūr al-Dīn never made easy concessions to lay readers.[44] However, the received wisdom that declares *Bustān al-salāṭīn* to have been considerably less popular is rather exaggerated. In fact, some parts of *Bustān al-salāṭīn* attracted considerable attention. For example, Book VII on intellect, medicine, physiognomy, women and "strange and miraculous stories" (*hikayat yang ajaib dan gharaib*) is preserved in more than twenty manuscripts, indicating keen interest.[45] Book III, by contrast, dealing with just kings and wise ministers, is only known through a *codex unicus*, which was finished in the month of Rabīʿ al-ākhir 1231/March 1816, belonging to the library of University Malaya in Kuala Lumpur, Malaysia (call number UM

38. For practical reasons I have used the edition of Dipodjo and Asdi 1999 where chapter 21 can be found on pp. 201–3.

39. "... supaya segala raja-raja yang Islam di bawah angin mengetahui segala perintah yang berlaku atas segala rakyat yang kafir itu." Dipodjojo and Asdi 1999, 201.

40. Braginsky 2004, 434.

41. Braginsky 2004, 435.

42. Hooykaas 1947, 173.

43. Florida 2000, 180.

44. Braginsky 2004, 451 comes to a similar verdict.

45. Harun 2009, 45.

41). The text of the latter Book, of which the cataloguer Petrus Voorhoeve in the 1950s still assumed that it was lost or perhaps never written, has been published, fairly recently, in 2008, by Jelani Harun.[46]

Books IV and V of the *Bustān al-salāṭīn* have been adapted in Javanese narrative poetry, developing into variegated versions, which calls Hooykaas' rather negative judgment, that the *Bustān* was not a popular work, into question, but this Javanese reception has hitherto hardly attracted scholarly attention.[47] In Javanese Nūr al-Dīn's work remains "hidden" behind rather cryptic titles: the designation *Serat (Imam) Nawawi* (Book of the Imam Nawawi) of one of its adaptations is not exactly a give-away. This title is due to the circumstance that the *Bustān* happens to open with a saying attributed to the Muslim scholar Yaḥyā b. Sharaf al-Nawawī (d. 676/1277–8).[48] Such a title as *Serat warna carita saking Ngarab* (Anthology of stories from Arabia) is much too general to be of indicative value.[49]

Nevertheless, Hooykaas is right that in Malay literature Nūr al-Dīn unabashedly played the role of *encyclopédiste*, studding his dense text with bookish knowledge of a highly specialist nature, perhaps of interest for historians or theologians, but offering tough going for the non-literati.[50] Braginsky even goes so far as to call Nūr al-Dīn "a pedant."[51] In contrast to Bukhārī's rather compact Crown of Kings, the contents of *Bustān al-salāṭīn* indicate that Nūr al-Dīn did not just intend his work to be a mirror for princes, but rather aimed at a more ambitious, highbrow encyclopedic work. It consists of no less than seven books, which in their turn are divided into several sections called chapters (*fasal*). The rather long book titles may give a good idea of the subjects contained:[52]

I. Book One concerns the first that was created by God Most High, the seven layers of the heavens and the seven layers of the earth and what appertains to them.

46. Voorhoeve 1951, 360; Voorhoeve 1955, 154; Harun 2008. A few years later, Voorhoeve 1961, 482, however, rectified his earlier pronouncement, mentioning the Kuala Lumpur manuscript, and also drawing attention to the fact that Nūr al-Dīn regularly refers to Book III in the other Books of his *Bustān al-salāṭīn*. As Jelani Harun discovered in 1997, the unique manuscript is now also "lost," but a photocopy and microfilm are fortunately still available, see Harun 2008, xlv; Harun 2009, 46.

47. See e.g. Poerbatjaraka 1950, 100–2; Behrend 1990, 352–3.

48. Jones 1985, 46. A synopsis in Dutch is provided by Vreede 1892, 303–5; see furthermore Pigeaud 1968, 32 (under LOr. 1812).

49. Behrend 1990, 247–8; Voorhoeve 1961, 482. In the text itself, however, the title given is *Sirat al-Sulatin* (Way of Kings), see Jones 1985, 46.

50. Hooykaas 1937, 168.

51. Braginsky 2004, 451.

52. I follow Grinter 1979.

II. Book Two concerns the history of the prophets and apostles of God, relating some of their deeds from the time of the prophet of God Adam to our Prophet Muhammad (may God bless him and grant him peace); and relating some deeds of kings in former times including their affairs and reigns from the time of Sultan Kiyau Murti to the time of our lord his majesty Sultan Iskandar Thānī, the shadow of God upon the earth.

III. Book Three concerns the appointment of kings and their employees, including their duties; and the conduct of caliphs and just kings including their duties; and also the qualities required of wise viziers and their conduct.

IV. Book Four concerns the conduct of ascetic kings and the pious saints of God.

V. Book Five concerns the conduct of oppressive kings and unjust viziers who commit treason against their kings.

VI. Book Six concerns the conduct of magnanimous and noble, brave and gallant men.

VII. Book Seven concerns intellect and science and their excellence; the science of physiognomy, anatomy and medicine; and the conduct of women and relates some wonderful and strange stories.

Or to summarize in more succinct terms:[53]

I. Creation of Heaven and Earth (30 sections)

II. Prophets and Kings (13 sections)

III. Just Kings and Wise Ministers (6 sections)

IV. Ascetic Kings and Pious Saints (2 sections)

V. Unjust Kings and Oppressive Ministers (2 sections)

VI. Noble, Generous Persons and Brave Men (2 sections)

VII. Intellect and Various Sciences (5 sections)

The remaining parts of this article focus upon the second section of

53. Shiraishi 1990, 42–3; Harun 2004, 28–9.

Book VI, which deals in Saya Shiraishi's poetic rendering, with "Dashing and Daring Heroes."[54] This is indeed, more or less, how Nūr al-Dīn announced it in the introduction of the *Bustān al-salāṭīn*, viz. "Brave and Notable Persons."[55] However, the actual heading is more concrete: "Chapter Two concerns the excellence (*fadilat*) of holy war in the cause of God (*perang sabilillah*) and concerns the wars (*ghaza*) of the Prophet (may God bless him and grant him peace) and the wars of his Companions (may God be pleased with them), and concerns some of the battles (*perang*) of kings of former times including the orders given by them."[56] In manuscript Cod. Or. 1694 of Leiden University Library (hereafter abbreviated as BS), the structure is as follows:

1. The excellence of holy war (pp. 168–173).
2. The wars of the Prophet (pp. 174–341).
3. The wars of the Companions (pp. 341–346).
4. The wars of (Persian and Arab) kings from the remote past (pp. 346–465).

Nūr al-Dīn's discourse on war is much understudied, even in the works of recent researchers. For example, Jelani Harun merely relates that it is a section on bravery, providing role models for kings and court officials "to follow the examples of heroes of the past, particularly in protecting their religion, people and country."[57] According to Paul Wormser, Nūr al-Dīn wished to convey a rather nuanced message: while highlighting the merits of holy war, he also wanted kings to act carefully and patiently, seeking the advice of ministers and wise men before waging war, because armed conflict constituted a serious affair, engaging the life and prosperity of a great number of Muslims.[58]

Apparently, indigenous Malay readers were little impressed by Nūr al-Dīn's deliberations on war, because merely three manuscript copies of Book VI have come down to us, exclusively produced as reading matter for foreign Malayists, and kept in the Leiden University Library (in chronological order):

1. Cod. Or. 1973.

54. Shiraishi 1990, 43.

55. The Malay text reads "segala orang yang berani yang besar-besar," see Steenbrink 1993, 5; it seems that the conjunction *dan* (and) is missing after *berani* (brave). Although the word *orang* is gender-neutral, Nūr al-Dīn was probably only thinking of men.

56. Grinter 1979, 33

57. Harun 2004, 42.

58. Wormser 2012, 71.

2. Cod. Or. 1694.

3. Cod. Or. 1974.

Cod. Or. 1973 must be the oldest, but it is in a very poor condition due to ink corrosion and hence not available anymore for inspection. On the flyleaf there is a note in Javanese with the date 1150/1737, but this may be unrelated to the main text.[59] Although this manuscript is extant, it is now practically a closed book. Manuscript Cod. Or. 1694 is a copy made by a certain Ramli ibn 'Abd Allāh at the General Secretariat, the official Dutch Indies scriptorium, in Batavia (present-day Jakarta), who finished his work on Saturday, 25 July 1835.[60] He probably used (the now defunct) manuscript Cod. Or. 1973 as his *Vorlage*.[61] Finally, manuscript Cod. Or. 1974, which is dated 15 April 1843, is merely a copy of Cod. Or. 1694 and thus philologically irrelevant.[62]

All in all, this leaves us with only one single manuscript (Cod. Or. 1694), copied some two hundred years after the initial composition. The text is highly corrupt. For example, the third subsection contains a remarkable scribal error. Despite the announcement of covering the wars of the Companions, this subsection in fact merely tells a story about 'Abd Allāh, the son of 'Umar I, leading an expedition against the Magians or Zoroastrians (*kaum majusi*) in Persia in order to convert them. It is told that Persia is ruled by a queen who is "very beautiful" (*terlalu elok parasnya*) and "her religion is most holy" (*mahasuci agamanya*). The latter qualification is of course rather puzzling, because why should she be converted if that were the case? However, as the context makes clear, the original word must have been *majusi* (Magian), but the copyist was perhaps misled due to his subconscious association of religion with "most holy" (*mahasuci*).

Attempting to reconstruct Nūr al-Dīn's original text is one thing, but trying to recover his meaning is quite another. Even if we were to possess a reliable text edition (still a pious wish), the intentions of the author would still remain subject to speculation, mainly because of his "recourse to narrative as a device in his expository writing,"[63] giving, in principle, the reader "joint responsibility for the production of a meaning."[64] The moral of the story with 'Umar's son in Persia above could be a starting point. Should more be read into the phenomenon of a female ruler, because after the death of Nūr al-Dīn's patron Sultan Iskandar Thānī, in 1641, his widow, the daughter of

59. Wieringa 1998, 200.
60. Wieringa 1998, 35–7.
61. Voorhoeve 1955, 155.
62. Wieringa 1998, 203.
63. I owe this phrase to Riddell 2001, 226 who uses it in a completely different context.
64. Fish 1980, 3.

Iskandar Muda, ascended the throne as Sultana Tāj al-ʿĀlam Ṣafiyyat al-Dīn (r. 1641–1675)? Was this to the liking of such an orthodox theologian as Nūr al-Dīn? Does he reveal his thoughts on female rulership through a parable?

In the speculations surrounding his abrupt departure from Aceh in 1644, it has been suggested that one of the factors causing his fall from grace at court may have been his disapproval of Aceh's female ruler.[65] However, there is no evidence that Nūr al-Dīn was opposed to the appointment of Tāj al-ʿĀlam and recent historical research suggests that until 1643 the Sultana and Nūr al-Dīn enjoyed amicable relations.[66] It seems more likely that Nūr al-Dīn's time was up: Iskandar Thānī's unexpected death initiated a backlash against his harsh rule, and Nūr al-Dīn, who was the main catalyst driving the court's strict adherence to orthodoxy, narrowly escaped with his life from a vengeful mob.[67] In retrospect, Iskandar Thānī's rule was no more than a brief "foreign" interlude in Acehnese politics. Iskandar Thānī, a Malay prince from Pahang, had been a very unpopular foreign autocrat whose sudden death may have been caused by poisoning.[68] After his death, the Acehnese *orang kaya* (notables) concluded a secret pact never to allow a foreigner to rule Aceh again.[69] The bullying tactics of Iskandar Thānī's foreign right hand man Nūr al-Dīn against the local clerical establishment must have done little to endear the latter to the Acehnese elite. In light of this virulent nativist climate, continuation of support for Nūr al-Dīn was politically inopportune for Tāj al-ʿĀlam, who rather swiftly began "to reverse most of her late husband's policies and reverted to the policies of her late father, Iskandar Muda, instead."[70]

In his *Tibyān fī maʿrifat al-adyān* (Exposition in Understanding Religions), dedicated to Tāj al-ʿĀlam, Nūr al-Dīn still contemptuously called the adherents of the *wujūdiyya* "would-be mystics" (*yang bersufi-sufi*), and also stated that "they are cursed by God and His prophets and the angels with several curses,"[71] but, when in 1643, another doctrinal dispute on mysticism broke out, Nūr al-Dīn's downfall was just a matter of time. Eventually, in a majority decision at the court council, a Sumatran theologian was chosen to replace him as *Shaykh al-Islām*, and Nūr al-Dīn had to take his leave.[72]

Although Nūr al-Dīn may not have opposed the appointment of Sultana Tāj al-ʿĀlam, his aforementioned story on a Persian queen during the era

65. Daudy 1978, 17.
66. Khan 2012, 103–4.
67. Reid 1993, 183.
68. Khan 2012, 104.
69. Khan 2012, 104.
70. Khan 2012, 104.
71. Van Nieuwenhuijze 1945, 206, 201.
72. Khan 2012, 105.

of 'Umar I does not necessarily betray a view that is well-disposed towards female rulers. In fact, if one so wishes, the story on the fire-worshipping Persian queen could be summarized as "the only good queen is a dead queen." Upon 'Abd Allāh's arrival, she immediately complies with his wishes for surrender and adopts Islam. After uttering the Islamic profession of faith, she declares tearfully that now that she has finally embraced the right religion, God should better immediately take her life, so that she could not commit any more sins. She dies on the spot and 'Abd Allāh comments: "Never has a Persian woman been seen who was so utterly wise as this woman."[73] Nūr al-Dīn refrains from additional comment. Clearly, the primary moral of the story is that Islam is the only right religion to follow, but, as this anecdote is embedded in a mirror for princes, it is also noteworthy that the very first act of the newly converted queen should be her prompt "abdication."

This raises questions about the topicality of *Bustān al-salāṭīn* as a mirror for princes. Put differently, was Nūr al-Dīn concerned with the practicalities of statecraft? Restricting myself to the subject of war, to which the second chapter of Book VI is specifically devoted, the answer must be negative. In keeping with the Middle Eastern tradition of the genre, his text is largely of "dubious practical use,"[74] mainly referring to stories from the earliest times of Arabic Islamic history and pre-Islamic Persian kingdoms. The author does not devote a single word to the use of such new technology as cannons, which at least since the fifteenth century had entered the archipelago, nor does he discuss new techniques of warfare that were used by the bellicose European trading companies.[75] For example, in discussing the tactics of taking a fortress the attackers make use of a catapult, described as "stone slinger" (*ayunan pelontar batu*), whereas the defenders shoot arrows.[76] The "practical" use of the rather dated examples seems to be restricted to their inspirational character, according with traditional Southeast Asian conceptions of warfare which stressed individual bravery and the role of supernatural powers. According to the historian Anthony Reid, "Southeast Asians, and in particular Indonesians from Aceh to the Moluccas, had a considerable reputation for individual bravery if not for military discipline."[77] Furthermore, "Southeast Asian chronicles and inscriptions were concerned to magnify the grandeur and charisma of rulers, and they therefore tended to attribute victory to supernatural rather than technical factors."[78]

73. The Malay text reads, "Tiada kelihatan seorang perempuan daripada Ajam hamba terlalu bijaksana daripada perempuan itu." BS 345–6.

74. Van Gelder 2001, 332.

75. On developments in warfare in this period, see Reid 1988, 121–9.

76. BS 433.

77. Reid 1988, 124.

78. Reid 1988, 125.

Stylistically, the four subsections (see above) of Nūr al-Dīn's chapter on war are quite diverse. The rather short subsection on the excellence of holy war functions as the chapter's introduction, providing theological arguments by heaping citation upon citation from the Qur'an and *sunna* (sayings and deeds of the Prophet). The prescriptions concerning holy war are part of Islamic law and here the author follows the conventions of legal handbooks. The second subsection is devoted to the Prophet's wars, drawing mainly on Ibn Isḥāq's (d. 151/767) chronologically ordered biography. Nūr al-Dīn acts as a precise historian who is concerned with getting his facts right: for example, concerning the raid on Banū Qurayẓa (in 5/627) it is stated that "the number of Jews who were killed were about six hundred; according to one story seven hundred; according to one story eight hundred, and according to one story nine hundred Jews."[79] In the battle of Badr (in 2/624) the Islamic forces are supported by "about a thousand angels" (*kira-kira seribu banyaknya*) and ninety Muslim jinns (*sembilan puluh daripada jin Islam*).[80] The place al-Ghāba is said to be located "about two miles" (*kira-kira dua mil*) from Medina.[81]

Frequently punctuating his story with references to Qur'anic verses in Arabic with Malay translations, Nūr al-Dīn makes it clear that the wars of the Prophet are part of "sacred history" (*Heilsgeschichte*). Strictly speaking, however, the Malay renditions of sacred writ are not always accurate, but tend to be rather free, inserting certain specifications about the historical context. For example, at the end of the episode on the expedition to Khaybar (in 7/629) it is told that Qur'anic verses 48: 18–9 were revealed, which are translated as follows: "God knew what was right in the hearts of the Companions, and He provided them with determination of heart and blessed them, and He rewarded them with victory over Khaybar; and they got considerable booty from the Jews. God is All-knowing about the deeds of His slaves."[82] Neither Khaybar nor the Jews are mentioned in the Arabic original.

The second subsection is rather long, but Nūr al-Dīn informs his readers that he could easily have expanded it still more: "Furthermore, I will not

79. "Syahdan adalah sekalian Yahudi yang terbunuh itu kira-kira enam ratus, pada suatu riwayat tujuh ratus dan pada suatu riwayat delapan ratus dan pada suatu riwayat sembilan ratus Yahudi." BS 266.

80. BS 178.

81. BS 267. The word *mil* or *mel* is spelled m-y-l. As this word is of European derivation (Dutch *mijl* or English *mile*), one wonders when it first entered the Malay language.

82. "Ketahui Allah barang yang ada kebenaran dalam hati segala sahabat daripada hati mereka itu maka dianugerah Allah taala akan mereka ia tetapi [read: itu ketetapan?] hati mereka itu dan keridlaan mereka itu akan Tuhan mereka itu dan memenangkan Allah akan mereka itu mengalahkan Khaibar dan beberapa daripada rampasan diperoleh mereka itu daripada harta segala Yahudi. Bahwa adalah Allah taala amat mengetahui segala hal-ihwalnya dan segala hambaNya." BS 283.

completely discuss the wars of the Prophet (may God bless him and grant him peace), but will merely be brief, because if I would be complete, my account would certainly be too long. Therefore I now begin with something from the wars of the Companions and the wars of the kings of former times and their statecraft."[83] The subsequent third subsection, already discussed above, contains only a relatively short story set in the time of 'Umar I. While still following the historical style of the previous section and quoting an obscure authority as its source, it already follows the more legendary narrative style of the fourth and final subsection.[84] Nūr al-Dīn mentions "storytellers" (*sahibulhikayat* and *yang empunya cerita*) as sources for the accounts of kings from the remote past, duly emulating their narrative style.[85]

Remarkably enough, this final subsection opens with the story of the flight of the (seventh-century) Persian king Khusruw Parwīz in order to avoid a war.[86] This decidedly unheroic act must have posed a problem to the more attentive readers, because many pages previously, at the very outset of his chapter, Nūr al-Dīn in his role as interpreter of Islamic law had stipulated: "And it is forbidden for a Muslim to flee when he is confronted with an infidel."[87] What lesson, then, could be drawn from a story about a pre-Islamic fleeing king? Unfortunately, the manuscript copy is very corrupt, but the drift of the Persian king's defense seems to be that normally "fleeing from war is a disgrace for kings and army commanders,"[88] but in a hopeless situation this tactic constitutes a minor evil that in the end may prove to be more advantageous for the state. To this Nūr al-Dīn adds the opinion of the "sages" (*hukama*, from Arabic *ḥukamā'* "sages, wise men, the judicious, philosophers, doctors") who, if I understand the rather enigmatic (because highly corrupted) text correctly, advise to consult with knowledgeable persons about organizing the defense, and further warn against the risk of chaos if troops flee in all directions.[89]

The example of the behavior of Khusruw Parwīz, which merely takes up three pages in the manuscript (pp. 346–8), leaves more questions than answers. What happened to the chapter's main theme of bravery? What about

83. "Syahadan tiadalah fakir mengabiskan ghaza Nabi s.a.w. sekedar mengambil pendeknya jua, karena jika dihabis-habiskan, niscaya ia lanjutlah perkataannya. Maka dimulai fakir setengah daripada ghaza sahabat dan peperang<an> segala raja-raja yang dahulu kala dan perintah segala peperangan mereka itu." BS 341.

84. The source is said to be a certain 'Ata al-Qakra (?), BS 341.

85. For a list of the stories, see Wormser 2012, 276–9.

86. In the manuscript copy the name is garbled beyond recognition.

87. "Dan haram atas seorang Islam itu lari tatkala ia bertemu dengan orang kafir." BS 168.

88. "... adalah lari daripada perang itu aib pada segala raja-raja dan segala hulubalang. BS 347."

89. See also Wormser 2012, 171 for a discussion of this almost incomprehensible passage.

God's help for the faithful? Had the rather exhaustive previous subsection on the Prophet's warfare not amply demonstrated that Muslims could win, even if they were outnumbered, God willing of course? However, Nūr al-Dīn offers no further explanations and continues with the story of the (sixth-century) Sasanian king Anūshīrwān (pp. 348–52), who "did not move from his throne and did not waver in his heart"[90] when a furious elephant went fully berserk in his palace complex. Apparently, this time the implied lesson seems to be that a king needs to be steadfast and unafraid in the face of grave danger, thus presenting a great contrast to the previous story, but again Nūr al-Dīn refrains from comment.

If the stories have to speak for themselves, little constraints seem to be imposed upon their readers. However, Nūr al-Dīn does not advocate that kings should completely think for themselves. Time and again, he emphasizes the most important need for kings of consulting wise men. In his *exempla* of the behavior of former kings Nūr al-Dīn quotes profusely from the words of sages (*hukama*) who function as the author's mouthpiece and perform a role similar to the chorus in ancient Greek drama. Entirely in character for wise men, they regularly pronounce such proverbial wisdoms as "whoever tries to deceive another, will be deceived himself," comparable to "whoso diggeth a pit shall fall therein" (Proverbs 26: 27 in the King James rendition).[91] Another trope from wisdom literature is the use of *onomastica* or wisdom lists. For example, in a short digression on *bakti*, a Sanskrit loanword (*bhakti* "homage, love, worship"), which can be used in Malay in the political sense of "loyal, submissive, faithful," the pundits are said to have drawn up the following list of seven categories: (1) *bakti* towards one's parents, (2) reciprocal love in one's family, (3) loving one's place of birth, (4) being most reluctant to leave one's place of origin, (5) loving one's youthful years (?), only doing wise things, (6) wearing ugly clothes, and (7) being content with one's condition.[92]

However, rather than dwelling on concrete examples of political wisdom as prescribed by the sages, Nūr al-Dīn constantly hammers at the idea

90. "(Kalakian maka Raja Nusyirwan pun) tiada bergerak daripada tempatnya semayam itu dan tiada berubah-ubah hatinya dan tetap." BS 351.

91. "Barang siapa mencari suatu tipuan dia akan seseorang maka berpalinglah tipu dianya itu kepada dirinya jua." BS 376.

92. "Pertama berbuat bakti kepada ibu-bapanya. Kedua berkasih-kasihan dengan keluarganya. Ketiga mengasihi negeri tempat jadinya. Keempat sangat keluh-kesahnya sebab meninggalkan negeri kejadiannya. Kelima sayang akan muda[h]nya tiada berbuat kebajikan. Keenam memakai kain yang buruk. Ketujuh sabar pada halnya." BS 374. For the fifth category I have followed the emendation by Arief (1989): "Kelima saying akan masa mudanya tiada berbuat melainkan kebajikan." On the development of the Sanskrit loanword *bhakti* in Malay, see Gonda 1973, 538–9.

that kings should always lend their ear to the sages and then act accordingly. As he puts it: "Whoever does not listen to advice will help his enemy."[93] In the story about the Umayyad caliph al-Walīd (r. 705–715), he cites from a "chronicle" (*kitab tawarikh*) to give the following advice (*nasihat*): "Likewise when kings run into difficulties in their profession they should consult with people who are handpicked and wise. In the deliberations the king should choose what would bring him benefit. In the deliberations he should be patient and steadfast, while entrusting himself to God the Most High in order to receive good fortune in this world and the next."[94] For the trust in God Nūr al-Dīn adduces Qur'an 3: 159, "when thou art resolved, then put thy trust in God" (Pickthall). Another wisdom list enumerates five signs for the fall of a kingdom: (1) entrusting the kingdom to a worthless person, whose rule is a disgrace, (2) doing wrong to ones who are loyal, (3) failing to consult with one's troops, (4) equivocation and following one's passions (*hawa nafsu*), and (5) assembling "heedless" (*ghāfil*) people in order to ask their advice.[95] The underlying fault of these five emblems is ruling foolishly, i.e. ignoring the good advice of prudent men, and thus losing the kingdom.

Needless to say perhaps, the ruler's advisers should be Muslims, because, "as the sages have said" (*kata segala hukama*): "Don't put hope in consulting infidels."[96] The sages (and hence their alter ego Nūr al-Dīn) moreover dismiss women as possible advisers: "*akal* (reason, from Arabic *'aql*) can be compared to a man and *nafsu* (lower instincts, from Arabic *nafs*) can be compared to a woman who is his wife."[97] Following one's lower instincts would be fatal for a king: again according to the sages, "*Nafsu* acts as an army using force against reason with the result that all right words are eclipsed."[98] The great

93. "Barang siapa tiada mendengarkan nasihat bahwasanya ialah menolongi saterunya." BS 404.

94. "Sebagai lagi segala raja-raja apabila datang kepada suatu kesukaran daripada pekerjaannya maka hendaklah ia musyawarat dengan segala orang yang pilihan lagi bijaksana. Maka dipilihnya daripada segala bicara itu yang ada memberi manfaat akan dia. Hendaklah ia sabar lagi tetap di dalam bicaranya itu serta dengan menyerahkan dirinya kepada Allah taala supaya diperolehnya bagi [read: bahagia?] di dalam dunia dan akhirat." BS 380–1.

95. "Pertama menyerahkan kerajaannya pada orang yang hina yang tida membicarakan akan aib pekerjaannya. Kedua menyakiti orang yang mengashi dia. Ketiga melarang musyawarat akan segala lasykarnya. Keempat mengubahkan niatnya dan mengikut hawanafsunya. Kelima menghimpunkan segala orang yang gapil yang member nasihat akan dia." BS 403–4.

96. "Tiada dapat diharap bicara segala kafir." BS 398.

97. "Akal itu upama laki-laki dan nafsu itu upama perempuan akan jadi isterinya." BS 436. This fragment is also discussed in Wormser 2012, 191

98. "Hawa nafsu itu suatu tentara yang mengerasi akal maka tertutuplah segala perkataan yang benar." BS 401.

danger posed by *nafsu* is reiterated in many variants: for example, it is "like fire, when flaring up, difficult to extinguish,"[99] or "like water, when massive, difficult to keep back."[100] The untrustworthiness of *nafsu* is also due to its intrinsic fickleness: "It is the nature of *nafsu* to want to keep on changing."[101] In this respect, *nafsu* resembles "the deeds of a woman who does not obey her husband's commands."[102] In yet another aside, Nūr al-Dīn combines the leitmotifs of foolish kings who (1) are immune to advice and (2) obey their lusts and desires (*nafsu*), by citing the sages that "the most evil men are of two kinds: firstly, kings who rule without the consent of learned men; secondly, lascivious old men."[103]

Intriguingly, Nūr al-Dīn shows himself here as a precursor of religious thinking in Aceh. As the anthropologist James Siegel has shown in his classic study of Aceh in the nineteenth and twentieth centuries, the key themes of *akal* or rationality and (*hawa*) *nafsu* or instinctive nature are firmly entrenched as key themes in Acehnese discourse.[104] However, the sexist and misogynist view that ranks woman below man, equating men with common sense and women with irrationality, which is in keeping with traditional Islamic views,[105] can be regarded as yet another example of the very theoretical, pedantic nature of Nūr al-Dīn's mirror for princes. As we have seen (above), it was on Nūr al-Dīn's watch that a sultana was appointed to rule in Aceh.

It would be wrong to conclude that Nūr al-Dīn's constant reiteration of the role of wise men in politics, while offering little to no practical thoughts on statecraft and administration, is somehow a gratuitous advice. There is more to it than the simple lesson that kings should think carefully about the possible results or consequences before doing something, and that "he that walketh with wise men shall be wise, but a companion of fools shall be destroyed" (Proverbs 13: 20). In accordance with the Persian and Arab models that Nūr al-Dīn hoped to emulate, "practical," as Geert Jan van Gelder

99. "Bahwa hawa nafsu itu upama api, apabila nyala ia niscaya sukarlah memadami dia." BS 412.

100. "Bahwasanya nafsu it seperti air, apabila besarlah ia maka sukarlah menahani dia." BS 412.

101. "Adat nafsu itu menghendaki berpindah-pindah jua daripada suatu hal." BS 437.

102. "... seperti perbuatan perempuan yang tiada menurut kata suaminya." BS 437.

103. "Seperti kata hukama bahwa yang sejahat-jahat manusia itu dua orang: pertama segala raja-raja yang mengerjakan yang tiada muafakat dengan segala orang yang budiman; kedua [segala orang] segala orang tuha berahi." BS 418.

104. Siegel 1969.

105. Incidentally, this is a thought which still finds its adherents in the twenty-first century. For example, in a Saudi Arabian publication on women in Islam its author can write that "[t]he woman is controlled more by her emotions than by reason," but he is not viewing this as something negative, because "this is obviously an asset in the home," see Hasan 2004, 27.

explains, does not mean here "particularly relevant for the addressee."[106] Far from being of direct use for supreme commanders, Nūr al-Dīn's Book on War has a homiletic nature, preaching a sermon about the qualities and virtues desired in rulers. Rather than with the actual practice of statecraft, Nūr al-Dīn is concerned with political ethics.

As Erik Ohlander suggests, "the medieval Islamic *Fürstenspiegel* were composed at a time of major crisis, a period characterized by intense competition between powerful regional dynasties for public recognition of their self-perceived role as guarantors of proper, right, and universal justice as expressed in the creation, maintenance, and perpetuation of a perfect (Islamic) state – a state which ensures first and foremost that its citizens achieve prosperity in both this world and the next."[107] Nūr al-Dīn's mirror for princes, too, was written at a critical juncture in Acehnese politics, when a foreign-born ruler wanted to change the course of his predecessor Iskandar Muda, whom historians regard as "the greatest of Aceh's rulers."[108]

Ohlander's suggestion that medieval Islamic *Fürstenspiegel* may be interpreted as "a larger meta-critique of contemporary problems,"[109] would also seem to apply to *Bustān al-salāṭīn*. It may be argued that Nūr al-Dīn, the foreign missionary, was not content with Acehnese society in which he found himself, and hence attempted to Islamize it in accordance with his Arabophile templates. However, he stopped short of criticizing the ruling sultan, who was his powerful patron, making it rather difficult in Nūr al-Dīn's case to imagine Ohlander's argument, which is also being made in several contributions to this volume, namely that mirrors for princes were often intended to provide a searching critique of contemporaneous kingship. Although the non-Acehnese Sultan Iskandar Thānī was disliked by the Acehnese grandees, who probably perceived him as a tyrant, Nūr al-Dīn was a faithful and loyal *Shaykh al-Islām,* who knew that he completely owed his position to the sultan. Hardly popular himself, he could not risk the loss of royal favor. Moreover, his position as the chief clerical authority made him into a co-wielder of executive power, working in tandem with the sultan.

In fact, Nūr al-Dīn must have been thrilled by a sultan whom Reid describes as a "pillar of orthodoxy."[110] This was a devout man who had "executed some scores of Portuguese who did not accept Islam in 1637, who excluded Chinese traders from Aceh because for them 'pigs are a must' ..., and who abolished the age-old practice of trial by ordeal in favour of

106. Van Gelder 2001, 336.
107. Ohlander 2009, 240.
108. Ricklefs 2001, 38.
109. Ohlander 2009, 246.
110. Reid 1993, 183.

witnesses, as prescribed in the shari'a."[111] Nūr al-Dīn bolstered the idea of the king as *Fidei Defensor* or Defender of the Faith: in his *Bustān al-salāṭīn* he faithfully followed the overarching theme of the "Just Ruler" of medieval Islamic mirrors for princes who enacted justice and ensured salvation.[112] In an explicit advice (*nasihat*) he urges kings "to uphold Islamic law like prayer, fasting and giving alms or other things like that."[113] To support this injunction he cites Qur'an 22: 40, based on the reciprocal principle of *do ut des*: "Verily God helpeth one who helpeth Him." However, he also reminds kings of the next verse, in which God gives the following command (according to the Malay rendition): "We have established kings in the land in order to make them pray and pay alms and we ordered them to let people do right things and forbid iniquity. And to God everything will be returned."[114]

It seems to have been Sultan Iskandar Thānī's wish to have a majestic mirror for princes that would glorify and legitimize his leadership.[115] Nūr al-Dīn complied all too happily while pursuing, at the same time, an agenda of his own. By constantly reiterating the claim that "the wise" are the sole arbiters of legitimate rulership, he advanced a potent argument in favor of his own position. If anything, *Bustān al-salāṭīn* as a gigantic "omnium-gatherum"[116] testified that its learned compiler not only belonged to the intellectual pantheon, but was a scholar's scholar and a sage's sage himself. Read in this way, the sultan was - at least in Nūr al-Dīn's proposed theory - perhaps even more dependent on his chief adviser than the other way around.

Ironically, it was under a woman's rule that Nūr al-Dīn learned a lesson in harsh *realpolitik*, namely that political theory and practice are not the same. It must have been particularly bitter for this self-appointed sage's sage to be dismissed by a woman sovereign, considering the fact that in his *Bustān al-salāṭīn*, in Chapter 4 of Book VII, specifically dedicated to the topic of women, he had cited the Prophetic saying (on the authority of Mu'ādh b. Jabal, d. 18/639) that "when God the Most High created reason (*akal*), He distanced women from it, and when he created stupidity, He drew them near."[117] But then, this too, may have been a simple comforting afterthought.

111. Reid 1993, 182–3.

112. Ohlander 2009, 237. The theme of justice is highlighted by Harun 2004.

113. "... mengerjakan hukum syarak seperti sembahyang dan puasa dan member zakat atau barang sebagainya." BS 416–7.

114. "Segala raja-raja yang kami tetapkan dalam bumi dikerjakan mereka itu sembahyang dan memberi mereka itu zakat dan <di>suruhkan mereka itu orang berbuat kebajikan dan ditegahkan mereka itu orang yang berbuat kejahatan. Bahagi Allah kembali segala pekerjaan itu." BS 417.

115. Cf. Wormser 2012, 208 on the possible reasons for its composition.

116. I owe the term to Van Gelder 2001, 337. The Malay copyist of Leiden Cod. Or. 1694 entitled it an "anthology of stories" (*Hikayat Bunga Rampai*), see Wieringa 1998, 37.

117. Cited in Wormser 2012, 191.

Bibliography

Manuscripts

Manuscript Cod. Or. 1694, Leiden University Library.
Manuscript Cod. Or. 1973, Leiden University Library.
Manuscript Cod. Or. 1974, Leiden University Library.
Manuscript UM 41, University Malaya, Kuala Lumpur.

Printed Works

Arief, Abdus Salam (1989), *Bustanus-Salatin Bab VI, fasal 2*, Yogyakarta.

Behrend, T. E. (1990), *Katalog induk naskah-naskah Nusantara jilid 1: Museum Sonobudoyo Yogyakarta*, Jakarta.

Braginsky, V. (2004), *The heritage of traditional Malay literature. A historical survey of genres, writings and literary views*, Leiden.

Bray, J. (2010), "Al-Tha'alibi's *Adab al-muluk*, a Local Mirror for Princes," in: Y. Suleiman (ed.), *Living Islamic History: Studies in Honour of Professor Carole Hillenbrand*, Edinburgh, 32–46.

Crone, P. (1987), "Did al-Ghazālī write a mirror for princes? On the authorship of *Naṣīḥat al-mulūk*," *Jerusalem Studies in Arabic and Islam* 10: 167–91.

Daudy, A. (1978), *Syeikh Nuruddin ar-Raniry: Sejarah, karya, dan sanggahan terhadap wujudiyyah di Aceh*, Jakarta.

Dipodjojo, A. S. and Endang Daruni Asdi (1999), *Taju'ssalatin Bukhari al-Jauhari. Naskah lengkap dalam huruf Melayu-Arab beserta alih hurufnya dalam huruf Latin*, Yogyakarta.

Drewes, G. W. J. (1955), "De herkomst van Nuruddin ar-Raniri," *Bijdragen tot de Taal- Land- en Volkenkunde* 111: 137–51.

—— (1986), "Nūr al-Dīn al-Rānīrī's charge of heresy against Hamzah and Shamsuddin from an international point of view," in: C. D. Grijns and S. O. Robson (eds.), *Cultural contact and textual interpretation*, Dordrecht, 54–9.

Fish, S. (1980), *Is there a text in this class? The authority of interpretive communities*, Cambridge (Mass.) and London.

Florida, Nancy K. (2000), *Javanese literature in Surakarta manuscripts. Volume 2: Manuscripts of the Mangkunagaran palace*, New York.

Gonda, J. (1973), *Sanskrit in Indonesia*, New Delhi.

Grinter, C. A. (1979), *Book IV of the Bustan Us-Salatin by Nuruddin ar-Raniri: A study from the manuscripts of a 17th century Malay work written in North Sumatra*, London.

Harun, J. (2004), "*Bustan al-Salatin*, 'The Garden of Kings': A universal his-

tory and *adab* work from seventeenth-century Aceh," *Indonesia and the Malay World* 32: 21–52.
—— (2008), *Bustan al-Salatin (Bab ketiga). Kisah raja-raja yang adil*, Kuala Lumpur.
—— (2009), *Bustan al-Salatin. A Malay Mirror for Rulers*, Pulau Pinang.
Hasan, A. G. (2004), *Women in Islam*, Riyadh.
Hooykaas, C. (1947), *Over Maleische literatuur*, Leiden.
Iskandar, T. (1966), *Bustanu's-Salatin bab II, fasal 13*, Kuala Lumpur.
Jones, R. (1985), *Hikayat Sultan Ibrahim ibn Adham. An edition of an anonymous Malay text with translation and notes*, Berkeley.
Khan, S. B. A. L. (2012), "What happened to Sayf al-Rijal?," *Bijdragen tot de Taal-, Land- en Volkenkunde* 168: 100–11.
Marlow, L. (2007), "Advice and advice literature," in: *EI*[3] 2007–1: 34–58.
—— (2009), "Surveying recent literature on the Arabic and Persian Mirrors for Princes genre," *History Compass* 2007–1: 523–38.
Niemann, G. K. (1907), *Bloemlezing uit Maleische geschriften. Tweede stuk*, 's-Gravenhage.
Nasir, M. N. M. (2010), "Presence of God according to Haqq al-Yaqīn, a seventeenth-century treatise by Shaykh Shams al-Dīn al-Sumatra'ī (d. 1630)," *Journal of Islamic Studies* 21: 213–34.
Ohlander, E. (2009), "Enacting justice, ensuring salvation: The trope of the 'Just Ruler' in some medieval Islamic mirrors," *Muslim World* 99: 237–52.
Peacock, A. C. S. (2007), *Mediaeval Islamic historiography and political legitimacy. Bal'amī's Tārīkhnāma*, London.
Pickthall, M. M. (1953), *The meaning of the glorious Koran. An explanatory translation*, New York.
Pigeaud, Th. G. Th. (1968), *Literature of Java. Catalogue raisonné of Javanese manuscripts in the Library of the University of Leiden and other public collections in The Netherlands. Volume II*, The Hague.
Poerbatjaraka, R. M. Ng. (1950), *Indonesische handschriften*, Bandung.
Reid, A. (1988), *Southeast Asia in the age of commerce 1450–1680. Volume One, The lands below the winds*, New Haven and London.
—— (1993), *Southeast Asia in the age of commerce 1450–1680. Volume Two, Expansion and crisis*, New Haven and London.
Ricklefs, M. C. (2001), *A history of modern Indonesia since c. 1200*, Houndmills.
Riddell, P. (2001), *Islam and the Malay-Indonesian world. Transmission and responses*, London.
—— (2003), "Ar-Raniri, Nur ud-Din (d. 1658)," in: N. K. Singh and A. Samiuddin (eds.), *Encyclopaedic historiography of the Muslim world*, Delhi, 817–8.

Roolvink, R. (1975), *Bahasa Jawi. De taal van Sumatra*, Leiden.
Shirasihi, S. (1990), "A study of Bustanu's-Salatin (The Garden of Kings)," in: G. Kahin (ed.), *Reading Southeast Asia*, New York, 41–55.
Siegel, J. T. (1969), *The rope of God*, Berkeley and Los Angeles.
Steenbrink, K. (1993), *The Bustanus Salatin by Nuruddin ar-Raniri*, Montreal.
Takeshi, I. (1984), *The world of the Adat Aceh: A historical study of the Sultanate of Aceh*, Canberra.
Van Bruinessen, M. (1998), "Studies of Sufism and the Sufi orders in Indonesia," *Die Welt des Islams* 38: 192–219.
Van Gelder, G. J. (2001), "Mirror for princes or vizor for viziers: the twelfth century Arabic popular enyclopedia *Mufīd al-'ulūm* and its relationship with the anonymous Persian *Baḥr al-fawā'id*," *Bulletin of the School of Oriental and African Studies* 64: 313–38.
Van Nieuwenhuijze, C. A. O. (1945), *Šamsu'l-dīn van Pasai. Bijdrage tot de kennis der Sumatraansche mystiek*, Leiden.
Voorhoeve, P. (1951), "Van en over Nūruddīn Ar-Rānīrī," *Bijdragen tot de Taal- Land- en Volkenkunde* 107: 353–68.
—— (1955), "Lijst der geschriften van Rānīrī en apparatus criticus bij de tekst van twee verhandelingen," *Bijdragen tot de Taal- Land- en Volkenkunde* 111: 152–61.
—— (1959), "Nūruddīn ar-Rānīrī," *Bijdragen tot de Taal- Land- en Volkenkunde* 115: 90–1.
—— (1961), "Supplement op de lijst der geschriften van Rānīrī,"*Bijdragen tot de Taal- Land- en Volkenkunde* 117: 481–2.
Vreede, A. C. (1892), *Catalogus van de Javaansche en Madoereesche handschriften der Leidsche Universiteits-Bibliotheek*, Leiden.
Wieringa, E. P. (1998), *Catalogue of Malay and Minangkabau manuscripts in the Library of Leiden University and other collections in The Netherlands. Volume One, comprising the acquisitions of Malay manuscripts in Leiden University Library up to the year 1896*, Leiden.
—— (2005), "Punning in Hamzah Pansuri's poetry," in: Th. Bauer and U. Stehli-Werbeck (eds.), *Alltagsleben und materielle Kultur in der arabischen Sprache und Literatur. Festschrift für Heinz Grotzfeld*, Wiesbaden, 391–8.
—— (2011), "Ein malaiischer *Codex unicus* der Geschichte von Sayf al-Mulūk (BSB München Cod. Malai. 2)," in: U. Marzolph (ed.), *Orientalistische Studien zu Sprache und Literatur. Festgabe zum 65. Geburtstag von Werner Diem*, Wiesbaden, 357–82.
Wormser, P. (2012), *Le Bustan al-Salatin de Nuruddin ar-Raniri. Réflexions sur le rôle culture d'un étranger dans le monde malais au XVIIe siècle*, Paris.

A Proposal for the Classification of Political Literature in Arabic and Persian

Folk Narrative as a Source of Political Thought?

Mohsen Zakeri

MY MAIN GOAL HERE is to present *Samak-i ʿAyyār*, a medieval Persian popular romance written in 585/1189, as a sample for yet another heretofore unconsidered category of the so-called mirrors for princes (henceforth: Mirrors). It is a preposterous proposition, of course, for it opens a Pandora's Box of not easily answerable questions. Should we treat all Persian "popular romances" as Mirrors? Is *Amīr Arsalān Rūmī* (written shortly before 1305/1887–88), or *Ḥamzanāma* (composed at an unknown date), a Mirror? Surely, each individual title should be evaluated on its own terms. The *Alexander Romance*, a comparable case, is certainly a good example for a Mirror and it has been received as such.[1] To contextualize this proposal within the setting of political literature, it is better, I think, to start with a review of what a mirror for princes is or can be, in which forms it has emerged, and where it is located within the plethora of political literature.

In recent times, Arab scholars familiar with European literatures have coined the expression *mir'āt/marāyā al-umarā'* for Mirrors for Princes, or *Fürstenspiegel*,[2] even though Arabic has known this branch of literature under a dozen more or less technical terms from earlier centuries. The use of the metaphor of "mirror" appears in the title of a few medieval Arabic books such as in Sibṭ b. al-Jawzī's (d. 654/1256) book of history entitled *Mir'āt al-zamān* (The Mirror of Times), or al-Yāfiʿī's (d. 768/1367) biographic-historical dictionary *Mir'āt al-janān* (Mirror of the Soul). However, I know only of two occasions where "mirror" is used for a manual of gnomic advice addressed to rulers: two works with the title *Mir'āt al-muruwwāt* (Mirrors of Manly Virtues), one by Abū Manṣūr al-Thaʿālibī (d. 429/1037) and the other by Ibn Jaʿdawayh al-Qazwīnī, who dedicated his work to the Saljuq vizier

1. Cf. Venetis 2006.

2. One such example is Damaj 1994. This is an Arabic translation of the *Qābūsnāma* based on R. Levy's English version which is called *A Mirror for Princes* (Levy 1951).

Niẓām al-Mulk (d. 485/1092).[3] Persian on the other hand knows the use of *āyīn*, a word closely related to *āyena* (mirror) as title of pamphlets of political guidance, appropriate manners, and description of court decorum from pre-Islamic times. A celebrated example is the *Āyīnnāma* (Book of Manners) translated by Ibn al-Muqaffa' (d. ca. 139/756). Partial contents of several lost *āyīn-nāmas* have been reconstructed and are available to us now.[4] Whether this branch of Middle Persian literature, which became widespread in Arabic as books of *ā'īn*, *rusūm*, *qawānīn*, *ādāb*, etc. and some of which – through Hebrew and Spanish translations – reached Europe from the tenth century onwards, has had an impact on the use of *speculum* in Latin literature remains to be investigated.[5]

As in the West where the diversity of forms and contents of the Mirrors for Princes has been acknowledged, popularity of political instruction in the Muslim world has also given rise to diverse forms and ideas. Classical writing on political thought in the genre of Mirrors in Persian and Arabic is indeed impressive; it is profuse and multifaceted such that identification and classification of this literature has proved to be a formidable task for the scholars who have tried to tackle it. Louise Marlow is right when she says: "The extension of the term 'mirror for princes' points to the extremely widespread production throughout the pre-modern era of literary works that offered advice to rulers; it is the function rather than the form of the literature that elicits the label."[6] However, this is again a fine distinction easier to formulate than follow in practice. Among others, it causes the legitimate question of what are the forms that have shaped this literature. Contrary to expectation, it still remains an urgent question as to what a Mirror in the area of Arabic and Persian literatures really is.

We have neither a working definition of the Mirror nor any book of reference to outline its parameters. All we have is a few bibliographical surveys of Arabic and Persian works on political thought which include Mirrors for Princes, especially by Mīkhā'īl 'Awwād,[7] Muḥammad Taqī Dānishpazhūh,[8] and Naṣr Muḥammad 'Ārif.[9] A conspicuous factor in these and other similar listings is that neither a definition of *Fürstenspiegel* is offered nor any criteria for inclusion or exclusion of texts have been outlined. The inventories

3. Ed. al-Ḥusayn 2004.
4. Muḥammadī 1338 sh/1959; Muḥammadī 1964.
5. Steele 1920, Introduction, especially p. x-xi, xl, lii.
6. Marlow 2009, 524.
7. In: al-Ṣābī 1383/1964, 48–63 (lists some 200 titles).
8. Dānishpazhūh 1339sh/1961, 211–27 (lists 164 titles); Dānishpazhūh 1988, 213–39.
9. 'Ārif 1994 (lists 307 titles up to the twentieth century).

by these authors present only a potpourri of all the sources that have one way or another to do with political theory and administration. ʿAwwād for example introduces books on the vizierate (administrative history) next to al-Māwardī's (d. 450/1058) *Aḥkām al-sulṭāniyya* (juristic; on constitutional law), al-Qalqashandī's (d. 820/1418) *Ṣubḥ al-aʿshā* (an encyclopedic administration guide addressed to professional bureaucrats), as well as the Arabic translation of Aristotle's *Politics.* To be sure, in all these books, one may find references of relevance to the demeanor of the king in different life situations or to political history, but few of them are Mirrors.

I define a Mirror with reservations thus: A manual of proper political and social conduct composed with an intention to exhort, addressed to a current ruler, prince, or administrative official (fictive or real) whom the author has in some way tutored or guided, or by an aging ruler to his son; using a variety of literary forms, it discusses the ruler's duties in administering state affairs and protecting his subjects, his practice of warfare, kingship and government, advices him how to choose his officials as well as his friends and women consorts, and describes his religious obligations, need for self-control, and function as a role model for his subjects.

Moral and political advice prescribed for the caliphs, princes, or magistrates in literary form is documented from the beginnings of the Umayyad period (41–132/661–750). The tradition continues from thereon steadily all the way to the early twentieth century. Abū Ṭālib Bihbahānī's Persian *Minhāj al-ʿulā* (The Path of Sublimity: A Treatise on the Rule of Law), written in 1875 and addressed to the Qājār monarch Nāṣir al-Dīn Shāh (d. 1896) is a good example of a late mirror for princes with all the characteristics of the classical genre, but with visibly modern features.[10] Next to the sententious sayings of ancient kings such as Alexander, Anūshirwān, and of early Muslim sages, we have references to the deeds of Napoleon, Charles I, Peter the Great, and other celebrated rulers. The author is still wary of abandoning the established tradition and takes recourse in the formula known in Middle Persian literature as the "circle of justice," this time on the authority of Aristotle (Bihbahānī has taken this notion from Ibn Khaldūn [d. 808/1406], whose *Muqaddima* is one of his sources).[11]

By following the example of the above mentioned scholars, I have succeeded without much difficulty to identify over a thousand books (these are published works, manuscripts, and bare titles) of direct political contents and interest for political thought and institutions in Arabic and Persian

10. Ed. Tehran 1389sh/2010.

11. See Bihbahānī, *Minhāj*, 87. On the circle of justice, see Darling 2007; a Pahlavi version of the circle of justice can be found in the *Dinkard*, ed. Fazilat 2005, nr. 134.

from the early days of Islam to the nineteenth century.[12] Alone for the period from the fall of Baghdad to the Mongols in 656/1258, which put an end to the Abbasid Caliphate, to the fall of Constantinople to the Ottomans in 857/1453, I have noted some 200 Persian and Arabic books on political principles, the art of government, and mirrors for princes (the collection is still growing). Only about one-third of these are listed by Naṣr ʿĀrif, whose focus was on Arabic sources. Many of these texts remain still in manuscript form. Geographically this literature spreads from India to Anatolia and from Central Asia to Spain. Historically they witness monumental political and cultural changes in the Muslim world.

Given the lack of an established generic term for Mirrors for Princes in Arabic and Persian, a typology and classification of this literature is called for. I have grouped the collected titles provisionally in six categories: 1. political philosophy; 2. political and administrative history; 3. juristic or constitutional traditions of politics; 4. anthologies of *adab* material and encyclopedias; 5. socio-political treatises; and 6. mirrors for princes. The criteria used for determining the categories of this classification will be given briefly under each rubric.

1. Political Philosophy

Books translated primarily from classical Greek (Aristotle, Plato, Themistius, etc.) and the Muslim works which discussed these or evolved out of them, such as those by al-Kindī (d. 259/873), al-Sarakhsī (d. 285/899), al-Fārābī (d. 339/950–1), al-ʿĀmirī (d. 381/992), the Ikhwān al-Ṣafāʾ (active probably sometime between 328/940 and 348/960), Ibn Sīnā (d. 428/1037), Ibn Bājja (d. 532/1138), Ibn Rushd (d. 595/1198), Ibn Ṭufayl (d. 580/1185), etc. Being philosophical speculations, these are more of a theoretical nature and their impact on actual contemporary politics could not have been all that significant. Greek contribution in the field of Mirrors for Princes is negligible.[13] In contrast to their neighbors, Greeks of the classical era had generally shunned the institution of kingship, and organized themselves according to various kinds of collective government. In fact the idea of divine kingship itself seems to have arrived in Greece in the Hellenistic period as Oriental influence.[14]

12. The collected titles, a brief synopsis of their contents, and the whereabouts of the available manuscripts and publications will be provided as an Appendix to a monograph I am preparing on the early mirrors for princes.

13. See the contribution by Matthias Haake in the present volume.

14. Cf. McEwan 1934.

2. Political and Administrative History

Books which concentrate on the political history of the caliphate and its administrative institutions such as Ibn Abī Ṭāhir's (d. 280/893) *Ta'rīkh Baghdād* (History of Baghdad, contains also Ṭāhir b. al-Ḥusayn's [d. 207/822] *'Ahdnāma*, A Political Testament to his son 'Abd Allāh), al-Dīnawarī's (d. between 281/894 and 290/903) *Akhbār al-ṭiwāl*, al-Jahshiyārī's (d. 330/942) *Kitāb al-Wuzarā'* (On the History of the Vizierate), Ibn Ṭiqṭaqā's (wr. 701/1302) *al-Fakhrī fī ādāb al-sulṭāniyya* (On the System of Government). Some sections of these books could be regarded as Mirrors. *Al-Fakhrī* for example is arranged into two distinct parts. It starts with a preamble on praise of knowledge and wisdom with focus on political concerns, moral values, and the best way for a king to carry out official affairs and his private life. The second part is a narrative of the Islamic history from the beginning to the fall of Baghdad to the Mongols in 656/1258. The author's attention is focused here on ministers of the caliphs rather than themselves. He presents his ideas on each issue first and then elucidates them by means of historical examples.

To this class belong numerous handbooks pertinent to administrative organs, financial institutions, or profession of law such as *Kitāb al-Kharāj* (On Taxes), *Kitāb al-Amwāl* (On Finances), *Kitāb al-Ḥisba* (On the Supervision of Market Activity), as well as *Adab al-qāḍī* or *Aḥkām al-quḍāt* (On Rules and Regulations for Judges). One of the long chapters of Qudāma b. Ja'far's (d. 337/948) *Kitāb al-Kharāj*[15] deals with the duties of the king and his entourage towards the subjects. This chapter consists of twelve sections and is presented in the best manner of the Mirrors: Persian kings and viziers, Alexander and Aristotle as well as early Muslim saints and politicians are presented as model rulers and advisors.

3. Juristic or Constitutional Traditions of Politics (*al-fiqh al-dastūrī*)

Articulations on politics based on legal and religious discourse to be called *sharī'atnāma* (Shar'ī Governance), a classical example of which is al-Māwardī's *al-Aḥkām al-sulṭāniyya* (Ordinances of Government). This is the first comprehensive legal theory of Islamic politics. The author details the dictates of the *sharī'a* in the best tradition of Muslim jurists (who discuss the rights and duties of the Caliph in accordance with the *sharī'a*, the sacred law to which his authority is theoretically subordinated, in a more idealized Islamic state).

15. Qudāma b. Ja'far, *Kitāb al-Kharāj*, 425–85.

Theorization about the nature and function of the caliph begins at a time when the caliphate as an institution had for the most part lost its entire former glance. Al-Māwardī's work is followed immediately by Abū Ya'lā al-Farrā''s (d. 458/1066) book of the same title, Imām al-Ḥaramayn al-Juwaynī's (d. 478/1085) *Ghiyāth al-umam fī l-tiyāth al-ẓulam* (The Savior of Nations and Removal of Darkness), Ibn Taymiyya's (d. 728/1328) *al-Siyāsa al-shar'iyya*, and a host of others.

Shī'ī juristic expositions on the Imamate, the political doctrines of the Khawārij, as well as discussions by Mu'tazilite theologians on the reasons for the need of political leadership may form subsections of this group, or even separate categories.

4. Anthologies of *adab* Material and Encyclopedias

General anthological collections of entertaining and pedagogical contents with substantial chapters pertaining to the sultan and his retinue: examples are Ibn Qutayba's (d. 276/885) *'Uyūn al-akhbār*, Ibn 'Abd Rabbih's (d. 328/940) *al-'Iqd al-farīd*,[16] al-Ābī's (d. 421/1030) *Nathr al-durr*, Ibn Ḥamdūn's (d. 1316 /1898) *al-Tadhkira al-Ḥamdūniyya*, 'Awfī's (d. 640/1242) Persian *Jawāmi' al-ḥikāyāt*, a substantial number of Abū Manṣūr al-Tha'ālibī's (d. 429/1037) impressive literary production, and many others.

The delineation between *adab* (belles-lettres) and *Fürstenspiegel* is fluid and never clearly defined, though *adab* is in general more inclusive, so that Richter can treat Ibn Qutayba's *'Uyūn al-akhbār* (an epitome of encyclopedic *adab*) as a *Fürstenspiegel* par excellence.[17]

What is often disregarded is that *adab* books of an encyclopedic scope are produced with objectives different from that of the Mirrors; their intended audience tends to be the educated public rather than the prince and his entourage. Often there is no relationship between the author of a work of *adab* and the caliph's or sultan's court. It is true, collections such a Ibn Qutayba's *'Uyūn al-akhbār* and al-Ābī's *Nathr al-durr* tell much about caliphs and politicians, the ruling class, and the workings of politics and administration in form of aphorisms and amusing anecdotes, but neither in their purport, nor in general content they are conceived as advice for rulers. Nonetheless, they surely constitute a rich source for the study of political thought in Islam.

Encyclopedias are a special case by themselves. However, since they only testify to the existence of literature on the art of government but do not add anything substantial to political thought, there is no need to mark them as

16. See Isabel Toral-Niehoff's contribution in this volume.
17. Richter 1932, 38–60.

a distinct class. They generally assign sections on *'ilm al-siyāsa* (science of politics) with subtitles on a range of themes pertaining to political discourse and the issues related to the ruling apparatus. Ibn Farīghūn's (mid 4th/10th century) *Jawāmi' al-'ulūm* (Compendium of Sciences),[18] and Fakhr al-Dīn al-Rāzī's (d. 606/1210) *al-Sittīnī* (Sixty Chapters) belong to this category.

5. Socio-Political Treatises

Ibn Khaldūn relies on al-Mas'ūdī's (d. 345/956) *Murūj al-dhahab* (Meadows of Gold), and al-Ṭurṭūshī's (wr. 515–6/1121–2) *Sirāj al-mulūk* (Lamp for Rulers) as well as on al-Māwardī's *Aḥkām al-sulṭāniyya* and the much earlier Ibn al-Muqaffa' for his elaborations on the forms of political rule.[19] His detailed analysis is a remarkable document of Arab-Islamic socio-political doctrine. However, as Erwin Rosenthal puts it: "If Ibn Khaldūn comes to the same conclusions as the authors of the 'Mirrors,' or even to the same or similar formulations, his aim is different, and for that reason alone, apart from other and more important considerations, his *Muqaddima* (Introduction to his universal history) contrasts with the 'Mirrors'."[20]

Each one of the above five categories can be subdivided further along theological, juridical, political, or literary frames for finer taxonomy. Classifications such as this, intended for the purpose of orientation and help in managing an immense amount of incongruent material, bring with them their weak sides too. The line of demarcation between these classes of writings is not always easy to determine and often a single author has written in several of these areas. Thus in his standard *al-Aḥkām al-sulṭāniyya*, al-Māwardī details his theory of state based on the rules of the *sharī'a* as a Shāfi'ī jurist, but in his *Naṣīḥat al-mulūk* (Advice for Kings),[21] *Tashīl al-naẓar* (Facilitating the Administration), *Qawānīn al-wizāra* (Rules of the Vizierate), and several other works, he expounds his political ideas mainly in line with the precepts of wisdom literature. Contrary to *al-Aḥkām al-sulṭāniyya*, the exposition in *Naṣīḥat al-mulūk* derives its inspiration from Sasanian tradition rather than from Islam.[22] Miskawayh (d. 421/1030) articulates his ethic-political philosophy on the basis of Greek philosophical explications in his *Tahdhīb al-akhlāq* (Refine-

18. See on this Hinrich Biesterfeldt's contribution in this volume.

19. Zakeri 2009, 169–78.

20. Rosenthal 1968, 69.

21. Not surprisingly one of the main sources of this book, the authenticity of which is questioned, is *'Ahd-i Ardashīr*; see al-Māwardī, *Naṣīḥat al-mulūk*, 58, 59, 87, 102, 142, 160, 202, 213, 228, 231, 235, 236, 268, 275, 280, 296, 343, 376, 388, 502.

22. Lambton 1980, 51.

ment of Character), but in his *Jāwīdān-khirad* (Perennial Wisdom), he shows his familiarity with and interest for the older Iranian political wisdom. He has preserved Arabic translations of several unique Sasanian political texts, including *'Ahd-i Ardashīr* and *Sīrat Anūshirwān*, in his *Tajārib al-umam* (Experiences of Nations). A similar approach is followed by al-Ghazālī (d. 505/1111) in his Arabic *Iḥyā' 'ulūm al-dīn* (Revival of Religious Sciences) and his Persian *Kīmiyā-yi sa'ādat* (Alchemy of Happiness), treated of late as a Mirror,[23] when compared with his *Naṣīḥat al-mulūk.*[24] Moreover, as Lambton observed, the political theories found in administrative manuals and Mirrors hold a position midway between the theories of the jurists on the one hand, and those of the philosophers on the other.[25] Their impact on both sides is amply evident in the constant borrowings of the jurists and philosophers from the fount of the Mirrors. This influence can be best seen in the *Rasā'il Ikhwān al-ṣafā'*, some sections of which constitute a philosophical *Fürstenspiegel*, as well as in Ibn Khaldūn's *Muqaddima.*[26]

6. Mirrors for Princes

As for form, the Arabic and Persian mirrors for princes are composed in a great variety of genres (or we may say transgress boundaries of genres), overlap and impinge upon one another. These again I have divided into six distinct groups: 1. *andarznāma, pandnāma*; 2. *āyīnnāma*; 3. animal fables; 4. epic narrations; 5. fiction; 6. chivalry romances (folk literature).

1. *Andarznāma, pandnāma*

The commonest Persian terms for aphoristic moral advice or wise saying are *andarz* and *pand*, both of Parthian origin, and probably even older. *Andarz* [<= *handarz* (Pahl.) <= *ham-darza* (OI), *han-darəza* (Av.)] originally meant "to tie or bond together, to agree with one another,"[27] and by extension, "agreed upon rules," or decorum. *Pand* [<= *pand* (Pahl.) <= *panthi* (OI), *panti* (Av.), *páthon* (Sk.)] is of the same root as the English path "way, road, route," and by extension means "the right way." Avestic also has *apanti* "the wrong way."[28] Whatever initial distinction had existed between *andarz* and *pand* was lost in

23. Hillenbrand 2004.
24. Binder 1955.
25. Lambton 1980, 47.
26. Zakeri 2009.
27. Bartholomae 1904, col 698, 1771.
28. Bartholomae 1904, col. 847; Nyberg 1974, 2: 150.

the course of time and they were used synonymously as "path, counsel." A good example is the well-known *Čītak handarž ī pōryōtkēšān* (Selections from the Wisdom of Early Teachers) (722/1322), which is also known as *Pandnāmag ī Zartušt* (Zoroaster's Book of Advice).

As a literary label *andarznāma* or *pandnāma* denotes the type of literature that is made of advice and injunctions for correct behavior, whether in matters of state, religion, or everyday life. In a wider sense either of the two may be applied to the whole range of *ḥikam* or wisdom literature.[29] Many early Arabic and New Persian Mirrors, especially the ones in form of anthologies or gnomologia, are dependent on the Middle Persian *andarz* literature. Hence not surprisingly collections of *andarz* are occasionally treated as *Fürstenspiegel*. A substantial amount of literature of this kind, known in Arabic, among other things, as *naṣīḥa/naṣā'iḥ* (counsel), or *waṣiyya/waṣāyā* (testament) was translated in the first centuries of Islam.[30]

To my great surprise and contrary to what has been generally assumed, the existing Middle Persian *andarznāma*s are for the most part apolitical in content and can be grouped in two categories as: wholly religious (pertinent to the duties of the Zoroastrian community of believers), or pedestrian moral advice, intended for the whole of mankind.[31] Nonetheless, in New Persian Literature, in particular in Firdawsī's (d. 411/1020) *Shāhnāma*, *andarz* or *pand* is usually delivered by the king to his prince or to the people, or by a wise man to the king. This change of emphasis seems to be a development in the Islamic period.

Numerous so-called *Ādāb al-falāsifa*, or collections of wise sayings attributed to philosophers and sages of the past (to be called florilegia or gnomologia), e.g. Miskawayh's *Jāwīdān-khirad* (Perennial Wisdom), al-Sijistānī's (d. 390/1000) *Ṣiwān al-ḥikma* (Depository of Wisdom), Ibn Hindū's (d. 423/1032) *al-Kilam al-ruḥāniyya min al-ḥikam al-Yūnāniyya* (Spiritual Words from the Wisdom of the Greeks), al-Mubashshir Ibn Fātik's (fl. mid 5th/11th century) *Mukhtār al-ḥikam* (Digest of Wisdom), and the anonymous *Khiradnāma* (Words of Wisdom) (6th/12th century) are better known representatives of this group. Needless to say, the constituent units of discourse, moral parcels and political advice alike, in all such collections are short pithy maxims and apophthegms.[32]

29. Asmussen 1971; Shaked 1987.

30. Henning 1956. For a good overall survey consult de Fouchécour 1986; see also Marlow 2009.

31. A standard example is *Andarz ī Ādurbād ī Mahraspandān* (The Admonitions of Ādurbād) (Jamasp-Asana 1897, 58–71). A part of this, probably based on a different Pahlavi redaction, is rendered as *Mawā'iẓ Ādurbād* and is preserved in Miskawayh's Arabic *Jāwīdān-khirad* (ed. Badawī, 26–8).

32. See Zakeri 2004.

2. *Āyīnnāma (On Rules and Regulations, Book of Etiquette, or On Policy)*

As mentioned at the outset, this is the closest equivalent for a Mirror in Persian and has entered Arabic unchanged as well in the form of calqued translations, but it has failed to become a generic term for this branch of literature. To this class of works, which is the most extensive, belong book with titles such as *'Ahdnāma* (Covenant, Testament, Commandment), *Tājnāma* (Book of the Crown), *Ādāb al-mulūk* (The Manners of Kings, or Rules of Royal Conduct), *Maḥāsin al-mulūk* (Good Qualities and Actions of Kings), *Naṣīḥat al-mulūk* or *Naṣīḥatnāma* (Advice for Kings), *Sulūk al-mulūk* (The Proper Conduct of Kings), *Siyāsat al-mulūk* (Politics of Kings), *Tadhkirat al-mulūk* (Memento of Kings), *Tuḥfat al-mulūk* (Precious Gift to the Kings), *Siyāsatnāma* (Book of Government). Muḥammad Rafīʿ al-Ṭabāṭabāʾī's (d. 1326/1908) *Kitāb Ādāb al-mulūk*, a Persian translation and commentary on ʿAlī b. Abī Ṭālib's (d. 40/661) alleged *'Ahdnāma* to his governor Mālik Ashtar, is one of the latest Mirrors from the Qājār-period that still follows the pattern established for the genre in the early Abbasid period. In form many of these are epistles delivered by a king to his prince or by a learned man to the king, vizier or other men in power.

Ibn al-Muqaffaʿ, the first translator of several such works into Arabic, was interested primarily in literature on government and the art of conducting public affairs. Among others, he translated *'Ahd-i Ardashīr* , perhaps the most celebrated and influential political testament in the Arabic language. In this originally late Sasanian document, addressed in some versions as an epistle to Ardashīr's son the Prince Shāhpūr, and in others to an unnamed "monarch," the author treats central questions of politics such as the role of the king, proper relationship between the king and his subjects, governing, conduct of war, appropriate ties with the enemies, justice, question of legitimacy and succession, and so forth. The contents of books such as this were absorbed by later historians, *adab*-encyclopedists, and authors who wrote for educational purposes or propaganda in an entertaining manner.

3. *Fables of the Kalīla wa Dimna type*

Kalīla wa Dimna, a book of fables, was conceived primarily as a mirror for princes, that is, ethical texts for instructing young royals in proper and virtuous behavior. Fables have been used to convey doctrines of statecraft (see Davidson's contribution in this volume). These entertaining and instructive tales communicate rules of conduct to guide princes from an early age to become wise and benevolent rulers. Other examples are Sahl b. Hārūn's (d. 215/830) *al-Namir wa l-thaʿlab* (The Panther and the Fox); the anonymous (ca. 500/1106) *al-Asad wa l-ghawwāṣ* (The Lion and the Diver); Ibn Ẓafar's (d. ca. 565/1169) *Sulwān al-muṭā' fī 'udwān al-atbā'* (Waters of Comfort), Sibṭ b. al-Jawzī's *Kanz al-mulūk* (Treasury of the Kings), Sa'd al-Dīn al-Warāwīnī's (fl. 7th/13th century) *Marzbānnāma* (The Book of Marzbān), addressed to Abū l-Qāsim Rabīb al-Dīn Hārūn, the vizier of Atābeg Uzbek b. Muḥammad b. Īldigiz, ruler of Azerbaijan from 607/1210 to 622/1225; Muḥammad b. Ghāzī Malṭīwī's (of Malṭawa, wrote in 598/1201) *Rawḍat al-'uqūl* (Garden of the Minds), which is a variant of *Marzbānnāma*;[33] and Ibn 'Arabshāh's (d. 854/1450) *Fākihat al-khulafā' wa mufākahat al-ẓurafā'* (Fruits for the Caliphs and Bantering Talk for the Refined), to note a few among many.

4. *Epic narration*

The pre-Islamic Sasanian [Middle] Persian Mirror par excellence was the *Khudāynāma* (Book of Kings), in Arabic *Sīrat al-mulūk* or *Siyar al-mulūk* (Conduct of kings), a forerunner of Firdawsī's *Shāhnāma*. Portions of this semi-historical and legendary collection were known to the Arabs already at the time of the Prophet and its numerous translations continued to fill the markets and excite the imagination of the Muslims for centuries. Muḥammad b. Ismā'īl b. Ḥusayn Nīshābūrī (ca. 450–525/1058–1131) of Bayhaq translated Firdawsī's *Shāhnāma* into Arabic about a century before al-Bundārī (586–643/1190–1245), who dedicated a new translation to the Ayyubid Sultan al-Mu'aẓẓam in 623/1226.[34]

The *Shāhnāma* was a vessel for the preservation of Persian royal values and cultural traditions. It contains instruction for the proper behavior of princes, counselors, and other government officials. The teachings and moral examples offered by the virtuous and upright characters of the *Shāhnāma*, in words and deeds, are among the aspects that explain its great success for over a millennium. Intended for the education of princes and sons of nobles, the poem offers models of conduct and governance that inspired generations of rulers and politicians.[35] The main objective of the poet was to offer a manifest of kingly manners and values to be followed by the kings of his days and those coming in the future. While relating the fate of mythic and historical rulers such as Jamshīd, Ḍaḥḥāk, Afrāsiyāb, Hurmuzd, or Shīrūya, he was warning the rulers of the fate of doom which was awaiting them. As such it can be easily considered a successful example of a mirror for princes. According to the eminent French scholar Charles Henri de Fouchécour,

33. Levy 1959; al-Warāwīnī 1992.
34. See al-Qifṭī (d. 646/1248), *al-Muḥammadūn min al-shu'arā'*, 128.
35. Meisami 1995; Meisami 1987.

Firdawsī has succeeded in bringing together and organizing the ancient wisdom in the form of a brilliant Mirror. The *Shāhnāma* is a *Fürstenspiegel* with a clear intention: to show the kings an ideal archetype to contrast their actuality with it; to hold a mirror up in front of them to see themselves. That is why the reading of stories about past kings was always advocated as a royal duty.[36]

The historical role of this branch of literature for conveying political wisdom may be substantiated by way of an example: In the year 420/1029 the Būyid prince Majd al-Dawla b. Fakhr al-Dīn b. Būya was the Iranian sovereign ruling in Rayy. He had given himself to women and studying of books and had left his mother to administer his kingdom. When the mother died, soldiers revolted against him and disrupted the peace. Majd al-Dawla asked the Ghaznawid Sultan Yamīn al-Dawla Maḥmūd b. Sabuktakīn for assistance. As the eastern army entered Rayy the first thing they did was to arrest and imprison Majd al-Dawla until Maḥmūd arrived. After the Sultan triumphantly took over the city and collected booty and taxes, he sent for Majd al-Dawla. Upon his entrance the Sultan said to him:

> Have you not read the *Shāhnāma,* which is the history of the Persians, and the *Ta'rīkh al-Ṭabarī,* which is the history of the Muslims? He said: Yes! He said: Your situation is not like that of one who has read them. Have you played chess? He said: Yes! He said: Have you ever seen a Shah enter upon a Shah? He said: No! He said: Then what made you deliver yourself to someone who is stronger than you?[37]

The wisdom communicated by this statement is straightforward: one should study books such as the *Shāhnāma* to learn proper manner of political and military conduct, and play chess to become skilled at strategy and tactic.

5. *Fiction*

The *Sindbādnāma*, some tales of the *Thousand and One Nights* (for example, its framework, where, at least in some redactions, a bad and blood thirsty prince is converted to a good and sublime ruler by way of storytelling),[38]

36. de Fouchécour 1996, 10, 16; de Fouchécour 1986; see also Askari 2013.

37. Ibn al-Athīr (d. 630/1233), *Kitāb al-Kāmil*, 8: 170.

38. As Robert Irwin explained, there is more political thought in the *Nights* than would appear at first sight. Political concerns are to the fore in the story collection's exordium. Some of the stories can be seen as belonging to the mirror for princes genre. Though criticism of tyranny and the positing of alternative societies are quite rare in Islamic literature, examples of both can be found in the *Nights* (Irwin 2004, 246); see also Loree Allen 2008.

Daqā'iqī of Marw's *Bakhtiyārnāma* (7th/13th century) could be included in this category. To Daqā'iqī is attributed also a *Sindbādnāma.* Isḥāq b. Ibrāhīm Sijāsī's *Farā'id al-sulūk fī faḍā'il al-mulūk* (Precious Pearls of Behavior: On the Virtues of the Kings), written in Persian in 610/1213, has adopted the path of *Kalīla wa Dimna* and *Sindbādnāma* in using fables and tales as vehicles for conveying instructive political thought.[39] In some stories the characters intermix freely with animals and natural phenomena passing through all physical boundaries without any barrier. *Bilawhar wa Būdhāsf,* the progenitor of the Christian legend of *Barlaam and Josaphat,* also known as *Book of the King's Son and the Ascetic,* is based ultimately on the life of Buddha and his alleged advisor Bilawhar, who delivers, among others, the wisdom of Buzurjmihr to his princely pupil;[40] as well as *Salāmān wa Absāl,*[41] are a few examples in this category.

6. *Chivalry Romance (Folk-narrative)*

Popular romances in the tradition of *Samak-i 'Ayyār,* the Alexander Romance, the *Dārābnāma, Fīrūzshāhnāma, Abū Muslimnāma* (all available in diverse recensions), *Amīr Arsalān,* and others. In these prose romances the model for moral and political instruction is usually a callow prince, who travels around the world in pursuit of his beloved. While describing the hero's journey across the world, the romance also depicts his inner journey toward social and moral maturity and the willingness to accept the responsibilities of adult life. In other words, the underlying moral purpose of the romance is to present a model for the education of a prince to become a king. Once separated from his family, he must overcome a series of challenges before being united with his beloved and returning home. These challenges serve to test his bravery, instruct him in administrative or military skills, and teach him sexual restraint and a proper attitude toward women. The romance typically ends with the hero being reunited with his beloved. They then marry,

39. Sijāsī, *Farā'id al-sulūk*; Öztürk 1976.

40. *Bilawhar wa Būdhāsf* is a Mirror, though its conception of a holy-wise king is not as close to real politics as for example the pseudo-Aristotelian *Sirr al-asrār* (4th/10th century). In addition to being filled with sermons, moral and ethical advice, this romance contains examples of good and fair kings as well as of repentance and spiritual transformation of ruthless kings who change into benevolent, righteous and just ones. Inclusion of the stories of seven or eight other kings with edifying and pragmatic lessons, plus the central frame story which revolves around a king, his prince, and the wise adviser, i.e. the sage Bilawhar, evince that the motives of its composer(s) had been to give indirect guidance to kings and rulers and lead them towards a benign rule.

41. On this see the insightful study by Lingwood 2011.

and he accepts the throne of his kingdom from his aged father. The new king and queen rule in peace and prosperity for the rest of their long lives.[42]

William L. Hanaway, who has studied this branch of literature intensively and has provided the above synopsis, noted that "The popular romances are a rich source for reconstruction of the social history of medieval Persia, a source only beginning to be investigated."[43] However, he then divides the classical Persian literary heritage into "popular" in prose and "courtly" in verse, and contrasts the traditional social and moral values of the Iranian common people with those of the courtly elite. Since he fails to substantiate this neatly arranged dual division by hard evidence, except that one is in prose and the other in verse, his suggestion remains only a speculation. He almost contradicts himself when he says: "We know that some of these romances were popular in court circles as well as with the general public, and this fact provides further evidence for the interaction of popular and courtly literary culture."[44] In other words, popular romances complement courtly romances in preserving and transmitting traditional values.

The traditional scholarship has unjustifiably classified popular narratives such as *Samak-i 'Ayyār*, *Dārābnāma*, or *Iskandarnāma* as folkloric (hence of less value) in comparison with the classical Persian literary works such as the *Shāhnāma*. The mere fact that these long oral stories were written down at the time when such undertakings were extremely costly and that many copies of some of them have survived is by itself good evidence that they were sponsored by the more affluent, hence courtly, sections of society which read or listened to them as everybody else did. There is nothing in a book such as *Samak-i 'Ayyār* that contradicts the "courtly culture," or can be viewed as vulgar and unsuitable for the court, princes or other members of the high society. Though clearly of an oral background, and close to common language in syntax and structure, it could have been delivered at the story-telling sessions as the court. From time to time the storyteller emerges as a superior orator in full command of his art and proceeds in the best manner of established classical literary writers. His capabilities in the use of a florid language emerge when he describes love and beauty, court ceremonies, the seasons of the year, or battle scenes. In the case of *Dārābnāma* and *Samak-i 'Ayyār* at least, this erudition evinces that the authors were decidedly well-educated men with good knowledge of the norms and ideals of the cultured society in which they lived. As Hanaway has remarked, the focus of these romances is on the moral value of kingship and the social value of relations between men

42. Hanaway 1991; Hanaway 1994.
43. Hanaway 1971, 140.
44. Hanaway 1991, 56.

and women.[45] In fact more original political thought is imbedded in popular romances than heretofore acknowledged. They communicate a more realistic and nuanced approach to the socio-political conditions of their times.

The medieval Persian romance *Samak-i 'Ayyār* is a prose narrative created, elaborated, and transmitted orally by professional storytellers over centuries until it was finally committed to writing by Farāmarz b. Khudādād Arrajānī in the year 585/1189. A unique manuscript of this text is kept at the Bodleian Library in Oxford.[46] Since then the book has been translated into French and Russian, and numerous studies both of the entire text as well as of specific aspects of its contents have appeared. A comprehensive pioneering study is done by Marina Gaillard.[47] More recently Roxana Zenhari has dedicated a dissertation to the study of the 80 colored illustrations in the Bodleian manuscript that have been left out of the printed text.[48]

Although a good instance of Persian popular literature, *Samak-i 'Ayyār* is at the same time in many ways unique among them all. We may say that *Samak-i 'Ayyār* is a prescriptive account of how to produce an ideal ruler of an ideal state. Moreover, *Samak-i 'Ayyār* is, or reads more like a standard handbook on *āyīn-i jawānmardī,* or the principles of Iranian "chivalry," to the extent that one may say no other Persian text can compete with it in this respect. This exceptional aspect of the book was recognized very early on and several studies have been devoted to extracting these principles from it. Not only does the book offer a glimpse into the social life and ethical mores of the common people, as well as of the court, but it also provides invaluable insight on the milieu of the *'ayyārs*[49] both male and female, their daily professional practices, and their highly elaborate moral code of con-

45. Hanaway 1994, 9.
46. Ed. Khānlarī 1959–74.
47. Gaillard 1987.
48. Zenhari 2012; see also Stockland 1993–5.
49. Dozens of terms have been used in modern literature to translate the name of these distinct social bands and organizations: vagabonds, drifters, stragglers, knight-errantry, chivalrous brigandage, brigands, adventurers, the ubiquitous bandits, scoundrels, vagrants, condottieri, gangs of ruffians, bandit de grand chemin, chevalerie insurrectionnelle, héroisme hors lois, etc. This diversity shows above all the lack of proper comprehension of these enigmatic groups, and that any attempt at rashly casting them under any of these categories will fail. *'Ayyār is* often used both as a positive appellation and an abusive epithet. At times of disturbance, the *'ayyārān* were always ready to serve as auxiliary troops. They show group solidarity, are well organized, and enter the scene as active arm of popular masses in the city quarters. When acting on the side of the central government, the official chronologists extol them as heroes and men of high morals, self-sacrifice and valor; when they fight in favor of opposite factions or defend local interests, they are disparaged as despicable and lawless bandits who show no respect for people's rights, honor and property. In any event, they are the main heroes of Persian folk-narratives. (See Zakeri 1995).

duct known as *jawānmardī* and *ʿayyārī*. The hero of the book is a humbly born trickster named Samak the *ʿAyyār*.[50] However, despite his lowly origins, Samak is in fact the expert master who adopts the inexperienced prince and instructs him in the path of adulthood and manliness. The didactic purpose of the romance is clearly as essential to the narrator as his celebration of entertainment. This is very much in line with the contemporary literary tradition, comparable with, for example, the courtly verse romances of the Saljuq period especially *Vis and Ramin* (4–5th/11th century) and the romances of Niẓāmī (d. 605/1209).

Samak-i ʿAyyār has the characteristics of what we may call a popular Mirror, in that in it are projected the desired qualifications of not only an ideal prince, but also those of perfect men in his service. The acting heroes are *ʿayyārs*, but the stories involve kings, princes, viziers and politicians at all echelons of political apparatus. The moral and social principles of *jawānmardī* (given in Arabic hendiadys *futuwwa* and *muruwwa*: "manliness," or "chivalry," or the sum total of moral and manly expectations from an ideal man) are presented in detail as ethical rules that the prince and his cohort should acquire and propagate. One of the main chapters of *Qābūsnāma* (472/1080), the classic example of a Persian mirror for princes from a century earlier, is assigned to an exposition of *jawānmardī*.[51]

One major criterion for the classification of any work of art is where the producer of the work wants it to be placed. The author of *Samak-i ʿAyyār* announces his intention unambiguously in these words: "I have included in this book stories of kings and peasants, emirs and heroes, commanders and chamberlains, viziers and boon-companions, viceroys and deputies ..., kingship and leadership; war and hunt; conducting armies, knowing how to proceed and to draw strategic plans;" and "I want this book to be a guidebook (*dastūr*) to kings in ruling, in implementing justice, and enacting the principles of kingship in such a way that it will be agreeable to the wise and the intelligent, to the shrewd and the learned and the men of acumen."[52] This objective is indeed followed consistently throughout the entire text.

Marzbānshāh, the arch-king of *Samak-i ʿAyyār* residing at Aleppo, has the glory and effulgence of kingship (*farr-i īzadī*), he is old, rich, holds an extensive empire, has a wise vizier and every desirable thing that a king could wish for, but a son to rule after him and eternalize his good name. The astute vizier Hāmān studies the stars and the books of the ancients and determines that the king of Iraq has a daughter who is predestined for the

50. Hanaway 1971, 140–3.
51. Kaykāwūs b. Iskandar b. Qābūs, *A Mirror for Princes: The Qābūs Nāma*, 239–62.
52. Ed. Khānlarī 1959–74, 1: 5; cf. Gaillard 1987, 163–4.

king. *Gulnār*, the widowed princess of Iraq, has already a two-year old son called Farrukhrūz, and agrees to become the queen of Aleppo. Marriage is consummated and the king goes on happily with conducting justice (*be dād u 'adl*) in the realm.[53] The day when the baby is born and brought to the king the sun is shining on his face, so they call him Khurshīd (Sun). Khurshīd grows up with his stepbrother Farrukhrūz. At the age of four he is sent to school. Moving up the ladder of knowledge (*'ilm u dānish*), he studies *adab* (manners) with several teachers, learns writing, reading, solving problems, and reads "all that which would be of use to kings."[54] At the age of ten, the king invites the experienced and expert masters in diverse fields of education to gather and examine the prince's learning. In addition he excels in the art of horsemanship, playing polo, throwing rings (*ḥalqa*), spears, archery, carrying a mace, lasso, gymnastics, swimming, wrestling, playground sports, and chess.[55] At the age of fourteen he develops a desire for learning music instruments and learns how to play harp (*chang*), *daff/duff* (a percussion instrument), *rabab* (a bowed, or string instrument), trachea (*nāy*), lute (*barbaṭ*), *'ajab rūd* (a wind instrument in traditional music of Iran) and others. He also receives training in singing, and reads love stories. His main hobby at the age of fifteen is hunting.[56]

This learning program offers an inventory of courses in a classical princely education current in Sasanian Iran. Similar catalogues can be found in the Pahlavi books *Kārnāmak ī Ardashīr* and *K̲usraw ī Kawādān ud rēdak-ēw* (late Sasanian period),[57] in the Christian-Syriac *Romance of Qardagh* (early 7th century),[58] in the *Sindbādnāma*, and a host of other books. These lists may be compared and supplemented also with the diverse examination courses that king Anūshirwān goes through.[59]

Up to this point the description of the prince's stages of upbringing is standard and almost a perfect recast of that of the prince of the *Sindbādnāma*. The circumstance in which the narrative of the *Sindbādnāma* unfolds is iden-

53. Ed. Khānlarī 1959–74, 1: 7

54. Ed. Khānlarī 1959–74, 1: 9.

55. Ed. Khānlarī 1959–74, 1: 9.

56. Ed. Khānlarī 1959–74, 1: 10.

57. The list of the study fields required from an educated prince is by no means complete here, and may be supplemented by *K̲usraw ī Kawādān ud rēdak-ēw* and other Sasanian texts. This unique example seems to have been primarily conceived to provide such a catalogue. Gutas summarizes the educational program of the sons of Sasanian nobility from the Arabic translation of *K̲usraw ī Kawādān ud rēdak-ēw* in al-Tha'ālibī's *Ghurar al-siyar* (Gutas 2006, 99).

58. The hero Qardagh is a noble Iranian who, in this Christian romance, personifies the ideal virtues and manly and martial traits of heroes as expected and propagated by Iranians under the Sasanians. See Walker 2006, for example 20–1.

59. Le Strange and Nicholson 1921, 86.

tical too: The old and prosperous king who has everything in the world except a son; prediction of the astrologers to the birth of a son, in whose horoscope there is much hardship and danger, but that at the end he will come out victorious; the prince's birth and his education in the hands of the most learned teachers. Here the antagonist villain is the lustful queen at the court; there the witch-nurse who attempts to eliminate the prince. In both the invigorating motive is love, though it is weight differently in each case; in the *Sindbādnāma* the seven wise viziers and others tell stories dotted with words of wisdom, here the actors demonstrate similar wisdom in practice.

Age seventeen: after a week of hunting the prince chases an onager alone, is lost, reaches a tent, finds a beautiful girl there, falls in love with her, but upon drinking water, he becomes unconscious. His retinue finds him abandoned in the desert half dead. The mysterious girl is gone but has left her ring on his finger. The ring has an engraving that nobody can read. The pain of lost love reduces the prince to bones.[60] After many months an old man appears who can read the note and inform the prince that the true owner of the ring is Mah Parī the princess of China who is under the spell of her witch-nurse.

Prince Khurshīd who is handsome and has awe and *farr-i pādshāhī*[61] (the glory or glance of kingship) sets off with his half-brother and a few companions for China. Upon arrival Farrukhrūz is kidnapped by the wicked nurse. Khurshīdshāh is left hopeless and wanders in the city. He befriends a cloth merchant, and encounters a band of *'ayyārān* led by Shughāl-i pīlzūr, the respected leader of *jawānmardān.* Shughāl is assisted by his young novice Samak-i 'Ayyār, the active head of the *'ayyārān.* While referring to these actors, the author makes no distinction between *akhī* and *jawānmard,* or *'ayyārān, rindān,* and *mardān.*[62] From now on, the page of the narrative turns, and the prince's role loses color and is pushed into the background. The true hero of the book, Samak the *'Ayyār*, is introduced who steals the reader's glance away from the young prince, as indicated by the title. Samak is a man of thousand tricks who functions as a problem solver, a man for all seasons. Moral lessons start with an oration on the principles of *jawānmardī.*[63] This may be best contrasted with the corresponding section of the *Qābūsnāma.*[64]

In addition to his spectacular acts in protecting and rescuing the helpless prince from dungeons and all sorts of threatening situations, Samak,

60. Ed. Khānlarī 1959–74, 1: 20.
61. Ed. Khānlarī 1959–74, 1: 174.
62. Ed. Khānlarī 1959–74, 1: 45.
63. Ed. Khānlarī 1959–74, 1: 47–8, 252–4; 2: 220.
64. Kaykāwūs b. Iskandar b. Qābūs, *A Mirror for Princes: The Qābūs Nāma*, 239–62.

despite his low origins, emerges as an all-knowing wise man on his side giving him advice on matters of leadership on every conceivable occasion: "One should not make servants of his retinue to hate him, for the greatest of all enmities is the enmity of the servants and one's entourage. This is because they are well-informed about all of one's secrets (so can cause serious harm)."[65] Or, later on in the narrative,

> The king ordered the messenger to be brought in. He entered. They presented to him rosewater (to perfume), and sat at the table with him and ate. Then the musicians came in, singers began singing and the cupbearers served wine. The king Farrukhrūz did not drink. Samak told him: "I know why you do not drink; you are still in mourning for your slain wives and the captivity of your son. It is not to say that I am any less sorrowful or have not observed the proper rites of mourning for them. After all, your slain wife Gulbuy was my daughter. *One cannot disregard and put the tradition of the ancient kings aside.* A King's bereavement is only a short period; if the lost person is a dear one, then maximum three days. Kings are used to receive messengers and listen to their message while drinking." Saying this Samak took a cup from the cupbearer, kissed it and gave it to the king, who now drank it. Then the messenger delivered his message.[66]

Samak's status rises above everybody else at the court, taking the place of the vizier. At one time a foreign delegation arrives for negotiations. Instead of asking his vizier 'Adnān, the King turns to Samak and says:

> "My dear Samak, give them the answer as you think suitable." The visiting Tūrān and all the heroes in his company were astonished and bewildered at Samak, to whom a king of Farrukhrūz' stature turns for an appropriate response when he has, in his service, a vizier as glorious as 'Adnān, under whose pen the entire world revolves. The King noticed their bewilderment and said: "My dear heroes (*pahlawānān*), be aware that I did not answer the messenger for we do not know what to say; we are concerned lest to say anything that may go against Samak's wishes. That is why we tell him to reply as he wills. All we wish is Samak's satisfaction, for he is to me like a dear father, and as far as my father was alive, he never did anything without consulting with him first and that is why he always made right decisions. I do the same in following his orders and in his pleasure and shall continue doing so. My kingship belongs to him, and indeed he

65. Ed. Khānlarī 1959–74, 3: 110.
66. Ed. Khānlarī 1959–74, 5: 538–9; abbreviated; emphasis is mine.

is the real king. We give orders and go to war, but he is the one who brings the state affairs into their right conclusions. Yes, he is the king and whatever he wills will be done. If he decides to remove me from my throne and replace me with someone else, he can do that. I am like his son, and the son should follow the orders of his father like a servant. Now you know with whom you are dealing."[67]

Extravagant examples such as this are abundant throughout the book, introduced perhaps in an attempt to alleviate the relationship between a local king and the *'ayyārān*.[68]

Kings such as Marzbānshāh and Khurshīdshāh love justice and take every measure to ensure that equity spreads throughout their realm. They always prefer peace to war and anytime a contentious situation escalates with an enemy, they step forward first with an offer to return to negotiations and try their best to avoid war.[69] When in war they do not allow mistreatment of captives from the enemy camp. After each victory and conquest of a city they proclaim, "Now there is peace and justice, the injustice is over; no one has any right to harm anybody;" or "There is no punishment, no confiscation, and the opponents are all free."[70] We read about Marzbānshāh that "he entered the city and let it be announced that if anybody takes a piece of bread or a handful of straw from someone by force, he will be severely punished."[71]

An unexpectedly large amount of information can be won from the book about the court, kingship and its supporting ideology; as well as the heroic ethos, the life in the palace and the royal household, the friends of the king, the hierarchy at the court, the royal pages and attendants, forms of official correspondence, diplomatic relations, and bonds between patrons and clients. To these may be added details of the ritual and ceremonial, the costume of the king, and the diadem to name but a few.

Just as in the *Kalīla wa Dimna*, in which political advice and wise injunctions are brought to the king via the medium of fables, and just as in

67. Ed. Khānlarī 1959–74, 5: 539–40.

68. The geographical location of *Samak-i 'ayyār* can be determined with a good degree of likelihood to be Shiraz or Isfahan. The date of the written composition is 585/1189. Slightly to the west in Baghdad in this period unique developments are taking place which prove to be of extreme significance for the intellectual and political history of central Islamic lands, namely: the Caliph al-Nāṣir's approach to *'ayyārī-futuwwa* organizations in his attempt to create a kind of political and spiritual unification of the empire under his aegis. Al-Nāṣir's initiation into the *futuwwa* took place in 578/1182, three years after he had assumed the title of Caliph.

69. Ed. Khānlarī 1959–74, 2: 181, 288, 370.

70. Ed. Khānlarī 1959–74, 3: 173; 2: 359, 583.

71. Ed. Khānlarī 1959–74, 2: 247.

Firdawsī's *Shāhnāma,* in which the bitter moral and practical lessons are wrapped in the garb of mythic and heroic legends, and just as in numerous books known as *naṣīḥat al-mulūk, ādāb al-mulūk,* or *maḥāsin al-mulūk* , in which the intended teachings are delivered in form of short, memorable, and pointed anecdotes and exempla, and just as in the pseudo-Aristotelian *Sirr al-asrār* (*Secretum Secretorum*), the *Bilawhar wa Būdhāsf,* the *Alexander Romance,* or some stories in the *Thousand and One Nights,* each with its own particular framework, setting and unique literary medium for presentation of their message, here too, the purposeful commands are imbedded within the context of the exploits of an ardent lover, an untried prince of the Empire in the West (i.e. Aleppo), who is captivated by his love for the princess of faraway China. He has to go through perilous stages that have the same function as the *haft khwān* (seven stations) of the *Shāhnāma* in order to become qualified for the rite of passage to gain his beloved princess and step on the throne. As in the case of *Thousand and One Nights,* the loose frame of the romance has certainly allowed the relaters of the stories throughout centuries to voice moral precepts, political comments, social criticism, as well as actual popular wishes of the ordinary people under the mask of events that take place in foreign lands, geographically vague regions, and under distant legendary monarchs.[72]

By introducing the *Samak-i 'ayyār* (a popular romance) next to the *Siyar al-mulūk* (Conduct of Kings) and the *Shāhnāma* (Book of Kings), that is, quasi-historical and epic narratives, as "mirrors for princes," I am not suggesting that all texts in these genres automatically fulfill the requirements for being Mirrors. Each candidate must be judged on its own right. As the few examples cited above should be sufficient, I hope, to show, the *Samak-i 'Ayyār* and the *Shāhnāma* are certainly good examples for being regarded as Mirrors, along with the *Kalīla wa Dimna, Sindbādnāma,* Alexander Romance, and many others.

72. For a comparable European case consult Robinson 2009.

Bibliography

'Ārif, N. M. (1994), *Fī maṣādir al-turāth al-siyāsī al-Islāmī,* Maryland.

Askari, N. (2013), *The Medieval Reception of Firdausī's Shāhnāma: The Ardashīr Cycle as a Mirror for Princes,* PhD dissertation, University of Toronto.

Asmussen, J. P. (1971), "Einige Bemerkungen zur sasanidischen Handarz-Literatur," in: *Atti del convegno internazionale sul tema: La Persia nel medioevo,* Rome, 269–76.

Bartholomae, Ch. (1904), *Altiranisches Wörterbuch,* Strasbourg.

Bihbahānī, Abū Ṭālib (1389sh/2010), *Minhāj al-ʿulā. Risāla-yi dar bāb-i ḥukūmat-i qānūn*, ed. Ḥ. Saʿīdī, Tehran.

Binder, L. (1955), "Al-Ghazālī's Theory of Islamic Government," *The Muslim World* 45: 229–41.

Damaj, M. A. (1994), *Marāyā al-umarāʾ*, Beirut.

Dānishpazhūh, M. T. (1339 sh/1961), "Fihrist-i pāra-yi az kitābhā-yi akhlāq wa siyāsat ba-Fārsī," *Nashriyya-yi Kitābkhāna-yi Markazī-yi Dānishgāh-i Tehran* 1: 211–27.

—— (1988), "An Annotated Bibliography on Government and Statecraft. Translated and Adapted by Andrew Newman," in: S. A. Arjomand (ed.), *Authority and Political Culture in Shiʿism*, Albany, 213–39.

Darling, L. T. (2007), "Social Cohesion (*ʿaṣabiyya*) and Justice in the Late Medieval Middle East," *Comparative Studies in Society and History* 49: 329–57.

Fazilat, F. (ed.) (2005), *Dinkard*. Book III, Tehran.

de Fouchécour, C.-H. (1986), *Moralia, les notions morales dans la littérature persane du 3e/9e au 7e/13e siècle*, Paris.

—— (1996), "Akhlāq-i pahlawānī wa akhlāq-i rasmī dar Shāhnāma," in: S. Meskoob (ed.), *Tan-i Pahlawān wa rawān-i khiradmand*, Tehran.

Gaillard, M. (1987), *Le livre de Samak-i ʿAyyār. Structure et idéologie du roman persan médiéval*, Paris.

Gutas, D. (2006), "The Greek and Persian Background of Early Arabic Encyclopedism," in: G. Endress (ed.), *Organizing Knowledge*, Leiden, 91–102.

Hanaway, W. L. (1971), "Formal Elements in the Persian Popular Romances," *Review of National Literatures* 2.1: 138–60.

—— (1991), "Amīr Arsalān and the Question of Genre," *Iranian Studies* 24: 55–60.

—— (1994), "Dārāb-nāma," in: *EIr* VII: 8–9.

Henning, W. B. (1956), "Eine arabische Version mittelpersischer Weisheitsschriften," *Zeitschrift der deutschen morgenländischen Gesellschaft* 106: 73–7.

Hillenbrand, C. (2004), "A little-known Mirror for Princes of al-Ghazali," in: R. Arnzen and J. Thielmann (eds.), *Words, Texts and Concepts cruising the Mediterranean Sea*, Leuven, 593–601.

Al-Ḥusayn, W. A. (ed.) (2004), *Mirʾāt al-muruwwāt, wa yalīhi kitāb Mirʾāt al-muruwwāt li-ʿAlī b. al-Ḥasan b. Jaʿdawayh*, Beirut.

Ibn al-Athīr (1987), *Kitāb al-Kāmil*, 11 vols., Beirut.

Irwin, R. I. (2004), "Political Thought in *The Thousand and One Nights*," *Marvels & Tales: Journal of Fairly-Tales* 18.2: 246–57.

Jamasp-Asana, D. (1897), *Pahlavi Texts*, Bombay.

Kaykāwūs b. Iskandar b. Qābūs (1951), *A Mirror for Princes: The Qābūs Nāma*, tr. R. Levy, London.

Khānlarī, P. N. (ed.) (1959–74), *Samak-i 'Ayyār*, Tehran.
Lambton, A. (1980), "The Theory of Kingship in *Naṣīḥat al-mulūk* of Ghazālī," in: ead., *Theory and Practice in Medieval Persian Government*, London, 47–55.
Le Strange, G. and R. A. Nicholson (eds.) (1921), *The Fārsnāma of Ibnu 'l-Balkhī*, London. [Reprint: Tehran 1384sh].
Levy, R. (1951), *A Mirror for Princes: The Qābūs Nāma*, London.
—— (1959), *The Tales of Marzubān (Marzubān-nāma)*, Indiana.
Lingwood, C. G. (2011), "Jāmī's *Salāmān va Absāl*: Political Statements and Mystical Advice Addressed to the Āq Qoyūnlū Court of Sultān Ya'qūb (d. 896/1490)," *Iranian Studies* 44: 175–91.
Loree Allen, S. (2008), *Narrative, Authority and the Voices of Morality: An Intertextual Journey of Key Themes in The Thousand Nights and One Night and Islamic Mirror for Princes*, PhD dissertation, Pacific Graduate Institute.
McEwan, C. W. (1934), *The Oriental Origin of Hellenistic Kingship*, Chicago.
Marlow, L. (2009), "Surveying Recent Literature on the Arabic and Persian Mirrors for Princes Genre," *History Compass* 7.2: 523–38.
Al-Māwardī (1986), *Naṣīḥat al-mulūk*, ed. M. J. al-Ḥadīthī, Baghdad.
Meisami, J. S. (1987), "Romance as Mirror: Allegories of Kingship and Justice," in: ead., *Medieval Persian Poetry*, Princeton, 180–236.
—— (1995), "The Šâh-nâme as Mirror for Princes. A Study in Reception," in: C. Balaÿ et al. (eds.), *Pand-o Sokhan*, Tehran, 265–73.
Miskawayh (1952), *Jāwīdān-khirad* [*al-Ḥikma al-khālida*], ed. 'A. Badawī, Cairo.
Muḥammadī, M. (1338 sh/1959), "Ā'īnnāma," *al-Dirāsāt al-adabiyya* 1: 15–39.
—— (1964), *al-Tarjuma wa l-naql 'an al-Fārisiyya. Kutub al-Tāj wa l-Āyīn*. Beirut.
Nyberg, H. S. (1974), *A Manual of Pahlavi*, 2 vols., Wiesbaden.
Öztürk, M. (1976), *Farā'id al-sulūk fī faḍā'il al-mulūk*, PhD dissertation, Sorbonne, Paris.
Pellat, C. (1976), *"Conseilleur" du calife*. Paris. [Ed. and transl. of Ibn al-Muqaffa', *Risāla fī l-ṣaḥāba*.]
Al-Qifṭī (1970), *al-Muḥammadūn min al-shu'arā'*, ed. Ḥ. Ma'marī, Paris.
Qudāma b. Ja'far (1981), *Kitāb al-Kharāj*, Baghdad.
Richter, G. (1932), *Studien zur Geschichte der älteren arabischen Fürstenspiegel*, Leipzig.
Robinson, K. D. (2009), *Reflections of Royalty: Late Middle English Arthurian Texts and the Mirrors for Princes Tradition*, PhD dissertation, Purdue University, Indiana.
Rosenthal, E. (1968), *Political Thought in Medieval Islam*, Cambridge.

Al-Ṣābī, H. (1383/1964), *Rusūm dār al-khilāfa*, Baghdad. [Translation: Elie A. Salem (1977), *The Rules and Regulations of the Abbasid Court*, Beirut 1977.]
Shaked, S. (1987), "A Facetious Recipe and the Two Wisdoms: Iranian Themes in Muslim Garb," *Jerusalem Studies in Arabic and Islam* 9: 24–35.
Sijāsī, Isḥāq b. Ibrāhīm Shams (1990), *Farā'id al-sulūk*, ed. ʿA. N. Wiṣāl and Gh. R. Afrāsiyābī, Tehran.
Steele, R. (ed.) (1920), *Opera hactenus inedita Rogerii Baconi*, Fasc. V, Oxford.
Stockland, W. (1993–5), "The Kitāb-i Samak 'Ayyār," *Persica* 15: 143–82.
Al-Ṭarsūsī, Abū Ṭāhir (2005), *Alexandre le Grand en Iran. Le Dārāb Nāmeh d'Abu Tāher Tarsusi*, tr. M. Gaillard, Paris.
Venetis, E. (2006), "Kingship and divine intervention in the Iskandarnama prose romance," *Archiv Orientální* 74: 255, 271–81.
Walker, J. T. (2006), *The Legend of Mar Qardagh. Narrative and Christian Heroism in Late Antique Iraq*, Berkeley.
al-Warāwīnī, Saʿd al-Dīn (1992), *Contes du prince Marzban*, tr. M.-H. Ponroy, Paris.
Zakeri, M. (1995), *Sāsānid Soldiers in Early Muslim Society: The Origins of 'Ayyārān and Futuwwa*, Wiesbaden.
—— (2004), "Ādāb al-falāsifa. The Persian Content of an Arabic Collection of Aphorisms," *Mélanges de l'Université Saint Joseph* 57: 173–90.
—— (2009), "'Mirrors for Princes' as Sources of Ibn Khaldūn's Political Theory," in: O. Bakkar and Bahrudin Ahmad (eds.), *Ibn Khaldūn and his Significance*, [Kuala Lumpur, Selayang], 169–78.
Zenhari, R. (2012), *The Persian Romance Samak-i 'Ayyar: Analysis of an Inju Illustrated Manuscript*, PhD dissertation, University of Göttingen.

Contributors

HINRICH BIESTERFELDT

Hinrich Biesterfeldt read Islamic studies, philosophy and ancient history at the Universities of Freiburg im Breisgau, Munich, Göttingen (PhD in 1970), and spent a postdoctoral year at Yale University. He worked at the German Orient-Institut in Beirut and at the Oriental Institutes of the Universities of Heidelberg and Bochum. His areas of research are: Arabic grammar and literature, Islamic intellectual history, in particular the history of philosophy and medicine in Islam. He published editions of, and studies on, the Arabic Galen, Abū Zayd al-Balkhī, Abū l-Ḥasan al-ʿĀmirī, and Ibn Farīghūn. He is co-editor of the series *Islamic History and Civilization. Studies and Texts* (Brill: Leiden).

CHARLES F. BRIGGS

Charles F. Briggs is Lecturer in History at the University of Vermont. His publications include *Giles of Rome's "De regimine principum": Reading and Writing Politics at Court and University, c. 1275–c. 1525* (1999); *The Body Broken: Medieval Europe 1300–1520* (2011); and, with Peter Eardley, *A Companion to Giles of Rome* (forthcoming). With David Fowler and Paul Remley he edited *The Governance of Kings and Princes: John Trevisa's Middle English Translation of the 'De regimine principum' of Aegidius Romanus* (1997), and he is currently working on an edition and English translation of the *De regimine principum*.

OLGA M. DAVIDSON

Olga M. Davidson earned her PhD in 1983 from Princeton University in Near Eastern studies. She is on the faculty of the Institute for the Study of Muslim Societies and Civilizations, Boston University, where she has served as Research Fellow since 2009. From 1992 to 1997, she was Chair of the Concentration in Islamic and Middle Eastern Studies at Brandeis University. Since 1999, she has been chair of the board, Ilex Foundation. She is the author of *Poet and Hero in the Persian Book of Kings* (1994; 2nd ed. 2006; 3rd ed. 2013) and *Comparative Literature and Classical Persian Poetry* (2000; 2nd ed. 2013).

REGULA FORSTER

Regula Forster studied German, Arabic, and Philosophy at the universities of Zurich, Tübingen and Birzeit. Since 2008, she is Junior Professor of Arabic at the Freie Universität Berlin. Her book, entitled *Das Geheimnis der Geheimnisse* (Reichert, Wiesbaden, 2006), deals with the Arabic and German versions of the Pseudo-Aristotelian *Sirr al-asrār / Secretum secretorum*. Her research focuses on classical Arabic prose, especially on the dialogue as literary form, on mirrors for princes, and on alchemical writings.

MATTHIAS HAAKE

Matthias Haake teaches ancient history at the Westfälische Wilhelms-Universität Münster. His main research interests are cultural history of Greek philosophy, Greek epigraphy and Hellenistic and Roman sole rulership. He is the author of *Der Philosoph in der Stadt. Untersuchungen zur öffentlichen Rede über Philosophen und Philosophie in den hellenistischen Poleis* (Munich 2007), and has published widely on the genre 'On Kingship' in Hellenistic and Roman times.

SEYED SADEGH HAGHIGHAT

Hagighat graduated in political thought from TM University in Tehran, and studied at the Islamic Seminaries between 1981–2004. His MA thesis on "Trans-national Responsibilities of the Islamic State," and his PhD dissertation on "Distribution of Power in Shiite Political Thought" are focused on Shiite jurisprudence. His research interests embrace Islamic political thought, methodology of political science, the Iranian Revolution and political Islam. He has published eighteen books, some of which have been translated into English and Arabic. In *Six Theories about the Islamic Revolution's Victory*, he has put forward a new theory about the Iranian Revolution. He has participated in several international academic conferences. His new book, *Methodology of Political Science*, deals with methodological and interdisciplinary issues. Currently he is a faculty member of the Department of Political Science at Mofid University in Qom. His articles and most full texts of his books can be accessed at: http://www.s-haghighat.ir

STEFAN LEDER

Stefan Leder is Professor of Arabic and Islamic Studies at Martin-Luther-University in Halle/Germany and currently director of the Orient-Institut Beirut. His research interests combine history, literature and textuality, applying textual criticism, discourse analysis, and intertextual analysis. His published work covers Arabic historiography, with particular attention given to narrativity; Islamic tradition, from the perspectives of authority of knowledge, transmission and moral politics; and the Bedouin patrimony in Arabic thought and discourse. He also writes on the history of oriental studies in Europe. His current research projects concern medieval political literature, and the intellectual and political role of the Ayyubid chancery exemplified by the critical edition of al-Qadi al-Fadil's correspondence.

JOHANNES NIEHOFF-PANAGIOTIDIS

Johannes Niehoff-Panagiotidis holds a chair in Byzantine Studies at Freie Universität Berlin, Germany. He studied classics, linguistics, and oriental studies and Indology in Tübingen and Pisa. In 1994, he earned a PhD (Tübingen) in comparative linguistics, with a thesis about Greek diglossia. His second book deals with the reception of *Kalīla wa Dimna* in its Byzantine Greek, New Greek, and Spanish versions. His special research interest is in the interaction between Byzantium and its neighbors, especially the Jewish, Christian Oriental, and Arabo-Muslim world.

HANS-JOACHIM SCHMIDT

Studies in history, French language and literature, and pedagogy at the universities of Trier (Germany), Nantes (France) and Santander, PhD in medieval history 1985, assistant at the Freie Universität Berlin 1984–1990, assistant professor at the University of Giessen (Germany) 1990–1994; visiting scholar at the German Historical Institute in Rome and at the State University of California in Berkeley; habilitation in medieval and regional history 1994; guest professor at the universities of Trier and Giessen 1994–1998; since 1998 full professor at the University of Fribourg (Switzerland); since 2007 executive member of the Institute of Comparative Studies on Monastic Orders (University of Dresden, Germany).

ISABEL TORAL-NIEHOFF

Isabel Toral-Niehoff studied history and Arabic studies in Tübingen (PhD 1997), Habilitation 2008 (Freie Universität Berlin). Her main publishing and research fields are: Arabia and the Near East in late antiquity; cultural identity; cultural transfer processes; Arabic occult sciences; *adab* and historiography; al-Andalus. Her monograph, *Al-Ḥīra. Eine arabische Kulturmetropole im spätantiken Kontext,* appeared in 2014. She is currently a senior researcher in the Courant Research Centre "Education and Religion" (EDRIS) at the University of Göttingen.

EDWIN P. WIERINGA

Edwin P. Wieringa (PhD Leiden 1994) is Professor of Island Southeast Asian Philology with Special Reference to Islamic Cultures at the University of Cologne, Germany. He has wide-ranging comparative interests in both literary and religious studies, and has published extensively on Malay and Indonesian literatures. His recent publications include a volume edited along with Arndt Graf and Susanne Schröter, *Aceh: History, Politics and Culture* (Singapore: Institute of Southeast Asian Studies, 2010).

NEGUIN YAVARI

Neguin Yavari's *Advice for the Sultan: Prophetic Voices and Secular Politics in Medieval Islam*, was published in 2014. She is currently working on a biography of Nizam al-Mulk in which the legacy of the celebrated Saljuq vizier, as reflected in historical accounts, is probed to exhibit the manifold ways in which historical context and historiography interact in premodern political discourse. Read from this perspective, the work argues, the medieval vita of the great vizier points to important currents and trends that have left deep imprints on Iranian history.

MOHSEN ZAKERI

Zakeri finished his studies in Near Eastern history at the University of Utah, Salt Lake City in 1993. The title of his dissertation was *Sasanian Soldiers in Early Muslim Society: the Origins of the 'Ayyārān and Futuwwa* (Wiesbaden 1995). He taught Persian and Islamic history at the Universities of Utah, Halle, Jena, and Göttingen. His *Persian Wisdom in Arabic Garb* (Leiden 2007) was awarded the International Book Prize of Iran in 2009. Zakeri has published many articles related to Persian/Arabic literatures in the early Islamic period. His main research interest is focused on translators and their translations from Middle Persian into Arabic.

Index